M000083410

The *Leadership in Action* Series

ON STRATEGIC LEADERSHIP

Center for Creative Leadership

The Center for Creative Leadership is an international, nonprofit educational institution founded in 1970 to advance the understanding, practice, and development of leadership for the benefit of society worldwide. As a part of this mission, it publishes books and reports that aim to contribute to a general process of inquiry and understanding in which ideas related to leadership are raised, exchanged, and evaluated. The ideas presented in its publications are those of the author or authors.

CENTER FOR CREATIVE LEADERSHIP

WWW.CCL.ORG

Stephen Rush, Editor
With an Introduction by Katherine Beatty

The *Leadership in Action* Series

ON STRATEGIC LEADERSHIP

CENTER FOR CREATIVE LEADERSHIP
Greensboro, North Carolina

CCL Stock Number 195

Published by CCL Press
Sylvester Taylor, Director of Assessments, Tools, and Publications
Peter Scisco, Manager, Publication Development
Stephen Rush, Editor
Karen Lewis, Editor

Design and layout by Joanne Ferguson

Library of Congress Cataloging-in-Publication Data

On strategic leadership / Stephen Rush, editor ; with an introduction by Katherine Beatty. — 1st ed.
p. cm.
Includes bibliographical references and index.
ISBN 978-1-60491-112-1 (print on demand) — ISBN 978-1-60491-113-8 (e-book) 1. Leadership. 2. Creative ability in business. 3. Organizational learning. 4. Organizational effectiveness. I. Rush, Stephen, 1954-

HD57.7.O5 2012
658.4'092—dc23

2011037747

CONTENTS

INTRODUCTION

In the words of the title of a book by a great scholar, colleague, and author, David Campbell, *If You Don't Know Where You're Going, You'll Probably End Up Somewhere Else*. Such is true in organizations and in life—it pays to have a vision for your organization, goals for your performance plan, a map for your drive to a new destination, and a definition of what you are attempting to develop as a leader. When leaders who are attempting to enhance their strategic leadership capabilities are asked to define what they mean by strategic leadership, a plethora of answers focusing on a wide variety of topics are received, including being visionary, having a plan, and gaining commitment from people to the plan. But most people agree that the focus of strategic leadership is the long-term success of the organization.

Unfortunately there is not much comfort in that agreement, as long-term organizational success is no small challenge. Given the turbulence of the current environment—the first-ever downgrading of the U.S. credit rating, strife and challenges to leadership in countries throughout the Middle East, the introduction of new technologies that allow for the mapping of the human genome, products such as the iPad that are changing the way people work, and trends in social networking that provide access to information across the globe at a moment's notice—our world is moving and conditions are changing at an unprecedented pace. Every era has its complexities (leaders are not typically heard to say that "these are simple times"), and today's life is no different for leaders trying to navigate these waters to help their organizations succeed. So this fieldbook is intended to help you explore a wealth of perspectives on strategic leadership, and as you do so, I invite you to create your own definition of strategic leadership.

You're going to hear many different views in the content that follows—each piece provides a sort of lens on this fascinating topic. Your journey through this book—which is drawn from articles published in CCL's magazine, *Leadership in Action*, between 2000 and 2010 and is the first in a series on topics such as Leading Through Transition, Selecting and Developing Others/Managing Talent, Innovation and Creativity, and more—will feel a bit like looking through a kaleidoscope—at one time a beautiful picture that then is scrambled as the tube is twisted. But with patience and a bit of work, another beautiful picture emerges.

Here are some of the pictures you might see through this kaleidoscope:

- Katherine Beatty and Laura Quinn, in "Strategic Command: Taking the Long View for Organizational Success," provide a starting point for a *definition* of strategic leadership. But Andrew P. Kakabadse discusses how a focus on corporate social responsibility can even expand that definition—strategic leadership is not just about the success of the organization but also about the responsibility the organization has to the larger community and environment.
- Another cluster of pieces in the book (by Wilfred H. Drath; Jay A. Conger; and John B. McGuire, Gary Rhodes, and Charles J. Palus) attempts to expand the way we think of leadership of an organization—it is not just the individual skills and perspectives that are critical; we must think about *leadership as a social process of the collective as a whole.*
- Perhaps our focus should not be on strategy but instead on the gap between strategy and reality—the *strategy-execution gap*, as many have called it. Gary Yukl and Richard Lepsigner, as well as Beatty and Quinn, tackle this question and provide some interesting insights into ways to bridge that gap.
- The *ability to learn* is fundamental to helping organizations adapt to changes and challenges. Could this be a foundational element of strategic leadership? Beatty and Richard L. Hughes, and Günter K. Stahl, note this in different ways. Stahl, for example, analyzes this need in the context of

mergers and acquisitions, and concludes that leaders help create a successful partnership by fundamentally building a new company.

- *Learning is best accomplished while doing the work of the organization*, and must also be linked directly to organizational outcomes. Michael Beer and Magnus Finnström; Frank P. Bordonaro; and Scott Mondore, Shane Douthitt, and William A. Gentry provide different perspectives on this aspect of developing strategic leadership.
- Finally, we cannot forget the *individual leader skills and perspectives* that are needed to be strategic. Yukl and Lepsinger; Christopher Musselwhite; Lee G. Bolman and Terrence E. Deal; and Andrew Wilson highlight some critical areas for consideration.

So I invite you to sit back, relax, and dive into the pieces in this book. Take your time, but come out of this with newly formed thoughts on what strategic leadership is and how you might develop it in yourself and others. Organizations today are greatly in need of development in this area, and this book can help you help them achieve this goal.

Katherine Beatty
Director, Global Portfolio Management
Center for Creative Leadership

Strategic Command: Taking the Long View for Organizational Success

Katherine Beatty and Laura Quinn

Organizations can best gain an advantage over their competitors by practicing strategic leadership. But how is strategic leadership accomplished, and who in an organization should be responsible for it? Strategic leadership is a complex process of thinking, acting, and influencing, and it can be exercised not just by individuals but also by teams.

If you were to ask a group of executives to define *strategic leadership*, you'd likely get as many different answers as there were people in the room. One executive might describe it as *creating a shared vision of the future*. Another might view it as *linking the efforts of everyone in the organization to the organization's goals*, and still another might interpret it as *not just accomplishing objectives but also steadily improving the organization.*

The difficulty of arriving at a simple, cut-and-dried definition of strategic leadership is underscored in the literature on the subject. In their 1995 book *Strategic Management: Competitiveness and Globalization*, Michael A. Hitt, R. Duane Ireland, and Robert E. Hoskisson developed a model of strategic leadership that has six critical components. In a study based on that model and reported in a 1998 article in *SAM Advanced Management Journal*, Abdalla F. Hagen, Morsheda T. Hassan, and Sammy G. Amin found that U.S. CEOs ranked these six components in the following order of importance: determining strategic direction, developing human capital, exploiting and maintaining core competencies, sustaining an effective corporate culture, emphasizing ethical practices, and establishing strategic control.

What these various definitions and concepts make clear is that strategic leadership is extremely complex and multifaceted. Yet it is for that very reason that strategic leadership is critical to achieving individual and organizational effectiveness and success in a rapidly changing, increasingly globalized business environment that grows more complicated by the day.

Leaders who want to develop strategic abilities need to gain an understanding of the three parts of strategic leadership: *what* strategic leadership achieves, *how* strategic leadership is accomplished, and *who* in an organization has the main responsibility for leading strategically.

CCL's program Developing the Strategic Leader, designed to help senior managers gain a better understanding of the complexity of strategic leadership as it relates to themselves, their teams, and their organizations, examines all three elements of strategic leadership. To this end the program uses as a starting point this model: individuals and teams (the *who*) exert strategic leadership when they think, act, and influence (the *how*) in ways that enhance the organization's sustainable competitive advantage (the *what*).

GOING LONG

If strategy is defined as the patterns of choices made to achieve a sustainable competitive advantage, then strategic leadership involves focusing on the choices that enhance the health and well-being of an organization over the long term. Those last two words are key. Half a millennium ago the Japanese military leader Miyamoto Musashi said, "In strategy it is important to see distant things as if they were close and to take a distanced view of close things." That may be easier to fathom in theory than it is to achieve in practice, because operating from a perspective that emphasizes the long term does not always come naturally or easily to leaders. This is especially true in today's business environment, in which short-term results are increasingly exalted, frequently with little consideration and to the detriment of the big picture.

As a result, leading strategically often demands courage and a willingness to swim against the tide of conventional wisdom. A case in point is Darwin Smith, who was CEO of Kimberly-Clark from 1971 to 1991. As related in Jim Collins's book *Good to Great: Why Some Companies Make the Leap . . . and Others Don't*, Smith, soon after becoming CEO, concluded that the potential of the company's core papermaking business paled in comparison to what could be achieved by branching out into a wider range of consumer products. His strategy included selling the pulp and paper mills that were an integral part of the company's tradition. Business analysts were shocked and predicted that Smith was making a huge mistake. But Smith stuck to his guns and his strategy, and today Kimberly-Clark is a global manufacturer with annual revenues of $19.7 billion in 2010.

COMING UP SHORT

The lack of attention that some leaders pay to thinking and acting strategically for long-term organizational success was perhaps never so evident as during the late 1990s—the now-faded glory days of the dot-coms. For the leaders of many of these companies, the overriding interest was building to the point of an initial public offering of stock. There was little concern about or planning for what would happen after the IPO. The focus was on short-term objectives rather than strategic goals such as establishing and maintaining profitability, and the decisions made reflected this limited focus.

This is not to say that strategic leaders shouldn't be concerned with the short-term health of their companies. The important thing is that actions they take to address those short-term concerns also support and enhance the long-term viability of their organizations.

Strategic leadership requires leaders to focus on the far-reaching implications of their ideas, decisions, and actions for the entire enterprise, not just one or two business units or functions. Strategic leaders need to understand how the various parts of the organization's system work together, and they must integrate perspectives from across the organization. If they don't, they're likely to be frustrated in their attempts to create and accomplish organizational goals, because individuals in the organization won't have a clear perception or understanding of their roles in supporting and achieving those goals.

In addition to having a firm grasp of what's happening in their own companies, strategic leaders need to stay on top of and react to the rapid and constant changes occurring in the marketplace environment. Failing to do so can seriously hinder an organization's ability to arrive at the *what* of strategic leadership—a sustainable competitive advantage.

GATHERING INFORMATION

The *how* of strategic leadership is a complicated combination of *thinking, acting*, and *influencing*—and each of these three processes is complex in and of itself.

Today's organizations and leaders often operate under ambiguous or even contradictory circumstances. Anticipating and effectively reacting to these circumstances is a key to success.

To do this, strategic leaders must not only develop the organization's vision and mission but also continually think about and review the organization's direction to ensure the organization is staying on the right course as the competitive environment changes. Strategic thinking, then, involves gathering information, making connections among the various pieces of information, and filtering the information to form ideas and strategies that are focused, relevant, and sound.

Effective strategic thinkers constantly scan the internal and external environments for factors, trends, and patterns that may have an effect on the organization's business.

In the internal environment, strategic leaders pay attention to whether the organization is fulfilling its mission, the ways in which the organizational culture and values do or don't support the organization's work, employees' capabilities and talents, budgetary issues, and how the organization's various units and systems function and interrelate.

Information must be gathered from every corner of the organization. The best way to ensure this is to build networks, which in turn requires the ability to foster trusting relationships with people in all areas and at all levels of the organization and to encourage and accept their input and feedback.

Establishing such relationships can't be done in a day; it also requires thinking and acting strategically—planting seeds and nurturing them over the long term.

Perhaps the best example of how leaders can form and stay plugged into networks that yield rich and relevant information is *management by wandering around*. Spending time among and genuinely communicating with employees throughout the organization enables strategic leaders to win those workers' trust and see the business through their eyes. And as Yogi Berra said, "You can observe a lot by watching."

As strategic leaders scan the external environment, they should pay attention to market conditions, global economies, changing technology, industry innovations, and shifting supplies of resources. But perhaps most important, they must keep a keen eye on their customers and what drives those customers' purchases.

An example of a leader who tuned in to customers and took a cue from them to set a successful organizational strategy is Louis Gerstner, who was CEO of IBM from 1993 until 2002. When Gerstner took over as CEO, Big Blue was singing the blues: profit margins were down in its core businesses as other technology companies successfully applied competitive pressures. Gerstner decided that IBM couldn't continue on the same course and maintain its competitive edge. As he gauged the needs of customers, he concluded that their number one problem was their burgeoning information technology systems. Few companies had people with a thorough understanding of how their various IT products combined into a system, let alone an ability to solve system problems. Gerstner shifted IBM's strategic focus from providing products to providing services that most of IBM's competitors were incapable of—helping companies troubleshoot and get the most out of their IT systems. In doing so he created a business model that other technology companies are still trying to emulate.

LINKING UP

It's not enough for strategic leaders to capture information from a wide range of networks inside and outside the organization. Once they have gathered the information, they need to examine it to discover interdependencies and see how various pieces of information are linked to different parts of the organization. Doing so is a monumental information-processing challenge. A crucial part of meeting this challenge is comprehending the systemic nature of organizations—a dynamic involving individuals, teams, groups, the industry, and the marketplace.

Strategic leaders also need to take into account the relationship between the organization's history and its vision for the future. If there are conflicts between the two, they may be a hindrance to achieving long-term goals—a hindrance that needs to be addressed and resolved. For example, if a company's top management decides that the strategic focus should be on enhancing the use of new technology but the organization's culture has traditionally been averse to risk, the likelihood is high that there will be problems in keeping the strategy on track.

Strategic leaders should focus on linking all the information they gather so they can give their organizations the best chance of gaining or maintaining a competitive advantage.

DATA OVERLOAD

One of the biggest problems strategic leaders encounter after they become proficient at gathering information is dealing with the sheer volume of information collected. They need to differentiate the information, and filter and distill it down to what is essential for setting the organization's strategic direction.

However, deciding which information—out of an often overwhelming amount—deserves attention and which should be passed over is easier said than done. Sometimes strategic leaders simply don't have the resources to sift through it all. Sometimes they feel an urgency to act and just don't have the time. Whatever the case, strategic leaders who are unable or unwilling to separate out the crucial information and establish a sense of order can find themselves paralyzed.

There is no simple prescription for filtering the information that is most relevant and crucial to setting an effective strategic direction. But to make sound choices, strategic leaders should be aware of their own career connections and biases and not let them sway decisions. For example, a strategic leader with a background in customer service may look at the available information and conclude—and convince others—that the organization should invest heavily in customer service, when in fact the organization's strategic goals depend more heavily on other needs.

CARRYING IT OUT

The second part of the *how* of strategic leadership is acting. All the good strategic thinking in the world isn't worth much if leaders don't act on it (or, as is sometimes the more prudent course, if they don't withhold action, based on their strategic thinking). When a leader fails, it's usually not because of a flaw in his or her vision for the organization. Rather, the fatal error generally lies in an inability to take action on and effectively implement that vision.

Although strategic leadership is focused on an organization's long-term well-being, it should be balanced with attention to tactical, day-to-day operations. The two perspectives need to be integrated. Leaders often struggle with this balancing act. They're often inclined to concentrate on the problems that arise during the day's work—issues and details that seem immediately important, straightforward, and easily resolved. In other words their instinct is to go around putting out fires. But in every decision that leaders make, it's critical that they ask themselves how that decision will affect the organization in the long term. Tactical efforts need to be aligned with and supportive of the long-term strategy.

It's also critical for strategic leaders to lead by example. Their own consistent behavior in carrying out their strategic vision has a trickle-down effect on others in the organization; it sets a standard by which others can establish priorities that are in consonance with the strategy.

A large part of the acting of strategic leadership is making decisions about whether and when to act. If opportunities arise in day-to-day operations that bolster the long-term vision, effective strategic leaders recognize and run with them. Conversely, opportunities that promise short-term benefits but may be detrimental to overall strategy are shunned. Two of the most important qualities for strategic leaders are confidence and patience—they need to steadily take actions toward the strategic goal, even in the midst of an ever-changing and often chaotic business environment. Yet strategic leaders also need to be flexible, to view strategy as emergent and all their decisions as temporary ones that can be modified as new information from strategic thinking becomes available.

MAKING YOUR MARK

Although strategic leaders must take action based on their strategic thinking to enable the organization to achieve its long-term objectives, it is not enough for them to act alone. They also need to *influence* others in the organization to work toward the strategic goals.

The first step of the process of influencing is to help people in all areas and at all levels of the organization gain a clear sense of the strategy and how it applies to their specific jobs and roles. But strategic leaders can't stop there—they then need to connect the needs and aspirations of the employees to the possibilities presented by the strategic vision, creating a commitment to, passion for, and excitement about the cause. Exercising this level of influence on everyone in the organization might seem to be a daunting task, especially when the inevitable difficulties and setbacks in advancing the strategy occur, and disenchantment and frustration loom. But leaders can instill a dedication to and zeal for the strategic vision by communicating effectively, telling powerful stories, and sharing their own sense of enthusiasm for and allegiance to the organization and its goals.

Strategic leaders can further influence the organization by aligning their systems, culture, and organizational structure to ensure consistency with the strategy. For example, CCL is working with a small company in the tool industry that has the strategic imperatives of innovation, speed, and quality. The company has made a structural change—people now report to process directors rather than functional vice presidents. The company is changing from a command-and-control culture to one that emphasizes collaboration and focusing on individual initiative. The reward system encourages both individual and company performance. The resulting synergy is powerful: people receive consistent messages about the importance of innovation, speed, and quality and are influenced to behave in ways that support the strategy.

WHO'S RESPONSIBLE

Now that the *what* and the *how* of strategic leadership have been established, the final question is: *who* in an organization should have responsibility for the tasks of strategic leadership? The obvious answer is the people at the top—presidents, CEOs, and other senior officers. Certainly, when an organization fails, it is the people at the top who are held accountable.

But it would be a mistake to think that only senior officers can be strategic leaders. Individuals whose decisions have effects beyond their own functional areas often have opportunities to think, act, and influence as strategic leaders. For instance, a purchasing manager who is considering switching suppliers can anticipate the impact the move will have on the engineering and manufacturing divisions, or a human resource director in charge of crafting reward systems can do so in a way that encourages cooperation across key business units.

But because strategic leadership inherently involves multiple perspectives and a gathering of information from many sources, some organizations are beginning to see the responsibility for strategic leadership as lying not with one or a few individuals but with teams. The diversity of perspectives and opinions that naturally arises from a group can provide a clear advantage in what should be a collaborative process of strategic leadership.

But there are challenges in the team approach as well. Everyone has seen a team that is made up of talented, resourceful, and committed individuals but performs way below expectations and is less than the sum of its parts. Strategic leadership teams can avert this outcome by ensuring the presence of a number of factors and being aware of potential problems as they go through the strategic processes of thinking, acting, and influencing.

First, a team must have access to and stay attuned to all the information it needs to do its work—information from each individual on the team, from within the organization, and from the external environment, such as technological, cultural, and market trends. It is critical that all this information be shared with each member of the team and brought to bear on the task of strategic thinking.

Second, a team must be empowered to act strategically. Each member needs to have a clear idea of what the team can and can't do, and the team needs to take timely actions within those boundaries. Two of the biggest problems that strategic leadership teams run into are not having a strategic vision that is shared by each member and failing to balance near-term tactics with long-term strategy, so the team must establish and focus on these critical prerequisites for effective strategic action.

Finally, team members must trust and respect one another so they can engage in the final part of the *how* of strategic leadership—influencing. The team needs to be careful to send out a uniform message about its mission and strategy so that others in the organization become energized by and committed to—rather than confused about—the long-term goals and understand how their roles and their work are related to and support those goals.

WORKING TOGETHER

It's important to remember that the three processes of strategic leadership—thinking, acting, and influencing—are not independent but interdependent. No part of the process occurs in a vacuum, and each relies on the others. Nor is strategic leadership a linear process—strategic leaders should be thinking, acting, and influencing each day. And perhaps most important, strategic leaders must be proficient at each part of the process to be effective, for leaders who come up with brilliant strategic ideas but are unable to champion them and see them through will not find much success.

Strategic Aims: Making the Right Moves in Leadership

Katherine Beatty and Richard L. Hughes

Many leaders have become successful because of their operational skills. But today's business environment requires strategic leadership that is systemic, focused on the future, and oriented toward change. Leaders who can foster greater strategic clarity, make stronger connections between strategy and tactics, and broaden their own and others' perspectives will contribute to the enduring success of their organizations.

What if you could ensure the enduring success of your organization by giving it the agility to weather change and uncertainty? What if you could develop leadership in your organization that was capable of ever-deepening insight and increasingly high performance? The key is better strategic leadership. Strategic leadership enhances an organization's sustainable competitive advantage through not only its strategy but also its vision, values, culture, climate, leadership, structure, and systems.

To appreciate the nature and importance of strategic leadership, it is helpful to distinguish it from operational leadership. Strong operational leaders are known for their orientation toward results and their ability to marshal resources to get the job done. Most senior executives have progressed in their organizations because they have strong operational skills, but effective strategic leadership requires skills that are

Systemic. Organizations are interdependent and interconnected systems, so leaders who take actions and decisions in one part of the organization should be mindful of the impact of those actions and decisions on other parts of the organization.

Focused on the future. Strategic leaders operate with a far-reaching timetable, integrating short-term results and a long-term focus.

Oriented toward change. Strategic leaders are often drivers of organizational change.

Organizations that have not adequately developed strategic leadership skills in their managers may run into three kinds of problems:

A lack of strategic clarity and focus. This occurs when leaders fail to make tough decisions that clarify both what *will* be done and what *will not* be done. The resulting lack of strategic clarity and focus prevents people from seeing their part in achieving goals. Personal agendas form and take on a life of their own, politics run rampant, and diluted strategy saps organizational energy and effectiveness.

Poorly aligned tactics. Sometimes the priorities that guide day-to-day work in an organization are only loosely aligned with the actual strategy. People often don't understand what organizational strategy means for their specific department, region, or function—and thus for the decisions and actions they take on a regular basis. A strategy that exists in the minds of executives in the boardroom or is written in a formal strategic plan counts for little if it doesn't clarify the steps by which strategic success will be attained.

Limited perspective. Leaders often focus on short-term success at the expense of long-term viability. The tremendous pressure that many managers feel to deliver short-term results drives this trend. It is also fueled by the habits of success: managers generally rise through the ranks by being rewarded for their strong operational leadership. It can be difficult for them to shift their focus and do something different. Short-term success is important, but if an organization consistently disregards the long-term perspective it will suffer in the end.

Overcoming the challenges posed by a lack of strategic clarity and focus, poorly aligned tactics, and limited perspective is no easy task. However, by breaking down strategic leadership into *what it involves, who does it,* and *how it takes place,* managers can foster greater strategic clarity, make stronger connections between strategy and tactics, and broaden their perspective. This will in turn contribute to the organization's enduring success.

LEARNING ENGINES

Leading strategically involves discovering the few key things an organization needs to do well and can do well and then creating the conditions necessary to act collectively on the implications of that discovery.

For this to happen, organizations need to become continual learning engines. In many organizations, however, the process of making and implementing strategy hardly fits that description. Strategy often is set in long meetings and off-site retreats, resulting in a weighty strategic plan that sets out goals and objectives. What really matters is what happens between such meetings and retreats. Is the strategy actually implemented? How do you know the strategy is sound? Is the strategy creating differentiation, clarity, and focus?

If strategy creation is perceived to occur at relatively infrequent events, organizations and their leaders may miss critical information and opportunities that arise between these events. A more useful approach is for strategic leaders to think of themselves as continually developing and discovering strategy and holding it in an ongoing state of formulation, implementation, reassessment, and revision. This means that making and implementing strategy is best thought of as a learning process driven by strategic leadership.

This conceptualization of strategic leadership as a learning paradigm owes much to what Henry Mintzberg, Joseph Lampel, and Bruce Ahlstrand, in their book *Strategy Safari: A Guided Tour Through the Wilds of Strategic Management* (Free Press, 1998), call *the learning school* of strategy formation as an emergent process. CCL sees its work in part as an application of this perspective to the individual, team, and organizational competencies required to implement such an approach in organizations.

Making strategy a learning process has five primary elements:

Assessing where we are. Strategic leadership requires a clear understanding of the competitive situation facing the organization.

This involves collecting and interpreting information about the organization's external environment: its markets and competitors, the nature of its industry, and governmental, economic, and social influences. It also involves collecting and interpreting information about the organization's internal environment, such as its capacity to deliver valued goods and services; its market position and customer relations; its systems, processes, and structures; and its leadership and culture. This element has both a hard side and a soft side in its application. The hard side deals with how the tasks of environmental scanning, competitive analysis, and the like are assigned and conducted and how the results are disseminated as part of the organization's formal strategic planning process. The soft side deals with the fact that effective strategic leadership requires an appreciation of how the competitive situation affects the enterprise as an interdependent whole, not just knowledge of the situation facing the individual leader's own department or function.

Understanding who we are and where we want to go. Strategic leaders are the stewards of the organization's identity and aspirations, including its vision, mission, values, and possibilities ten or twenty years ahead. These factors represent a key lens through which different aspects of the competitive situation are filtered and key organizational priorities established.

Learning how to get there. Getting down to the nuts and bolts of strategic leadership involves drawing on insight, information, and vision to determine priorities and formulate strategy. One of the most important challenges of this element is identifying key *strategic drivers*—the relatively few but critical determinants of long-term success for a specific organization in a specific industry. Business strategy should be developed based on an understanding of these strategic drivers. Cirque du Soleil, for example, has created a phenomenon in what had been a dead segment of the entertainment market—circuses—by focusing on the key strategic drivers of performance talent, lavish production, and innovation, according to an article by Linda Tischler in the July 2005 issue of *Fast Company*.

But having a viable business strategy is not enough. It's also important to develop a leadership strategy for addressing the human and organizational capabilities essential to implementing the business strategy effectively. Organizational culture plays a role here, as strategic leaders need to understand and shape the spoken and unspoken culture of their organization and its leadership.

Making the journey. How does strategy translate into action? What tactics are needed to implement a given strategy effectively? How does strategy seep into the lifeblood of the organization so that tactical actions across departments and divisions are consistent with overall strategic priorities? For Cirque du Soleil, the task of attracting, training, and retaining artistic talent requires a team that scours the globe for fire jugglers, pole climbers, bungee jumpers, and more traditional world-class athletes. Cirque doesn't always recruit those who have won awards or medals—more often it recruits performers who have nearly the same level of skills as those who have won accolades but who still have something to prove. Moreover, Cirque looks for multidimensional talent and showmanship; during auditions, candidates may be asked to do something completely unexpected, such as sing a song after climbing to the top of a rope.

Checking our progress. Strategic leadership requires continually assessing the organization's effectiveness. This involves looking at indicators of current performance relative to expected performance and judging whether adequate investments are being made to ensure the organization's sustainable competitive advantage. Cirque du Soleil, for example, puts more than 70 percent of its profits back into new initiatives, challenging itself to reinvent its brand with each new production.

OPPORTUNITIES ABOUND

Strategy involves an ongoing discovery process that has both top-down and bottom-up elements. To put it differently, many people play a part in leading their organizations strategically. It's true that the CEO is ultimately responsible for deciding on a path for the organization and that the senior management team is usually also involved. But this does not mean that they are the only—or even the best—strategic leaders in the organization.

There are many opportunities to exercise strategic leadership for anyone whose decisions and perspectives have an impact beyond his or her own functional areas. For example, a purchasing manager can anticipate the impact on engineering and manufacturing of switching a supplier. Or a human resource director can develop systems to encourage cooperation across business units. Even people serving on the front lines of customer interface are in a unique position to scan the environment and make sense of information in ways that can enhance the strategic perspective of the entire organization.

In addition, it is not just individuals who are engaged in strategic leadership; often such leadership is a collaborative, team activity. A lot of CCL's work in this area has been with what it calls strategic leadership teams—groups whose collective work has strategic implications for a particular business unit, product line, service area, functional area, division, or company.

Readers of CCL's electronic newsletter, *Leading Effectively*, were asked about the strategic leadership teams they have served on. More than half the respondents indicated that their positions were below the senior management level, but 97 percent indicated that they had participated on at least one strategic leadership team in the past five years. This suggests that strategic leadership is enacted by many different teams composed of people from many levels and across many functions of an organization—not just by individual executives.

THREE SKILLS

At some point in their careers, many managers are told that they need to become more strategic. CCL has found that achieving this goal requires sharpening managers' skills in the areas of *strategic thinking, strategic acting,* and *strategic influencing*. These three processes work interdependently—in other words, the way one thinks affects the way one acts, and the way one influences largely determines the kind of information one gets from others and thus will have available to consider.

Collectively, these three skills drive a leader's progress through the five elements of strategy as a learning process.

Strategic thinking involves having a vision of what the organization can and should become; it offers new ways of understanding the organization's challenges and opportunities through scanning the internal and external environments for trends, patterns, and other factors that may influence the business both now and in the future. A particularly critical competency for strategic leaders is systems thinking, which allows leaders to discern the complex interrelationships among the variables that contribute to organizational success.

Strategic acting is taking timely, decisive, and coordinated action based on the insights and understanding derived from effective strategic thinking. Often, however, there is only limited time for strategic thinking before action is required, so strategic thinking and strategic acting go hand in hand—each informing the other to improve the overall outcome. Another important aspect of strategic acting is creating conditions that allow others in the organization to act strategically as well. One of the most effective ways to do this is to set clear priorities that facilitate coordinated action across the enterprise and provide a basis for acting decisively with both the short term and the long term in mind.

Strategic influencing creates conditions of clarity, commitment, and synergy throughout the organization. Again, it is important to appreciate the dynamic ways in which strategic thinking, acting, and influencing interact. For example, strategic leaders often need to draw on a group of diverse stakeholders to address a complex organizational challenge. This requires that these stakeholders make sense *together*, not just that one leader works things out in his or her own mind; it involves thinking and influencing simultaneously, creating in a collaborative way a common and shared understanding among different individuals who have different perspectives. Two strategic influencing skills pertain to the challenge of championing change in organizations: investing in relationships and navigating organizational politics. Few things have a more negative impact on a leader's credibility in the organization than clumsily trying to influence others without first building the necessary foundation of relationships. Strategic leadership happens in the white space on the organizational chart; it involves working on issues that cut across organizational boundaries. For that very reason, it helps to spend time developing relationships that do not naturally form from the organizational structure or the nature of the work itself.

Because shifts in strategy often equate to shifts in power in organizations, politics is an almost inevitable aspect of strategic leadership. Yet political behavior can easily be perceived as self-serving and damaging to one's credibility and potential influence. Therefore good strategic leaders need to develop the skill of navigating the political landscape of the organization while maintaining—and perhaps even enhancing—their own credibility as individuals.

ADVANTAGE GAINED

The skills of strategic thinking, acting, and influencing are what drive strategy as a learning process in organizations. Individuals and teams enact strategic leadership when they think, act, and influence others in ways that enhance the organization's sustainable competitive advantage. When CEOs and other top executives understand the strategic leadership process and build that same capacity in others, they will contribute to the organization's chances of enduring success.

Getting It Done: Four Ways to Translate Strategy into Results

Gary Yukl and Richard Lepsinger

A recent survey indicates that many of today's business leaders believe their organizations are not only inadequate at implementing strategy but also unlikely to get better at this critical challenge. Other research on managers has identified four leadership behaviors that are useful in enhancing the execution of business strategy.

A brilliant strategy is of little value unless it can be implemented effectively. The process of translating strategy into successful business results and maintaining efficient, reliable operations is commonly called *execution*, and it is one of the essential challenges for leaders in today's business environment, where rapid and complex change is the norm.

In a recent survey of more than four hundred leaders at the assistant manager level or above—including general managers, vice presidents, assistant vice presidents, directors, department heads, and managers—OnPoint Consulting found that 49 percent of the respondents said their organization was poor at execution and 64 percent of those managers did not believe the situation would improve.

Finding ways to improve execution is an important task for today's leaders. Our research indicates that four leadership behaviors are especially useful for enhancing execution: operational planning, clarifying roles and objectives, monitoring operations and performance, and solving operational problems.

OPERATIONAL PLANNING

This leadership behavior involves determining short-term objectives and action steps for achieving them; determining how to use personnel, equipment, facilities, and other resources efficiently to accomplish a project or initiative; and determining how to schedule and coordinate the activities of various individuals, teams, and work units. Operational planning facilitates the organization and coordination of related work activities, preventing operational delays and bottlenecks in work processes, avoiding duplication of effort, and helping people to set priorities and meet deadlines. By identifying and addressing potential problems that could lead to accidents, errors, and erratic performance, planning increases the reliability of work processes.

Planning is especially useful when a work unit is carrying out large, complex projects over a period of months or years, when there is a need to meet difficult deadlines and stay within tight budgets, when a work unit performs several different types of tasks, and when interdependent work units need to ensure close coordination. Planning increases a leader's ability to manage several initiatives simultaneously, especially when the initiatives involve shared use of facilities, equipment, and personnel. It is essential to ensure that interrelated projects are mutually supportive and carefully coordinated. Completing an activity early, missing a deadline, or failing to complete an activity successfully can cause problems for other people and require revisions of their plans.

During the initial planning stage the people who are accountable for a project that involves more than one team or subunit should meet to jointly review their plans, schedule interrelated activities, and ensure that shared resources—people, equipment, and facilities—will be available when needed. The initial planning should make an effort to anticipate potential problems and determine how to avoid them or deal with them effectively if they occur. However, even the most detailed and thoughtful plan will likely encounter unanticipated problems that threaten its success. Leaders who lack a plan will produce fragmented and incremental activities, but leaders who make a plan that is too rigid will also be in trouble. Plans are oriented toward a desired but unknown future, and to be effective they need to be flexible so they can be adjusted to new information or changing conditions.

Operational planning is just as important for top executives as it is for lower-level managers, although the planning specifics may be somewhat different. Executives are usually responsible for developing strategic objectives, general strategies for achieving them, and specific initiatives that will facilitate execution. Lower-level managers are usually responsible for developing and implementing action plans for a specific project, and the amount of discretion they have in this planning varies greatly depending on the nature of the project or initiative.

For example, as part of its strategy to enhance its worldwide consulting practice, a human resource firm decided to establish a standard set of consulting processes and solutions to be used by all its staff. For this initiative to succeed, the field consultants would need to have a high degree of commitment to it, which would be unlikely if most of the planning were done at the corporate level. Therefore the head of each field office was asked to take responsibility for the development of specific action plans for each element of the initiative, including training consultants to use the solutions and developing local marketing plans. In this way the unique needs of each location could be taken into account and the timing of events could be coordinated with other activities already planned for each location.

CLARIFYING ROLES AND OBJECTIVES

This leadership behavior involves the communication of responsibilities, role expectations, and performance objectives to direct reports, peers, and outsiders who make an important contribution to work-unit performance. Clarifying behavior includes setting specific task objectives, explaining duties and responsibilities, explaining priorities among different tasks or objectives, describing expected results, setting clear standards against which performance will be compared, setting specific deadlines for completion of tasks, and explaining when and how specific rules and procedures must be used. When top executives clarify expectations for direct reports who are also managers, they focus more on the performance of the person's unit than on individual performance.

Clarifying can improve employee satisfaction and performance by removing ambiguity about roles and priorities. High performance is more likely when people know what to do, how to do it, and when it should be done. To perform at a high level, people need to clearly understand their responsibilities with regard to different tasks, the expected results for each task, and the relative priority of the various tasks for which they are responsible.

Clarifying also improves cooperation and coordination among individuals and between organizational subunits. Work gets done more efficiently and output is of higher quality when people are clear about who needs to be involved in decisions and activities and the nature of that involvement. Ambiguity about responsibilities can result in territorial conflicts that undermine cooperation, and key activities may fall through the cracks when each person thinks someone else is responsible for those tasks.

Clarifying is especially useful when the work is complex and people are confused about what is expected of them. Such confusion is more likely when there are multiple performance criteria, when the nature of the work or technology is changing, when there is a crisis and people do not know how to respond, and when employees are new to the job and lack relevant prior experience. Clarifying is even more important when work-unit operations are frequently affected by changes in policies, plans, or priorities determined by higher management or clients. Because clarifying is a way to communicate plans, the situations where planning is especially important (for instance, where large, complex tasks are performed by multiple individuals or teams) are also those where clarifying is essential.

Setting specific performance goals or task objectives is also an important form of clarifying. Leaders who communicate specific, challenging objectives reap several benefits. These objectives focus people on important activities and responsibilities, encourage people to find more efficient ways to do the work, and facilitate constructive performance evaluation by providing benchmarks for comparison. Execution improves because specific objectives guide efforts toward productive activities and challenging objectives energize those efforts.

A common problem is that leaders clarify objectives for easily measured and quantified aspects of the work (such as sales) but not for more difficult to measure yet just as important aspects (such as service quality and customer satisfaction). In setting objectives for less tangible aspects of the work, it helps to remember that although only some objectives are *measurable*, the attainment of all objectives is *verifiable*. For example, the level of customer satisfaction can be determined by surveying or interviewing customers about their perception of key elements related to satisfaction (for instance, ease of use, freshness, speed, and performance). The extent to which service quality goals are being met can be verified by comparing actual service against a set of standards that define what quality service looks like in your organization (for instance, standards for responsiveness, handling of problems, on-time performance, and product availability).

Execution will suffer when people disagree about objectives or priorities. Picture the potential conflicts and inefficiencies that would result if one group in your unit was working toward reducing costs while another group was focused on bringing state-of-the-art products and services to market. Leaders need to ensure that clear priorities are established when there are multiple objectives that are not completely compatible.

MONITORING OPERATIONS AND PERFORMANCE

This leadership behavior involves gathering information about work activities, checking on the progress and quality of the work, and evaluating individual and unit performance. Monitoring can take many forms, such as following up to make sure a request has been carried out, walking around to observe how the work is going and to ask questions about it, checking on the quality of the work (for instance, inspecting the output, monitoring quality reports, and reviewing customer complaints), meeting with people to review progress on a task or project, checking work progress against plans to see if the task or project is on target, and evaluating how well a major activity or project was done.

The increasing emphasis on empowerment has led some people to conclude that monitoring, with its connotations of command and control, is no longer an essential leadership behavior. However, the primary purpose of monitoring is not to increase control but to facilitate performance of the work by others. Appropriate monitoring helps leaders to identify potential problems early and prevent disruptions in work-unit activities and service to customers. Monitoring provides the information needed for problem solving and decision making, evaluating people's performance, recognizing achievements, identifying performance deficiencies, assessing training needs, providing assistance, and allocating rewards such as pay increases or promotions.

The appropriate degree of internal monitoring depends on such situational aspects as the nature of the work and the people doing it. Monitoring is most important when employees are inexperienced or apathetic about the work or when operations are prone to accidents or disruptions and leaders need to detect emerging problems quickly to deal with them effectively. Monitoring is also essential when mistakes or delays will imperil project success and must be quickly remedied. The need for monitoring is increased by tight deadlines, difficult contractual obligations, and interdependent tasks that need to be closely coordinated.

The performance indicators most relevant for tracking and measuring will depend on the nature of the work and the determinants of success. A common mistake is to focus on a single indicator when information about other indicators is also essential to evaluating overall effectiveness. The processes used to produce outcomes should be measured in addition to the outcomes themselves. By measuring essential steps in operational processes, leaders can gain a better understanding of the causal relationships that determine effective execution. For example, quality problems can be dealt with more effectively by identifying the critical steps in the production or service process where most defects and mistakes occur.

Continuous measurement of the process in those steps makes it easier to eliminate common mistakes, detect deficient materials before they are used, and correct any defects immediately. Measures of the personnel, equipment, and resources involved in each step in the production process make it easier to analyze that process and find ways to simplify procedures, avoid delays, and reduce unnecessary costs.

There are two primary sources of standards for evaluating the performance of an activity. Prior performance of the same type of activity by an individual or unit can provide a basis for setting standards for future performance under similar conditions. However, even when a unit's performance improves, it may remain well below the performance of similar units in competing organizations. Thus a second source of standards is the performance of similar units within or outside the organization. In situations where information about competitors' performance levels is not available, it is often possible to develop standards of performance based on customer expectations of service and quality, safety and other government regulations, generally accepted standards of conduct (for instance, ethical behavior, fairness, and respect for individuals), and internal standards for quality and effectiveness.

In addition to monitoring the overall operations of the work unit, it is important to monitor the performance of direct reports and people who carry out key support activities for the unit. A common method for monitoring progress on assignments and projects is to request written reports from the responsible person or to schedule progress review meetings with him or her. The type of information and level of detail to be supplied in the progress reports should be determined when the project is initiated. Establishing clear reporting requirements in advance is also a form of clarifying, and it helps managers avoid monitoring too closely, which can communicate a lack of trust. The frequency and nature of reports will depend on task or project complexity and the competence of the individual responsible for the work. More frequent reporting is appropriate for people who are inexperienced or unreliable. Follow-up and reporting may involve written reports and formal progress review meetings, or they may be accomplished through informal discussions.

The success of monitoring depends on getting accurate information, sometimes from people who may be reluctant to provide it. For example, people may be hesitant to inform their boss or a senior manager about problems, mistakes, and delays. Even a person who is not responsible for a problem may be reluctant to report it if he or she might become the target of an angry outburst (the kill-the-messenger syndrome). Therefore it is essential that reactions to information about problems be constructive and nonpunitive. Questions about work problems should be open-ended and nonevaluative to encourage people to respond and to provide a more complete picture of the situation. In addition to seeking information, these questions should also communicate the leader's concerns and expectations to people.

SOLVING OPERATIONAL PROBLEMS

This leadership behavior involves identifying work issues, analyzing them in a systematic but timely manner, and acting decisively to implement solutions. Problem solving occurs in response to an immediate disturbance of normal operations, such as an equipment breakdown, a shortage of necessary materials, a customer with a complaint, a mistake in the work, an accident, an unusual request by higher management, or an action by direct reports or colleagues that jeopardizes the success of a mission.

Problem solving is reactive and occurs in a short period of time, as opposed to planning, which is more proactive and time consuming.

Leaders face an endless stream of problems and disturbances in their work, and solving operational problems is key to effective execution. Effective leaders take responsibility for identifying problems and dealing with them in a timely way. In contrast, ineffective leaders attempt to avoid responsibility for a problem by ignoring it, trying to pass it off to someone else, involving more people than necessary in making the decision (in order to diffuse responsibility), or delaying the decision for as long as possible. Although it is essential to deal decisively with an immediate problem, it is also important to diagnose the cause of the problem accurately and devise potential remedies. Solving the wrong problem can make things worse instead of better.

Because there are always more problems than a leader has time to address, it is important to look for relationships among them, rather than assuming they are distinct and independent. Taking this broader view of problems produces a better understanding of them. Relating problems to one another and to strategic objectives makes it easier to recognize opportunities for dealing with several related problems at the same time. Leaders will do a better job of finding connections among problems when they remain open-minded about problem definition and actively consider multiple definitions for each problem.

COMBINING BEHAVIORS

Operational planning, clarifying roles and objectives, monitoring operations and performance, and solving operational problems are closely intertwined, and effective execution often depends on using these behaviors in mutually supportive ways. Monitoring provides much of the information needed to formulate and modify objectives, plans, policies, and procedures. Clarifying is an essential process for communicating plans and accountabilities to others. Operational plans help leaders determine which work processes need to be monitored and guide progress evaluation by indicating when key action steps should be initiated or completed. Problem solving helps ensure that operations are not disrupted for too long and that plan implementation stays on track.

One example that illustrates the interrelationships among the efficiency-oriented behaviors involves a Japanese-owned pharmaceutical company that developed a drug to treat problems associated with aging. High demand for the drug put tremendous strain on the company's manufacturing facilities. The vice president of operations realized that it would take a highly organized effort to ensure sufficient supplies to meet the aggressive sales projections coming out of the field. The vice president worked with his leadership team to set specific productivity and quality goals for the year and identify the actions required to make those goals a reality. The team recognized the importance of establishing detailed production schedules so that everyone understood what to do, why it needed to be done, and when it needed to be done. After the goals and plans were formulated for the operations unit, they were translated into specific actions for each department and reviewed to ensure interdepartmental coordination. The people in each department set their own individual targets for the year, aligning them with the department's and the company's overall objectives. Periodic meetings were held to review progress, solve problems, and identify opportunities for the continuous improvement of production and work processes. Production quality and quantity were monitored daily to ensure targets were being achieved. If any deviations from established standards were discovered during these daily meetings, the team mobilized immediately to identify the cause and develop solutions to get production or quality back on track. The vice president of operations also kept in constant contact with the sales organization to ensure he had the most recent forecasts and organizational commitments. In this way, adjustments to production levels and quality could also occur on a planned basis.

TIME TO FOCUS

The OnPoint Consulting survey revealed a significant gap between strategy development and strategy execution in organizations. Even more dismaying, however, is the apparent lack of confidence among leaders that their organizations will be able to close this gap. By focusing on the four leadership behaviors described in this article, leaders can increase their chances of translating strategy into successful business results.

Making Strategy Real: Bringing People Together Toward a Common Cause

Katherine Beatty and Laura Quinn

The hardest part of strategic leadership is getting people throughout the organization—from the executive team to the people on the front lines—to think and act similarly when making or carrying out strategy, even as the business environment continually places new demands on the organization. For leaders, closing the gap between strategy and execution requires focusing on clear priorities, creating common understanding through real dialogue, and engendering a learning orientation in the organization.

As a leader facing the increasingly complex challenges of today's and tomorrow's business environment, have you ever found yourself thinking like this?

The competitive environment is more complex today than ever before.

Globalization has raised competition in our industry to an unprecedented level.

Today's challenges require more creative solutions and more complex organizations than I can ever remember.

Our customers' needs are becoming harder and harder to meet.

If you are like most leaders, your answer to our question is yes. None of these developments are exactly breaking news, yet today's leaders are just scratching the surface of meeting the challenges posed for their organizations. Perhaps the preeminent challenge is finding a way to close the gap between a well-thought-out business strategy and effective implementation of that strategy. Many organizations find it difficult to get all their people—no matter how smart and talented they are—to work together toward an overall strategy.

CCL, in its work with strategic leaders, has found that the hardest work of strategic leadership is getting people throughout the organization—from the executive team to the people on the front lines—to think and act similarly when making and carrying out strategy, even as the business environment continually places new demands on the organization.

For example, in the course of CCL's Developing the Strategic Leader (DSL)—a program for upper-level executives and

senior leaders whose work has long-term strategic implications for their organizations—participants are asked to answer these questions:

- What is the major challenge you face personally in becoming a better strategic leader?
- What is the major challenge your organization faces in the area of strategic thinking and planning?

CCL analyzed the responses of 291 executives who attended DSL. The categories that emerged were varied and complex. For example, strategic leaders frequently struggle with the challenge of influencing and communicating with others—trying to bring people together toward a common cause so that work is coordinated. Additionally, strategic leaders are challenged by the need to advance the *entire* organization, not just their own particular units. As the scope of work increases, new skills and processes and a better climate for developing and implementing strategy are required.

At the heart of leading the *entire* organization lies a barrier: the sheer difficulty of getting alignment throughout a broad entity. CCL has talked with executives who perceived that their counterparts in other parts of the organization were not aligning their activities. In some cases the resulting frustration ran so deep that it turned into real conflict and the labeling of a colleague as someone who was "just working her own agenda at the expense of others" or who "just cannot think beyond the silo."

Were these people really just out for themselves? Were they really incompetent? Of course, people with questionable intentions or inadequate skills do at times rise up in organizations. But more often, in CCL's experience, lack of alignment is a result of other, more subtle but powerful reasons.

Uncovering and remedying these reasons is where the work of the strategic leader begins. Strategic leaders must ensure that people have clear, shared priorities. They must work to develop a climate that generates common understanding. And they must create a learning orientation throughout the organization. These goals should not be approached sequentially; in fact, strategic leaders need to work to achieve them all simultaneously.

KEY DRIVERS

One of the best ways to ensure alignment throughout the organization is to set clear priorities and ensure they are understood. When all goals are perceived as equally important, urgent, and critical, people often have the misconception that all the work can get done if it is just sequenced correctly. The reality more often than not is that people's efforts and other resources just get diluted. When resources are limited—as they almost always are—most if not all of the goals do not receive the necessary attention. In fact efforts to achieve them may even work against each other.

One DSL participant said that the biggest challenge to working strategically in his organization was "coordination of each vice president's strategic and personal agendas to coincide with regional and global initiatives. Huge difficulties arise out of different objectives and priorities in each VP's organization."

Picture a massive and complex game of tug-of-war with no overarching goal: people work passionately to achieve their own goals but pull in different directions. It's hard for the whole organization to move forward under such circumstances.

So how do leaders set priorities at the organizational level? It starts with a common understanding of the key strategic drivers of the organization and the relative priority among these drivers. Strategic drivers are the determinants of long-term, competitive success for a particular organization in a particular industry; they are also known as factors of competitive success, key success factors, and key value propositions. Organizations typically have no more than three to five strategic drivers at any one time, a subset of the factors on which different companies in the industry compete. The key strategic drivers should represent the factors the organization has chosen to invest in and excel at in order to compete in the industry.

For example, the freight and delivery industry has a number of key strategic drivers. Some companies focus on price, speed of delivery, or global reach. Trucking company YRC chooses to compete on two other drivers: on-time delivery and reliability. The company learned that its customers value these attributes above all others: they want their goods delivered at the promised times (even if transit time is a bit slower than the competition's), and they want their goods to arrive undamaged. The YRC example highlights an important characteristic of strategic drivers: they reflect a deep understanding of the customer, the industry, the organization's current capabilities, and the capabilities it will need in the future.

FIRST THINGS FIRST

Once strategic drivers are understood, they need to be prioritized. Which single driver is most important? Which is second most important? The tendency is to say they are all equally important, but this is dangerous and can lead to a strategy that attempts to be everything to everyone. The reason for identifying a relatively small number of drivers and prioritizing them is to ensure that the organization becomes focused on the pattern of inherently limited investments that will give the greatest strategic leverage. Strategic leaders must make tough decisions so they can allocate resources efficiently. And they need to do so in a way that gets everyone on the same page about the prioritization.

ON THE SAME PAGE

So a key task of strategic leaders is to set clear priorities. But the real challenge for the top team and the organization lies in following through. In the end, do people have a common understanding of the priorities? Are the priorities communicated in consistent ways throughout the organization? Is everyone really on the same page?

Getting everyone aligned is a challenge for many reasons. First, people naturally have different theories, opinions, and experiences, which lead them to think differently about what makes the business successful and therefore what the strategic drivers are and should be. Often these differences are linked to the functional areas where people were trained.

In one of CCL's strategic leadership business simulations, people in marketing roles argued vehemently for additional investments in marketing that they said were sure to result in increased market share. But in reality, much must happen in conjunction with other areas of the organization for any investment in marketing to be worthwhile. Because people have such different backgrounds and experiences and come together with different information, they are naturally going to hold different ideas or theories about what will make the business successful. Therefore, *how* you go about having the conversations about priorities is critically important.

Leaders have often been trained to get their position across to others and get these others to buy into that position. Operating in this way has rewarded leaders, allowing them to stand out, be seen, and have a clear impact in their organizations. But this strength can become a weakness when the buy-in is for a specific organizational function rather than overall priorities. It can also be a weakness when an executive is so intent on influencing others to get on board with a position that he or she misses opportunities to listen and learn from others and to broaden his or her own view.

Consider the example of a top leadership team. It can be tough for this group to work as a true team, in part because team members are generally accountable as a group for the outcomes of the team's work (in this case the success of the organization). But most executives have excelled by being held accountable as individuals for the success of their units. It takes a major reorientation in mind-set to rely so much on others and collaborate with others for one's success. Ultimately, these executives need to be willing to be open to influence from others and to shift their own positions—because the best strategic positions are richer, fuller, and more exciting than any position any single person has put forth. How does a team or group of executives work to achieve this common understanding? It comes largely through genuine dialogue. In such a conversation, people

- Spend as much energy listening to and understanding others as they do helping others to understand them.
- Share openly and freely their hopes, worries, feedback, and thoughts, and do this in a constructive way.
- Hold a complex issue open to conversations and deliberation, without rushing to an answer.
- Work to learn from others, rather than always trying to get others to adopt their views.
- Walk away with a fuller understanding of the situation than they walked in with.

A simple way to gauge your own ability to enter into and engender this kind of dialogue is to count the number of inquiries you make during a meeting and compare that to the number of declarative statements you make. People with the power to engender dialogue spend at least as much time asking questions as they do providing answers.

A LEARNING PROCESS

The process of understanding strategic drivers and establishing priorities may take some time—it isn't easily sorted in a two-day, off-site meeting. Rather it requires actions over the course of months or even years, and then the organization must be able to learn from and respond to the consequences of those actions.

Formulating strategy is not an event followed by implementation. It is a learning process, much like the scientific process of hypothesis testing. Leaders, ideally with input from stakeholders, formulate theories about what it will take for the organization to be successful in its particular environment; they then test their theories using, in effect, business experiments in which they implement tactics arising from those theories. Through these experiments everyone in the organization learns about what is and is not working, and the leaders use that new information to amend their theories of the business.

This kind of language may sound strange when applied to business because it suggests that we don't know for sure what will make an organization succeed in the long run. That can be a scary proposition: the stakes are high in business—people's jobs and sometimes even their lives are dependent on leaders being right. In this environment being right can become the force behind leaders' words, actions, and reactions to others. Unfortunately, a perceived need to be right can also create a culture where the process of learning is significantly undervalued.

Following are two examples of language that indicates strategy is seen as an event in the organization rather than as a learning process:

- "The top team is away at their annual off-site meeting setting the strategy for the next three years." When strategy is set at an event, it may be revisited periodically, but where is the window of opportunity for *really* changing the strategy if new information arises? In what ways does the planning and budgeting cycle handcuff the organization and result in a lack of flexibility?
- "The new CEO has come in and is ready to unveil her strategy." Why is the organization's strategy associated with a particular person? This suggests ownership by that person, with the result that change may be difficult to implement until that person is gone. Review your own organization's history: how often has a shift in strategy been associated with a change in top leadership? If your answer is "frequently" or "usually," you are not alone.

Crafting strategy should be more of a discovery process than a process of determination—that is, rather than relying on a leader, especially a new leader, to put his or her personal mark on the organization's strategy, organizations discover their best strategies over a period of years, and these strategies reflect more about what is happening in the industry than they do about who is in charge at the top.

TO THE CORE

Strategic leaders are able to close the strategy-execution gap by focusing on clear priorities, creating common understanding through real dialogue, and engendering a learning orientation in the organization. When these things happen, strategy is a shared understanding that exists in the fabric of the organization.

Knowing and Doing: How to Put Learning Where the Work Is

Frank P. Bordonaro

The idea that knowing and doing should be tightly linked may seem like a management no-brainer. But progress in putting learning more directly on the path of work has been slowed by conventional thinking. How can leaders move learning to the places and people where it can most powerfully further the strategy of the company? First, they must put aside old habits and form a new perspective about where the most important learning takes place.

Where else would one want to have learning occur than at the places where it can most directly lead to better performance? For centuries people have been learning in studios, laboratories, and fabrication plants under tutelage and with tools and materials in their hands. During the Renaissance, plaster sculptures were hauled from one painting salon to another so students could use them as models while master painters coached. Similar arrangements connecting learning and work have developed in the crafts, skilled labor, and to some degree the sciences.

What about business? The idea that knowing and doing should be linked in the management and professional ranks is only now coming into its own. The obvious common sense of such linkage is still rarely discussed among leaders in most corporations. For the learning strategist, that spells opportunity.

Why has corporate executive education been separated from the work to begin with? In general, management and professional skills have not originated from the hands-on, applied branch of education. They have instead been an outgrowth of a second model, based on university traditions. Preparation for business leadership, like preparation for other socially elevated roles, has been thought to result from a long socialization process wherein conceptual material is read about, discussed, and explored by extended example. Even in today's better university executive programs and in corporate learning centers, management learners work under an implied *absorb-store-apply* model.

What is the practical implication of this? If you are a human resource or learning executive sitting in a corporate office, you are probably in charge of the most senior training and learning going on in the company. That's a nice opportunity for leverage but it's also a limitation. It means you have inherited the second model, the one removed from the work. You may even be in charge of a corporate university, a name that speaks volumes about the underlying model. And there is a further, closely connected barrier between you and the points of action: hierarchy. Senior people are organizationally distant from customers. So you are not only removed from the work in time and space but the roles of your audience lack the immediacy of customer impact. In a fast-moving world, this is a box you don't want to be in. After all, someone is in charge of learning that happens close to customers, and if it is based on local traditions and parochial impulses, if it is removed from the rallying cry of the company, then it too has disadvantages.

This article is about helping leaders of learning to break out of the historical box that confines them to the absorb-store-apply model and to move learning to the places and the people where it can most powerfully further the strategy of the company.

The timing is good to make such a shift. Recent advances in technology and the effects of financial struggles in the corporate world have conspired to bring about some refreshing departures from old habits. As the pace of work has increased and reinvention cycles have been shortened, the pressures to *use what I know* and *learn things I can use now* have increased. That's why the recent spate of innovations in *simultaneous knowing and doing* is welcome.

Thanks to these beginnings, today's learning planners are in a position to seek competitive advantages for their companies through thoughtful adaptations of these new practices.

PLANNING STEPS

But where to begin? The simple call to put *learning where the work is* won't help much if the work is happening everywhere. A few simple planning steps are needed:

First, assume for planning purposes that the rest of the organization exists to help the people on the customer front to win. Then lay out the other important work in order of its organizational distance from the customer.

This means you need to look at the organization horizontally instead of vertically. Picture the enterprise as a chain of four interconnected zones of work.

In Zone 1, *the customer front*, people have a number of ways in which they engage, secure commitments from, and retain relationships with customers. Typically, these customer facers locate, inform, educate, listen, counsel, interpret needs, set expectations, and exchange promises.

Zone 2, *operations*, is about servicing and supporting what is happening at the customer front: distributing information and communication devices, formalizing and recording commitments, converting verbal and written transactions into monetary ones, and carrying out follow-up activities with both customers and customer-facing individuals. This zone is also a carrier of messages (such as regulations and pricing policy changes) from further inside the organization and sometimes monitors Zone 1 activities on behalf of management.

Zone 3, *finding market opportunities and creating and designing products*, is concerned with offering products and devising services of potential value to customers. This is about scanning the universe of potential customers and, considering what the organization can reasonably expect to provide, selecting the markets and the value propositions that will be offered to them. Decisions made here end up placing customer facers in front of certain customers instead of others and with certain products and services instead of others. Depending on the industry, these products and services range widely, from financial abstractions to new tire treads, but the idea is to assemble and reassemble whatever existing or new parts one can get one's hands on and create something of potential value to a customer in a selected market.

Zone 4 is *interpreting reality and allocating resources*. This is the business of the top brass and their supporting experts.

ON THE PATH

These definitions ought to sound familiar; they account for most of the work that goes on to bring value to customers. They do not say much about work done just to maintain an organization's existence, which represents a huge share of most companies' resources. Those kinds of work have been purposely, if only temporarily, swept aside. Why? Because we tend to gravitate toward them when we plan learning, which is why corporate learning functions are so often preoccupied with supervision, management, and leadership. The point is not to discount the importance of those undertakings but *to encourage more concern for work that is directly on the path leading to the all-important customer.*

Consider the total learning field of play just described and use it to make an inventory of the learning investments going on in your organization today (staff, curriculum, population served, and gross annual dollars). This inventory may be as detailed as you like or it may be approximate. The idea is to get a feel for the distribution of resources being invested in the work that is on the path to the customer.

You might try this simple approach. Devote a single sheet of paper to each of your businesses. For each business, divide the sheet into rectangles, with each rectangle representing a zone of work (1 through 4). Now adjust the size of each rectangle to show the degree to which changes in role, process, and performance in each zone are important to the business strategy. For example, if the strategy calls for a shift in distribution channels but not a shift in products or markets, Zones 1 and 2 would become larger than Zones 3 and 4.

Within each rectangle, draw a circle to indicate the dollar amount currently spent annually on learning. Size the circles so you can compare at a glance the amounts spent in each zone. Inside each circle, put the current headcount for learning, training, and development. This exercise can give you a feel for allocations and misalignments quickly.

Next, make note of where across these zones your present corporate learning function has control and accountability. The common arrangement is for Zone 4 to be the concern of more senior positions, whereas Zones 3 and 2 are the concern of divisional and functional learning groups, and Zone 1 is in the control of local (operating unit) management. In companies dominated by a retail business model, the corporate office may be in charge of local training, and there are all kinds of matrix arrangements. For the moment, however, we are trying to answer basic questions:

- As we look at the learning work being done in the zones, where do we seem to be best addressing performance needs? Where do we fall short? Where are we uncertain of learning effectiveness?
- In light of the company's rallying cry, how would learning resources ideally be allocated, regardless of who is in charge of them?
- Which specific kinds of work and which target populations in each zone are most important to the strategy of the business?

NEW GROUND

Here are some examples, one for each zone, of companies that have begun to move learning and work closer together:

Zone 1: Century 21

Century 21, a residential real-estate powerhouse, with 88,000 brokers, knows all about the challenges of running a complex learning support system at the customer front. Before the company reinvented its field training, a staff of 4,500 trainers swarmed the 6,600-office operation, running classrooms of franchisees through manuals produced by a large central staff. Today, just 150 roving "master trainers," who collaborate with local manager-coaches and a handful of central-office designers, handle the same massive learning task. The learning load grows daily. To compete, brokers need skills in presentation software, digital photography, Web-based advertising, and wireless office management, to name just a few. Century 21's system handles it all.

How does the company do it? First, it figured out which content was absolutely crucial for brokers to produce income. All learning content and objectives were then geared to that simple goal. Media selections were made with an eye to optimum value and ease of distribution (for instance, no streaming video when stored video would do). The learning group made access easy, offering 120 hours of free online learning; holding live, online classes; and making virtual classroom learning at home an attractive option.

The company's final results are hard to fault. Attrition, the cost monster of all storefront businesses, was cut in half in the first two years of operation, while agent income grew by 16 percent. All of this saw the firm through a 145 percent expansion of agent population. The cost of training ran above prior years in the inaugural cycle, then dipped below historical levels—and stayed there.

Zone 2: Xerox

In the early 2000s, Xerox, which was determined to hang onto its next-generation executive talent, wanted to revise its methods of developing emerging leaders. Like many corporations, Xerox found value in deploying talented junior executives to tackle a host of internal issues. Operations supporting customer-facing groups were included in the problem-solving agenda. In pursuit of better efficiencies and longer reach for the action-learning model, Xerox brought in a longtime leadership development partner, CCL, to help out. CCL joined Xerox in taking a firm step into cyberspace. CCL recast the classic action-learning model as a blend of learning modalities. In-person interactions are now reserved for problem selection, team building, online workspace practice, presentations, and proposals. Online work is sandwiched between face-to-face sessions. Self-assessment tools have been repurposed for desktop use, and most of the project work is performed on-line by the geographically dispersed teams.

By orchestrating the modules for mutual support and providing coaches and tutorial help, the new model is achieving efficiencies. A six-month program replaced an earlier two-year version, and delivery and tuition costs have been reduced by 60 percent.

Zone 3: S. C. Johnson

Few consumer product companies can rival the brand and product production records of S. C. Johnson. Yet company insiders can tell you that the business of developing fresh ideas into popular products—much less doing so while servicing the tastes and customs of consumers in more than fifty countries—is a tall task. Scientists, marketers, country managers, financial analysts, and a host of others must fulfill individual roles while pursuing, in cooperation with others, a fierce desire to innovate for the worldwide market.

The first step in the process of moving learning and work closer together was to rethink the coordination of separate groups as a design problem, with creation of customer value as the end product and a small team representing the specialist groups as the operating engine. The company elicited help from outside experts who could blend knowledge of product development processes with expertise in group dynamics. Time was spent selecting design-team leaders who had knowledge of the company and its processes yet could bring an off-mainstream perspective—a European executive has been placed in charge of a U.S. team, for example. In turn, leaders of all design groups are receiving special support in their roles and meet as peers to sort out issues. Meanwhile, the design team members receive crash courses in one another's specialties, to lower fences between various professional perspectives. A policy of *slowing down to gain speed* has been put into place, meaning members are prevented from making group decisions until considerable front-end learning has been completed. Finally, the teams use rigorous decision-making and resource commitment processes.

One lesson from this example is that certain irreducible learning features tend to come together in Zone 3: the conception of the small work team as a performing unit, the dual-track attention to content and process, the practice of sharing expert information (in place of exchanging expert opinions), and the role of the leader as an objective broker all play a part in the ongoing quest.

Zone 4: Ameren

The work of top executives has not been exempt from the trend toward simultaneous knowing and doing. Think, for example, of the fingertip access today's executives have to data and news from inside and outside the company. There is no doubt that globalization and the relentless progress of consolidation in market and product families have conspired to make new learning more time sensitive and more connected to topics where decisions are pending.

A concrete example of placing new learning tools in the hands of executives is provided by energy holding company Ameren, which worked with visual-learning consultants Root Learning and management consulting firm Towers Perrin to place learning directly in the path of decision making. Using specially created simulations and visual models deployed at the desktop, business unit executives are able to calculate the cash flow impact of specific decisions they are considering. Supporting tools provide insights about the broader economics of the business, preserving the larger context of individual decisions. This example offers only a glimpse of the coming changes in the daily lives of executives. Technology advancements are playing a large role in the new linkage between work and learning at senior levels.

OUT WITH THE OLD

Once you have carefully considered the total possible strategic field of play for learning and have looked at a few examples of learning as it affects different zones of the enterprise, you can make deliberate choices about your location and degree of involvement. The overall message: put aside conventional ideas about where the most important learning work takes place. The old hierarchical model poses an implicit division of labor in which corporate learning functions are preoccupied with senior training. This may not be right for your company. A good learning strategy is to hold a firm opinion about the location of critical work *in all four zones* and to lay claim to certain hot spots where learning can best be put to use. Although your work will emphatically include senior management, it must address other zones as well.

The future will bring intense competition as companies race to knock down barriers separating learning from its immediate application to the work of the moment. Staking out new learning territory across the four zones will provide a good start to setting new priorities that place your managers and leaders on the long-neglected path of applied learning.

Learning by Design: Developing an Engine for Transforming Your Company

Michael Beer and Magnus Finnström

Traditional leadership development programs often fail to achieve the desired results because they don't focus on learning linked to the company's business strategy and the real day-to-day challenges facing managers. The experience of Sweden-based industrial group Cardo, which built its executive management program from scratch, shows how organizations can unleash the leadership capabilities required to drive transformation and strengthen business results.

Few would argue that the quality of leadership at all levels can make or break efforts to transform a company. Yet if developing great leaders is so important, why do most companies get it so wrong?

All too often, leadership development programs are delegated to human resources rather than seen as a lever for the CEO to develop and mobilize individuals in pivotal roles around a transformational agenda. This lack of senior line ownership leads to a focus on classroom learning—typically led by guest star performers—rather than on learning linked to the company's business strategy and the real day-to-day challenges facing managers. This is, in effect, teaching leadership skills in the abstract rather than in the context of the organization, the team, and the high-stakes performance goals against which managers are measured. Not surprisingly, the learning doesn't stick, in part because changed people return to unchanged organizations.

Based on our research and our work with clients, we believe there is a better approach to leadership development, one that engages people in working on genuine business priorities and

learning from their attendant successes and challenges in changing their own behavior, mobilizing their teams, and aligning the organization. Through this approach, companies can unleash the leadership capabilities required to drive transformation and strengthen business results.

In our view, effective leadership development programs are based on five basic design principles:

1. They are driven from the top of the organization through the business lines (not through the HR function) and address leadership development and organizational development simultaneously. The goal is to build leaders and the organization at the same time. Although strong support from HR is key to success, top management needs to take ownership of the program and not view it as something that happens on the sidelines of the business.

2. They are linked to achieving performance outcomes that matter to the business and to participants. Taking its cue from the work of management consultant Robert Schaffer—author of *The Breakthrough Strategy: Using Short-Term Successes to Build the High Performance Organization* (Harper-Collins, 1988)—much of the learning comes through individual and team work on *breakthrough projects*. These are stretch performance challenges that can have a demonstrable impact on business results within a clearly defined timeframe.

3. They set learning in the context of the organization and the team the participant is leading. Learning to be a better leader is not about focusing strictly on one's own strengths or shortcomings and mastering a set of skills in isolation. Reflection and learning must happen at multiple levels: learning to lead the organization, the team, and oneself.

4. They create a safe environment in which leaders can have honest, collective conversations about the real challenges they face on the job. Such conversations are critical to ensuring that leaders

can get good feedback about their organizational, team, and personal leadership effectiveness and the issues that may be getting in the way of that effectiveness.

5. They connect leaders who are undergoing a similar learning process, so that they can learn from each other and build a community of practice—a shared *leadership culture*–over time. One way to do this is by enlisting participants from the early programs as coaches for those who follow.

CLOSING THE GAP

To illustrate these principles, let's look at the case of Cardo, a Sweden-based international industrial group now running the third wave of its leadership development program. Faced with a decade-long decline in performance and with no improvement in sight, top management realized that unleashing the capabilities and commitment of Cardo's leaders was the key to unleashing the capabilities and performance of the business. The performance payoff from enhanced leadership has already been enormous—a return of ten to twenty-four times the program costs.

Now, flash back to late 2005 and early 2006. Peter Aru was in his first year as CEO, with a mandate from the board to transform Cardo from a highly decentralized holding company—an agglomeration of relatively small businesses acquired over the years and never fully integrated—into a more tightly managed entity with four operating divisions. Aru recognized that successfully making the transition would require closing a major gap in leadership capabilities.

Like many other organizations, Cardo had previously run traditional leadership development programs based on classroom learning, but it had seen little impact on actual leadership behavior or business performance. This time, Aru, Anita Hebrand (senior vice president of HR), and Per-Olof Nyquist (head of organizational development) decided not to buy an off-the-shelf program but rather to build a new *executive management program*

(EMP) from scratch and to make it a program that would support the new group strategy and could evolve over time to reflect learnings from previous sessions and changed conditions.

The idea was to design a program that would establish a common language and skill base around how leaders build high-commitment, high-performance organizations. Such businesses are able to achieve sustained high levels of performance by organizing and managing so as to effectively implement their strategies; elicit uncommonly high levels of commitment from employees, customers, and other key stakeholders; and enable ongoing learning and change. The EMP was intended to achieve this by driving strategy implementation through breakthrough projects and by creating a cross-division network of top managers who could model honest communication, cooperation, and coordination.

Each program runs for thirteen to fourteen months and consists of four building blocks: goal setting and self-managed learning, in-person learning modules, action learning, and reflection and connection.

Goal Setting and Self-Managed Learning

Before attending the first in-person session, EMP participants are asked to define the key developmental objectives for their organization, for their team, and for themselves. Participants complete a *from-to* analysis at each of these three levels as prework for the program and meet with their manager to discuss their assessment and confirm their objectives before moving forward. Throughout the program, they periodically take stock of progress in making the transition to the desired end states for each level.

For example, a manager from a regional organization in Cardo's Wastewater Technology Solutions division identified instability in the inside sales and service shop operations as a key challenge to sustaining sales growth and supporting products after the sale. The organization needed to move from being reactive to proactive, the manager's team needed to shift from silo behavior to taking a comprehensive view, and the manager himself had to go from making quick assumptions and jumping to conclusions to asking more questions. To that end, the organization made a number of critical personnel changes and beefed up sales training. The team members initiated cross-department meetings to review the challenges and discuss improvement opportunities, agreed to give each other positive feedback when things were working well, and organized get-togethers outside work to allow people to get to know each other better. And the manager vowed to use more inquiry and advocacy before taking action, thereby reducing the potential for misunderstandings and defensive thinking.

In-Person Learning Modules

The program is structured around five in-person learning modules (LMs) that take place quarterly, each lasting four days. They are designed to provide participants with relevant theories, tools, and frameworks and the chance to practice using them; to allow participant follow-up and group reflection on experiences from the action learning as well as the self-managed learning that takes place between the LMs; and to prepare participants for the next phase of action learning.

LM1 provides an overview of how to build high-commitment, high-performance organizations and how to have productive conversations. LM2 focuses on leading the organization and aligning structures, systems, and capabilities to the strategy. LM3 is about leading your team and building psychological commitment. LM4 centers on leading yourself and learning and change. LM5 includes an after-action review and looking forward.

Action Learning

Action learning occurs between the learning modules and takes two primary forms. First, each participant leads two consecutive ninety-day breakthrough projects. These projects are not make-work exercises; rather they address urgent issues already on the top of the agenda for the participant and the organization and they focus on achieving a measurable performance result. Moreover, they address problems for which a solution does not currently exist—in other words, the participant and his or her team members must work together and use their collective knowledge and experience to come up with creative new solutions.

The first breakthrough project is launched immediately after LM1 and completed before LM3.

The second form of action learning is initiated after LM2. It requires each participant to engage his or her team in a strategic alignment process—such as clarifying the business priorities and the requirements of the organization—and then to engage the larger organization in commenting on this strategic direction, including the barriers to implementing it and the organizational strengths to be leveraged. This becomes a learning process for both the participant and his or her team.

With an understanding of the priorities and readiness for change emerging from this strategic alignment process, the participants then launch their second breakthrough project, which starts after LM3 and needs to be finalized before LM5.

After each breakthrough project concludes, the team conducts an after-action review, using a structured process that makes it easier for the team to honestly evaluate how things have gone, without fear of retribution or recrimination. The team members discuss five questions:

- What did we set out to do?
- What actually happened?
- Why did it happen?
- What will we do differently next time?
- How will we sustain the results and spread learning to other parts of the organization?

For example, a breakthrough project team from the Belgian unit Door & Logistics Solutions (DLS), Cardo's largest division, set two goals: to cut days of sales outstanding (DSO, or tied-up capital) by 6.5 days, or 10 percent, by the end of 2008 as compared with the DSO at the end of 2007, and to increase awareness throughout the company of the need for efficient processes to optimize working capital. As a result of the project, DSO did drop but only by four days. In terms of raising awareness, the team estimated that it had achieved 80 percent of its goal. Through the review process, the team assessed what went well (for instance, the project kickoff involved people from the entire organization) and not so well (the original target was unrealistic, for example, and some deadlines were missed, especially on tasks involving external parties). Next time, team members agreed, they would set more realistic targets, back-plan (start with the end result and work backward to determine targets, activities, and resource requirements along the way), verify resource availability upfront, be stricter about deadlines, and increase external communication. To sustain the results and spread learning, they worked to embed changes into routine processes and launched four follow-up projects.

Reflection and Connection

The Cardo program contains explicit time for *learning how to learn*—both during and between the LMs. The participants are divided into groups of four; typically each group has a mix of people from different divisions so as to support the objective of building networks across units. This also helps participants realize that they all face the same kinds of people- and process-related problems even though their businesses are different. Each group is assigned a coach, who facilitates the group members' sharing of experiences from their breakthrough projects as well as from their personal development journeys.

Of the various EMP components, Cardo participants found reflection at the individual and team levels to be the most challenging cultural change, both when they were together and back home.

Yet despite the initial reluctance by some participants, feedback from the first two groups showed that the time spent on reflection was worthwhile, and it ranked as one of the top three program components in the final debrief. According to Maria Bergving, Cardo's senior vice president of communications: "Introducing individual as well as group reflection for my team has been very positive. Reflection is the best way to learn, and by sharing achievements, successes, and failures we also learn from each other and build commitment to and understanding of our common goals."

Cardo has been able to connect people undergoing a similar learning process and to build a community of practice over time by enlisting participants from the early programs as coaches and role models for those who followed. This has not only amplified the impact of the EMP but also yielded two additional benefits. First, because program graduates get the big picture, they can put questions from later participants into a larger context, in terms of both the content and the learning journey; this aids understanding and accelerates competence development. Second, because the coaches themselves need to stay abreast of the program content, they continue to learn.

A strong community of practice also supports individuals in taking courageous initiatives. In several parts of the organization, Cardo has seen evidence of accelerated performance improvement and culture change after two or three people from the same region have attended the program and created a community-of-practice *island*. For example, Mark Driscart, the manager of DLS in Belgium, launched his own strategic alignment process after participating in the second program. He relied completely on internal support from his fellow graduates, including his manager.

FOCUS ON BUSINESS

From the start, the members of the Cardo senior team have been involved and committed to the EMP. Over time, their presence in the program has further strengthened its effect as well as their own learning journeys. Aru, the CEO, takes the program very seriously, attending the learning modules and following up personally to track the performance impact of the breakthrough projects.

The experience of Cardo's troubled DLS division illustrates the value of having senior team involvement and linking the program to core business priorities. In parallel with the EMP, the DLS senior team decided to launch a *strategic fitness process* (SFP). Through this process (which is similar to the action-learning alignment and learning process), the senior team clarified its business priorities and the organizational requirements for effective execution, then engaged the larger organization in a structured and honest dialogue around the strategic direction the senior team had defined, the barriers to implementing it, and the unrealized organizational strengths that could be built on. In response to this feedback, the senior team members showed that they were ready to accept accountability and made some tough decisions. This created a lot of momentum for the new Cardo culture and reshaped the learning context for the EMP participants from DLS.

The SFP took place right before the second breakthrough project and dramatically improved the conditions for project success. The priorities for the whole division had been clarified, and key people had been mobilized to support the change. The DLS participants gathered during LM3 and agreed that all their projects needed to be aligned with the priorities. When it came time to measure impact in LM5, much of the direct financial return came from the DLS projects launched after the SFP.

Because the EMP and SFP are both rooted in an underlying theory about what it takes to build high-commitment, high-performance organizations, it was easy to run them in parallel and easy for people to work effectively in both and to apply the learning concepts locally. This accelerated Cardo's transformation and put DLS on a faster path compared with the other divisions, a momentum that continues to this day.

FINDING SUCCESS

In terms of both the financial impact and the strategic payoff for the company, the EMP has been a resounding and immediate success. Based on the quantifiable results achieved through the breakthrough projects, the first program delivered a tenfold return on program costs; the second, a return of twenty-four times the costs. Amid the economic downturn, many of the projects have focused on freeing up working capital. As a result, though volumes are down, Cardo is enjoying increased margins and strong cash flow.

The financial return on investment is driven by a change in behavior and culture. "Among the participants we see increased collaboration across functions and geographies as well as greater sharing of best practices," observes Nyquist, the head of organizational development. "We now have sixty-two managers globally who are skilled at using the same management toolbox. There is also another level of performance focus. Breakthrough projects have become a way of approaching change for many of the participants. And when things get stuck, people engage in more open and honest conversations, which help to resolve blockages. Managers have a better understanding that their unit is part of a larger system and of how they contribute to overall effectiveness."

What's next? Cardo plans to roll out a core leadership program, built on the same principles and theories, to six hundred additional managers over the coming years. In addition, the company is initiating SFPs in two more divisions to run in parallel with the third wave of the EMP. Cardo leaders have discovered that they have expanded their capacity to drive business initiatives and are regularly finding opportunities to leverage the current wave of EMP as well as to involve previous participants.

HIGH STAKES

Our experience at Cardo and elsewhere has shown that leadership development can be a powerful engine for business transformation, but it requires going beyond traditional approaches. Only by confronting the efficacy of one's own organization within the context of its strategy and performance goals can leaders improve the quality of their management and leadership. People learn how to be effective leaders *when the stakes are high*—when they have committed to substantial improvement in their organization's performance and seek to learn what stands in the way.

However, to make this learning possible, senior line leaders need to foster a safe environment in which program participants can have honest, collective conversations about what it will take for the business to win and for them personally to be successful and energized. Leadership development can then drive organizational development, and the requirements for organizational development can shape leadership development.

Getting It Together: The Leadership Challenge of Mergers and Acquisitions

Günter K. Stahl

Mergers, acquisitions, and strategic alliances are supposed to create new, stronger organizations, but history shows that such combinations often fall far short of expectations. Cross-border integrations, such as those between Western and Eastern companies, are particularly difficult to manage. Here the CEOs of two multinational firms that have been there talk about the factors that set winning corporate combinations apart from the rest.

Every merger, acquisition, or strategic alliance promises to create value from some kind of synergy, yet statistics show that the benefits that look so good on paper often do not materialize. The result, more often than not, is value destruction. The literature on mergers and acquisitions indicates that failure rates typically range from 50 to 70 percent or even higher. A *BusinessWeek* study of megamergers conducted between 1998 and 2000 found that in more than 60 percent of the cases, shareholder value was destroyed. (Keep in mind that this was during an unprecedented boom phase when stock markets soared.) Alliances are on average more successful than mergers and acquisitions, but cross-border alliances in particular are difficult to manage, and their performance is often disappointing.

Why do so many corporate combinations that looked like such great opportunities end up in disaster? Recent research suggests that contrary to common belief, it is not poor strategic fit that most often causes mergers and acquisitions to fail but poor execution. The errors can be seen, for example, in instances of insensitive management, lack of trust building and communication, slow execution, power struggles, or a leadership vacuum following the deal. Research on alliances shows by and large a similar pattern. Even with this kind of information, most corporate combinations still place special emphasis on the strategic and financial goals of the transaction, whereas the cultural and people implications rarely receive as much attention.

To gain some insight into what sets winning corporate combinations apart from the rest and the leadership challenges involved in integrating organizations, I spoke with Carlos Ghosn, chairman and CEO of the Renault-Nissan Alliance, and Jean-Pierre Garnier, former CEO of GlaxoSmithKline and Pierre Fabre SA.

LEADERSHIP'S ROLE

"Academic scholars and most business analysts tend to view these business ventures only from financial and operational perspectives," says Ghosn. "They are often surprised when mergers struggle or even fail, when on paper they seemed sure to succeed."

Garnier concurs: "In any merger or acquisition, investment banks and equity analysts will provide you with a plethora of figures quantifying the synergistic strategic benefits of the union. Yet what determines whether a merger succeeds or fails is really its people. History, sadly, has been littered with far too many examples of failed acquisitions or mergers that did not create value for the companies involved. What lessons can we draw from them, and how can we avoid this?"

Perhaps one way to better understand what goes right or wrong in mergers, acquisitions, and strategic alliances is to first recognize how leadership plays a critical role in the process. Ghosn and Garnier shed some light on the crucial but often-neglected areas that they found needed specific attention during their experiences with mergers, acquisitions, and alliances.

"My experience with Nissan has reconfirmed my conviction that the dignity of people must be respected even as you challenge them to overturn deep-seated practices and traditions," says Ghosn. "The most fundamental challenge of any alliance or merger is cultural: if one does not believe anything can be learned from one's new partners, the venture is doomed to fail. I have always believed that an alliance, merger, or acquisition—in fact, any corporate combination—is about partnership and trust rather than power and domination."

In the Renault-Nissan Alliance, the two companies pursue synergies in several areas, including sharing the platforms on which vehicles are built. They also exchange research and technological innovations, including state-of-the-art engines, transmission engineering, and fuel cell research. To facilitate coordination and improve performance, part of the alliance integration plan called for employee exchanges between the organizations. In addition, some employees, while staying in their original companies, worked in Renault-Nissan alliance structures such as cross-company teams and functional task teams.

Yet even when common operating structures are well built and maintained, questions still arise about which identity will dominate when corporate identities are combined, coordinated, or blended. Embracing and respecting the differences between companies involved in mergers, acquisitions, or alliances goes hand-in-hand with allowing trust to grow between companies that have been, in some cases, long-time competitors.

Says Ghosn: "People will not give their best efforts if they feel that their identities are being consumed by a greater force. If any partnership or merger is to succeed, it must respect the identities and self-esteem of all the people involved. . . . Two goals—making changes and safeguarding identity—could easily come into conflict. Pursuing them both entails a difficult yet vital balancing act."

DIFFERENT CULTURES

Mergers, acquisitions, and alliances involve blending people of different corporate cultures and even various national cultures into one company, which tends to complicate matters further. Instead of melting everyone together, a leader must capitalize on the cultural differences between employees and try to diminish the psychological distances between them.

Ghosn says: "I have been asked, 'Is Renault-Nissan bicultural?' My reply is that our alliance is both global and multicultural. We are French and Japanese, certainly, but our corporate culture also includes American, Chinese, Brazilian, Mexican, and many other cultures. We are always evolving, always adapting, always pursuing synergies that will improve our performance, based on our internal learning from one another."

At the same time, whether or not a firm is multinational, the CEO must also be attentive to the internal differences in corporate culture that people feel when going through a merger or acquisition or entering an alliance.

"One of the key issues I faced with the [2000 merger of SmithKline Beecham and Glaxo Wellcome into GlaxoSmithKline] was to have employees thinking and behaving as GSK people and not Glaxo people or SmithKline people," says Garnier. "We had to decide and collectively answer some very fundamental questions from the start. Why did we exist as a business? How did we work and treat each other as colleagues? Where were we going as a business in the future? How were we going to get there?"

To answer these questions, GSK formed a corporate executive team that collected input and consultation from the various departments and eventually distilled the essence of what the new GSK stood for. The team outlined the new vision and guiding principles in a document and distributed it to all the employees. "However," Garnier adds, "these principles would have remained little more than words unless each member of the GSK family adopted them and decided to act accordingly."

REINFORCING VALUES

To drive change, the CEO must espouse visionary, or value-based, leadership. In this kind of leadership the leader reinforces the values inherent in the organization's vision and exhibits characteristics such as articulating a clear and appealing vision; using strong, expressive forms of communication to do so; displaying strong self-confidence and confidence in the attainment of the vision; communicating high expectations for followers and confidence in their abilities; role-modeling behaviors that emphasize and reinforce the values inherent in the vision; and empowering people to achieve the vision.

One can see that some of these concepts have been applied by Garnier, for example, when he set forth GSK's mission: "to improve the quality of life by enabling people to do more, feel better, and live longer." He also took it upon himself to communicate the company's spirit in a broadcast to all GSK employees. The message was straightforward: deliver performance with integrity.

"Performance with integrity for GSK meant not taking shortcuts or pride in the way we generated profits for shareholders," Garnier says. "When faced with a choice of either maximizing profits for the company or doing good, we would choose to do good first. Of course, words had to be backed up by action in order to be credible and to demonstrate that we walk our talk."

The action was visible in part in the company's efforts to provide low-cost drugs to poor, developing nations. Garnier says, "We also committed ourselves to an ambitious program, in conjunction with the World Health Organization and regional institutions, to eradicate lymphatic filariasis, a grievous disease afflicting the poor in underdeveloped countries, as a public health problem by 2020."

These elements, coupled with communication of the company's core values (innovation, performance, integrity, passion, and commitment), enabled GSK employees and stakeholders to understand how their roles in the company could affect people's lives. "This was something that everyone understood, and it served to energize our people and create excitement for the new company," Garnier says. "More important, employees would get a chance to participate in the process of executing the winning game plan that was being created."

This approach has helped the company advance in achieving its strategic goals, which include becoming the indisputable leader in the pharmaceutical industry—but again, not at any price, only within GSK's value system.

Ghosn also exemplifies value-based leadership. He says Nissan's mission is to provide "unique and innovative automotive products and services that deliver superior measurable values to all the stakeholders in alliance with Renault," and its vision is "enriching people's lives." In addition to the value created through its core business, Nissan is exploring many community-based activities, some designed to encourage and develop young people's creativity and others aimed at promoting better understanding of environmental protection. The company's philanthropic work, which is focused toward education, the environment, and humanitarian relief, includes raising its employees' awareness of community involvement and partnering with various nonprofit organizations. For example, about twenty students participate each year in the Nissan-NPO Learning Scholarship Program, which was established to help students develop knowledge and management skills by interning in specialized environments. The goal is to promote human resource development.

Reinforcing his belief in making the company's values a reality (another quality of value-based leadership), Ghosn made headlines worldwide as he laid his job on the line in October 1999, declaring that he and his management team would resign if Nissan did not fulfill any of the critical commitments of the Nissan Revival Plan, which was aimed at breathing new life into the company. He set out clearly marked progress measures in the three-year plan, so that the change process would be transparent and understandable for everyone involved. When the Nissan Revival Plan commitments were delivered one year ahead of schedule, that plan was immediately followed by the NISSAN 180 plan, which is described by the company as "a comprehensive blueprint for Nissan's continuing revival, calling for growth, profit, and zero debt." In the first two years of NISSAN 180, two of the three commitments (an 8 percent operating profit margin and zero net automotive debt) have already been attained.

BUILDING THE NEW

Given their high failure rates, mergers, acquisitions, and alliances can be rather frightening propositions for those involved. Even though there is no standard for success in building harmonious organizations, understanding the role of leadership in the process can help the numbers of merger, acquisition, and alliance success stories proliferate.

Garnier says GSK has been fortunate in that it has a heritage of managing alliances and mergers. "Each of these occasions has represented an opportunity for us to learn and improve," he says. "One big lesson: build a truly new company that is different from either of its predecessors. After all, we can hardly hope to build a new company if we are duplicates of each other."

Analyze This: Six Steps to Leveraging People Investments

Scott Mondore, Shane Douthitt, and William A. Gentry

Connecting employee data on such things as skills, behaviors, attitudes, competencies, and demographics to tangible outcomes is not so difficult that it should preclude leaders from attempting to focus on it. A six-step process can help leaders discover the people drivers in their organizations.

Whether the economy is strong or weak, leaders must constantly look for competitive advantages to ensure success for their organizations. Maximizing the performance of people has typically been an elusive factor in organizational success. It is not easy to show the return on investment of people initiatives and to demonstrate a cause-and-effect connection between people data and organizational outcomes. It has become a cliché for leaders to say that "our people are our most important asset," but leaders rarely if ever back up that statement with any data or analysis. Ironically, those "most important assets" are the first to be cut when the economy slows down.

If we accept that the links between employees' behaviors, skills, abilities, and attitudes on the one hand and organizational outcomes on the other can be recognized and quantified—and that we can examine those links more closely to discover the specific drivers of organizational outcomes—we should consider the resulting benefits to organizations:

1. Dollars being spent today on the wrong employee initiatives (such as the latest "silver bullets" that promise to make

employees more engaged and productive) can be reinvested in more beneficial employee initiatives—specifically, ones that affect critical organizational metrics and outcomes.

2. People investments based on strong analytics will result in specific, tangible outcomes that benefit customers, shareholders, and employees.

3. Returns on investments in people—the impact of those investments on the organization's bottom or top line—can be quantified, monitored, and tracked.

4. Human resource departments can be held accountable for affecting organizational outcomes, the same way line-of-business or product leaders are held accountable.

5. People investments will be seen as tangible because the numerous impacts of people investments on organizational outcomes can be quantified. Leaders will then look to HR as a real player in the organization and will include HR in devising organizational strategy.

6. Last but not least, after all this work with analytics and investments, employees might just end up being "satisfied."

There are even more benefits, but these six alone are compelling enough to encourage organizations to apply the approach outlined here.

GOING FOR IT

Connecting employee data on such things as skills, behaviors, attitudes, competencies, and demographics to tangible outcomes is not so difficult that it should preclude leaders from attempting to focus on it. It does take advanced statistical knowledge, but this should not be a strong enough barrier to keep leaders from taking on the challenge and realizing the opportunities. We have put together a six-step process that you can use to discover the people drivers in your organization. Though this process incorporates advanced statistical analytics, what is more important is that it is made up of many organizational development and change methodologies with which most leaders are already familiar.

Step 1: Determine Critical Outcomes

An organization must first determine the top two or three critical outcomes or priorities that it anticipates will be accomplished through its employees. For example, outcomes such as improved sales, productivity, and customer satisfaction and reduced turnover and incidence of errors are commonly desired. These outcomes can be gleaned by reviewing strategic documents and plans. Interviews of key stakeholders such as board members, the CEO and CFO, and other organizational leaders, such as the director of sales, are also useful in the process. Once this information has been collected and summarized, the outcomes identified must be prioritized; the top two or three will then be included in the analysis. It is a near certainty that the organization's level of focus on these outcomes will change year by year, but it is helpful to maintain some consistency in order to track progress and keep the organization as focused as possible. A disciplined approach to measurement and analysis year to year is important for gleaning all the benefits from this process. Ideally, the same two or three outcomes will be critical to the organization year to year.

Step 2: Create a Cross-Functional Data Team

Once the owners of the critical organizational metrics have been identified, a cross-functional data team needs to be organized. This team should consist of the appropriate statistical and measurement experts, key line-of-business leaders or metric owners, and HR leaders who own the people data. The measurement experts are needed to determine the data required to empirically link the necessary data sets, and then to conduct the necessary statistical analyses. Leaders may also find it necessary to make adjustments to the existing measurement approach for the critical outcome measures. Measurement characteristics such as the level or frequency of measurement may need to be altered in order to make the appropriate linkages across the various data points. This cross-functional team should also facilitate and sponsor the analytics initiative. Therefore it is important to include in this process organizational leaders with influence and decision-making authority in order to facilitate buy-in.

Step 3: Assess Measures of Critical Outcomes

Once leaders have convened the cross-functional data team and identified the two or three most critical outcomes, the next step is to understand how data are currently captured in the organization. For example, most organizations measure customer satisfaction at regular intervals, such as monthly, quarterly, or annually. Several characteristics of each outcome measure must be assessed:

- The level of measurement (such as by work unit, by line of business, or by organizational level)
- The organizational owners of each outcome measure (such as the department or leader of customer satisfaction measurement)

- The frequency of measurement (such as monthly, quarterly, or annually)

It is critical to understand each of these measurement characteristics before making any linkages to people data. Ideally, measures will be "apples to apples," with the people data being measured at the same level and frequency as the outcome data.

Step 4: Objectively Analyze Key Data

Advanced statistical knowledge plays a key role in this step of the process, where the various data sets are empirically linked via statistical methodologies. Many large organizations employ statisticians or social scientists with a statistical background. Hiring a consultant or full-time statistician for this step is necessary if your organization currently doesn't have this type of resource. Most leaders are familiar with the concepts of relationships (via correlation) and prediction (via regression) but are likely not familiar with a more advanced and far more robust technique called *structural equation modeling*. Correlation is not sufficient. Regression is inadequate. Structural equation modeling is the preferred approach for the types of data linkage analyses needed here, as causality can be inferred and measurement error can be taken into account. Structural equation modeling might allow leaders to state, for example, that particular employee attitudes about work-life balance are a causal driver of increased customer satisfaction. When leaders make people-related investments, they want a level of certainty similar to what they have when they make capital investments. Structural equation modeling also makes it possible to use implied causality for calculating return on investment.

The statistical component of this step sounds complicated but is really just a tool for accomplishing three things:

- Understanding the relationship between meaningful outcomes and employee data

- Prioritizing specific types of interventions that will lead to meaningful outcomes
- Estimating return on investment to determine the levels of investments to be made and the expected returns

This work is designed to enable leaders to discover which levers to pull, from a people perspective, and how much to invest in each area. The final results generated from these employee data analyses will be the priorities that will drive the desired outcomes. For example, the analyses might show leaders that increasing managers' competencies around executing effectively will lead to increased cost effectiveness and customer satisfaction and decreased employee turnover—and by how much.

Step 5: Build the Program and Execute

Once the critical drivers of meaningful outcomes have been identified, the next step is to implement the types of interventions that will have the desired effect. This stage of the action-planning phase can be focused at the system (organization-wide) level, the line-of-business level, or the work-unit level. Even without analytics, this step encompasses the largest amount of work for leaders. The investments that are being made are focused on those employee demographics, processes, and attitudes that have a proven, empirical impact on the organization's desired outcomes, as gleaned from the previous step. In this process, an expected return can be used to guide the amount of investment made on a particular intervention. Basically, leaders can move away from just taking action to try to make employees happier and move toward investing in their people to provide greater shareholder value.

Organizational leaders who focus on people as a priority have likely developed a strong process for action planning at all levels. The key to implementing this approach is to leverage any existing, useful processes and at the same time enhance them. For example, leaders may be effective at incorporating an efficient process and tools for action planning at the work-unit level but less effective at the overall system level. It is often the case that leaders will push results of people analyses to individual managers, who then own the action-planning process for their departments. Solid action planning for leaders requires action planning at both the work-unit level and the system level. Using analytics to prove the worth of people initiatives will result in buy-in from senior leaders to implement the initiatives systemwide.

One trap during this step is the temptation for leaders to look for a people intervention that is a silver bullet. Best practices are great for guiding some aspects of action planning. However, leaders who simply replicate others' best practices will not get their organizations very far. This concept holds true for the diagnostic steps as well as the intervention steps. Analyses that were conducted at other organizations, even ones similar to your own, will not necessarily yield the same results for your organization. There is no one size-fits-all analysis or intervention.

Leaders need to understand that their people interventions must be based on their own organization-specific analytics, customized, and placed in the context of their organization's unique culture. Creating a sense of urgency around building and executing an intervention requires that leaders provide clear expectations for the return on investment and tangible goals, tied to performance incentives.

Step 6: Measure and Adjust

The final step is establishing strong routines in measurement and assessment by re-measuring to examine progress and calculate return on investment. Most leaders understand the importance of measurement and setting goals; they also understand the importance of creating a culture of accountability. For example, measuring employee attitudes through an employee survey every three years does not create a sense of accountability among leaders regarding these attitudes. Maintaining a culture of accountability is the primary reason that customer satisfaction is measured nearly continuously in most organizations. Similarly, financials are not reported only on an annual basis, and with good reason. Leaders do not need organization-wide employee attitude surveys every month, but measuring those attitudes annually is a reasonable increment for creating accountability. Learning management systems provide employee training data at a high frequency of measurement, usually in real time. In those cases where high-frequency measurement is available, a leader's ability to drive accountability and monitor progress is improved.

As is the case with any organizational initiative, leaders must be able (and willing) to make adjustments based on the results from analytics and measurement. Most leaders understand that change is frequent in any business environment or economy and that the level of people's impact on important outcomes can shift as situations change. Select two or three priorities and build action plans around those priorities. Measure the organization's progress against those plans (at both the work-unit and system levels) two or three more times, then recalculate the data set linkages and reprioritize. Leaders should conduct this analysis process, and it should be done annually for maximum effect.

GETTING FOCUSED

Leaders spend numerous days discussing succession planning, benefits, talent management, compensation, 401(k) plans, training plans, and so on, and such strategy and budgeting meetings regarding people investments have the potential to be effective at plotting a course for the coming year that will drive outcomes. Unfortunately, such meetings also have the potential to turn into discussions that focus solely on finding ways to cut costs from the HR budget. This is a fact of life because it is likely that every function will be asked to cut costs, particularly when economic downturns occur. Where HR is viewed only as a cost function, cost cutting will be the only topic that leaders discuss. Conversely, leaders who use the described analytical process to unveil the critical levers that can be pulled to positively affect organizational outcomes will see HR as a key function, one that drives strategy and incorporates investments that are based on analytics and return on investment.

Strategic planning is never easy, and it is made more difficult for leaders when HR is not aligned with their strategies. The stakeholder interviews that leaders should conduct at early steps in the process will provide a basis for aligning the strategic-planning process with the rest of the organization's priorities. After implementing this process, which will show leaders where the strongest and most effective investments in people should be made, strategic-planning meetings can be focused on how to leverage investments in people to add to the financial health of the organization, as opposed to how much can be cut out of the HR budget this year. In serious economic situations, cost cuts will be necessary; the process of prioritizing investments in people, however, will show leaders where to cut and where to invest most effectively.

Leaders can also align the six-step process with their strategic-planning process. Leaders typically conduct an annual strategic- and financial-planning process, starting approximately one quarter before the beginning of the next fiscal year. We recommend that this process of identifying critical people levers be performed during that planning process. The analyses should be conducted three to four months before the beginning of the fiscal year. This will give leaders enough time to complete all the steps in the process and make decisions on prioritizing their focus. The results of the process will inform strategy, metric setting, and budgeting for people initiatives, so it is appropriate for leaders to incorporate the process into their existing strategic-planning process. This ensures that people initiatives will be aligned with key organization-wide strategic priorities, will be funded appropriately, and will be associated with an expected return on investment. When this occurs, people investments are clearly linked to the strategic priorities of the organization.

Leadership is about using information to drive action. People investments should be a part of this protocol. The six-step process can help leaders prioritize their people initiatives, based on analytics and return on investment. It may be a broad shift in an organization's typical approach to people investments, but it is a necessary one to gain competitive advantage.

Leading Together: Complex Challenges Require a New Approach

Wilfred H. Drath

Leadership has become more difficult because of challenges that are not just complicated but also unpredictable. Such challenges demand that people and organizations fundamentally change, and make it virtually impossible for an individual leader to accomplish the work of leadership. What is needed is a more inclusive and collective leadership, a prospect that although difficult to achieve holds much potential.

People in organizations want and need to work together effectively and productively. Individuals long to be part of a bigger picture that connects them to a larger purpose. This is what they expect leadership to accomplish. They expect leadership to create the direction, alignment, and commitment that will enable them, working together, to achieve organizational success.

The trouble is, it's getting harder and harder to make this happen. Creating direction, alignment, and commitment—the work of leadership—is becoming more difficult than ever. There are a number of reasons for this. As organizations break down functional silos and develop greater global reach, people more often work with others who are not like them. It's harder to get people who don't share a common set of values and perspectives to get behind a common direction, to align, and to commit to one another.

Adding to this difficulty, people don't work side by side as much anymore. People working together might be scattered over several regions and time zones, even over different countries. Subtle and not-so-subtle barriers to communication and trust are created by the lack of simply being in the same room together. It's harder to shape a common purpose and get people aligned, and it's more difficult for people who don't see each other face to face to commit effectively to one another.

It's also getting harder to make leadership work because of changes in the attitude toward traditional ways of practicing leadership. Increasingly people without formal authority want to be involved in setting their own direction and in designing their own work and how they will coordinate with others. They are less willing to commit themselves to work in which they have had no say. Yet people may not be prepared to participate effectively in leadership this way. They may knock on the door demanding to be let in on leadership without actually knowing how to enter into it. It's harder to create direction, alignment, and commitment when there are different and sometimes competing ideas of how to best accomplish this leadership work and when people have differing levels of readiness for participating in leadership.

FACING THE UNKNOWN

In general, leadership is more difficult today because of what Ronald A. Heifetz, in his book *Leadership Without Easy Answers*, calls *adaptive challenges*, which can also be thought of as complex challenges. A complex challenge is more than just a very complicated problem. Complexity implies a lack of predictability. Complex challenges confront people with the unknown and often result in unintended consequences.

This unpredictability also means that a complex challenge is quite different from a technical problem. Technical problems are predictable and solvable. Using assumptions, methods, and tools that already exist, people can readily define the nature of a technical problem and prepare a solution with some confidence in the results. So, for example, if a key supplier changes the pricing on critical components, and such changes are expected to happen from time to time (the problem is already understood), and there are established ways of responding (tools for solving the problem already exist), then this is a technical problem. A technical problem arises and is solved *without any fundamental change* in assumptions, methods, or tools. Also, the people who solve a technical problem don't themselves have to change.

A complex challenge cannot be dealt with like this. Existing assumptions, methods, or tools are no good in the face of a complex challenge and may even get in the way. To be faced successfully, complex challenges require altered assumptions, different methods, and new tools not yet invented. Complex challenges require people and organizations to change, often in profound and fundamental ways. This is where things get unpredictable. Some examples of current complex challenges are the need for companies that have merged to bring about culture change, for the health care industry to address the nursing shortage, for many companies to make the transformation from product push to customer pull, and for social agencies to get diverse constituents with differing perspectives to work together on such deep-rooted issues as reducing the number of youthful offenders.

Complex challenges are made even more difficult by the fact that no one can say with any authority or accuracy just how things need to change. This is where leadership starts to get a lot harder. Because the complex challenge lies beyond the scope of existing assumptions, the frameworks that people use to try to understand the nature of the challenge itself are not adequate. So, for example, it's not just that people in an organization that needs to undergo a culture change don't know how to make the change happen. It's worse than that. They have no way of being sure what sort of new culture is needed. No one who is part of the existing organization has any kind of especially gifted insight into the needs of the new, changed, still-unknown organization of the future. Everyone has ideas, of course, and everyone has a point of view and may be quite attached to it. Only by virtue of position and authority are anyone's ideas given special status. Unfortunately, although having a lot of authority may make it possible for a person to make sure his or her views hold sway, that doesn't guarantee the effectiveness of those views.

If all of this makes it sound as though a complex challenge requires a lot of talk and reflection among a lot of people in an organization, it does. And all that talk and reflection takes a lot of time. Because the complex challenge is not only complex but also a challenge, however, it demands a response now, not someday. So facing a complex challenge puts people in a bind and ensures that they will experience some stress as they try to think and reflect together without letting analysis lead to paralysis.

NO GOING IT ALONE

In the face of complex challenges, a leader, no matter how skilled and otherwise effective, cannot simply step into the breach, articulate a new vision, make some clarifying decisions, and proclaim success. Because a complex challenge requires a whole system and all the people in it to change, it lies beyond the scope of any individual person to confront. Complex challenges make it virtually impossible for an individual leader to accomplish the work of leadership, and individual leadership therefore reaches a distinct limit in the face of complex challenges.

Since about the 1920s (in the writings of Mary Parker Follett) there has been talk of the possibility of distributing or sharing leadership and making leadership more inclusive and collective. If leadership is still needed (and who can deny that it is), and if no individual alone can provide leadership in the face of a complex challenge, then perhaps what is needed is the collective action of many people. It's conceivable, even compelling, that everyone in an organization could contribute in some way to facing a complex challenge. The possibility that a more inclusive and collective way of leadership could help organizations meet complex challenges and be more effective is promising.

The problem has always been—and remains today—*how* to get more people involved in leadership, and *how* to make leadership more inclusive and collective.

Two critical problems continuously block the way. The first could be called the *too-many-chefs* problem: the effort to make more people into leaders seems doomed to collapse in a cacophony of differing visions and values as too many individuals exhibit leadership. The second could be called the *diffused accountability* problem: when people share leadership, it seems inevitable that accountability will also get shared until, as everyone becomes accountable, no one is really accountable at all.

Both of these problems are real. Attempts to make leadership more inclusive and collective have often—if not always—foundered on just these obstacles. Such failures have made many people realistically pessimistic about the utility of a more inclusive and collective approach to leadership. Yet the promise of such leadership grows brighter as complex challenges surpass the ability of the individual leader to respond.

The problem is how to develop more inclusive and collective ways of making leadership happen without running afoul of the twin problems of too many chefs and diffused accountability. Somehow we need to develop the whole process by which direction, alignment, and commitment are created—not just develop individual leaders. We at CCL call the development of individual leaders *leader development*; the development of the whole process for creating direction, alignment, and commitment we call *leadership development*. Both leader development and leadership development are needed. But even though leadership development is becoming more critically important every day, it lags far behind leader development in most organizations.

DEFINING THE TASKS

A good place to start developing a more inclusive and collective leadership is to think of leadership (both individual and collective) as a process that is used to accomplish a set of *leadership tasks*. This makes it possible to focus not on the way leadership is practiced but rather on what people hope to *accomplish* with leadership. A useful question is, What work is leadership expected to get done? As already suggested, leadership is expected to set direction, create alignment, and generate commitment—or some similar list of desired outcomes.

The too-many-chefs problem that often comes up in trying to share leadership is created when organizations try to get more people to act as leaders and exhibit leadership. This is subtly but importantly different from getting more people involved in the process of accomplishing the leadership tasks.

Getting more people to act like leaders does little more than multiply the individual leader approach. In the face of a complex challenge, simply having more people trying to say what should be done is unlikely to be effective.

In the same way, the diffused accountability problem is created when organizations make more people accountable by designating more people as leaders. This is also little more than a way to multiply individual leaders. Many ways of trying to share leadership in order to make it more inclusive and collective are actually still firmly rooted in the tradition of the individual leader—designating more leaders can just add to the difficulty of accomplishing the leadership tasks in the face of complex challenges.

So having more leaders is not the answer. Instead the answer is to create richer and more complex processes of accomplishing the leadership tasks. Focus on how to create direction, alignment, and commitment in the face of complex challenges, and forget about how many people are, or are not, leaders.

Putting the accomplishment of the leadership tasks at the heart of leadership frames different and more useful questions: What are the obstacles to clear direction, effective alignment, and solid commitment? What resources exist in the organization for creating direction, alignment, and commitment as a complex challenge is being confronted? What different approaches to accomplishing the leadership tasks are possible for the organization? How might people act in new and different ways to accomplish the leadership tasks?

Answering questions like these can help organizations avoid the traditional problems of shared leadership by getting them past the idea that more inclusive and collective approaches require making more people individual leaders.

THREE CAPABILITIES

Complex challenges require richer and more complex ways of creating direction, alignment, and commitment. The ways people talk, think, and act together—the culture of the organization along with its systems and structures—are what need to become richer and more complex.

At first this may seem to be a bad idea. When facing a complex challenge, surely the last thing needed is more complexity. Yet the very complexity of the challenge calls for an equally complex capacity to respond. A complex capacity to respond means something different from just a more complicated process. It means a more varied, less predictable, more layered process capable of greater subtlety. At CCL we believe that making the leadership process more collective, pushing the process beyond one that depends primarily on individuals, enriches the process of leadership to the level of sensitivity and responsiveness required by a complex challenge. Continuing to depend on individual leaders (no matter how many) to lead people through basic and profound changes is risky. This is because any individual leader, no matter how capable, may be unable to make such changes personally. Getting more people working together in more ways increases the likelihood that people who are able to make the needed changes themselves will become influential in the leadership process. We call this *connected leadership*.

Three collective capabilities can be useful for organizations needing to achieve connected leadership: shared sense-making, connection, and navigation.

Shared sense-making. Complex challenges do not come wrapped with an explanation. By their nature they cause confusion, ambiguity, conflict, and stress. They are immediate, so they press for a solution now. But they also force people to change toward the unknown, so they also require reflection. Moving too fast can make things worse. What seems to be required is the capability to engage in shared sense-making.

This is not problem solving; it's not even problem defining. It's a process that must come before a challenge can even be thought of as a problem with solutions. The outcome of this sense-making is shared understanding. It involves people in paying attention to both the parts and the whole of the challenge. It requires people to experience multiple perspectives and to hold conflicting views in productive tension. It answers the persistent question about difficult change: Why change? Without an understanding of why change is required, people are rightly suspicious of it.

Connection. The process of leadership is realized in the connections between people, groups, teams, functions, and whole organizations. Complex challenges threaten existing connections. Think of what happens in an organization seeking to become more customer focused. The existing structures and boundaries that differentiate and coordinate such entities as production, marketing, sales, and finance begin to be more like impediments than workable ways of organizing. Facing complex challenges requires people and organizations to develop and enrich their forms of connection.

The outcome is relationships made to work in new ways both within and between groups and communities. Getting relationships to work in new ways requires people to see patterns of connection (and disconnection) in order to explore the root causes of the complex challenge and clarify differing and sometimes conflicting values. Often, new language emerges.

Navigation. Because a complex challenge is not a familiar problem to be solved but a reality to be faced through change and development, the process is one of learning from shared experiments, small wins, innovations, and emergent strategies. No one can set a goal whose achievement will resolve the complex challenge. It is a journey whose destination is unpredictable and unknown. A key to success is the ability to be keenly sensitive to the forces of change as they happen, like mariners who sail a ship by making minute, mutual adjustments to one another and to the elements of wind and current.

These capabilities cannot be taken on by individuals. They can be developed only between individuals and between groups, functions, and whole organizations. Too often the move to more inclusive and collective approaches to leadership is attempted without making this move into the space in between. More inclusive approaches to leadership have often been expected to flow from a change in the competencies of individual leaders, such as when leaders are called on to be more empowering and inclusive and to share leadership. The persistence of the obstacles to more inclusive and collective leadership comes from the failure to let go of long-held and long-valued assumptions about the individual nature of leadership.

MAKING GAINS

In facing complex challenges, people, organizations, and communities can develop ways of accomplishing the leadership tasks that give more people a sense of being responsible for setting direction, creating alignment, and generating commitment. Successfully facing complex challenges will support a sense of shared power and collective competence.

It will also create the possibility for leadership strategy. Because strategy means making choices among alternatives, no strategy is possible without alternatives to consider. So if the development of connected leadership, of a more inclusive and collective leadership process, adds to the alternative ways that leadership can be carried out, it also creates the possibility that choices can be made about leadership. Leadership then would no longer be a matter of making a single kind of practice work for every context. Instead of seeing leadership as simply a natural force to which humans are subject and that comes in only one naturally determined version (such as the forceful leader taking charge), people would come to see leadership as a process that humans control and that can be shaped to human needs through intentional choices.

Inside Out: Transforming Your Leadership Culture

John B. McGuire, Gary Rhodes, and Charles J. Palus

Any organizational culture holds tremendous power. Culture is a system of closely held beliefs that require certain behaviors and exclude other behaviors. It sets norms on everything in the organization. To change the organizational culture, senior leaders must begin by acknowledging their place in the culture, engaging fully in the work of advancing the leadership culture, and standing up first so that others can follow.

Belief systems, explicit or not, drive behavior. When executives embark on an organizational change initiative—whether tied to new systems, products, markets, or approaches—they are asking people to alter their beliefs in some way. To implement a strategy that requires people to change the way they do things, leaders need to work beyond the operational plan and learn how to change the culture. External change in operations won't take hold without internal change in culture to back it up.

The challenge, then, is for an organization to use its leadership culture to create leadership beliefs and practices that support the new operational direction rather than undermine or stall it. Through our research and client work, we have found that when individuals and organizations intentionally unearth and examine beliefs, values, and assumptions, they are able to address the *culture factor* as a strategic imperative alongside operational tactics. They draw out hidden or unconscious drivers for what is happening—or not happening—in the organization.

By giving attention and weight to internal dimensions, leaders introduce the possibility of new thinking and new beliefs—and therefore new decisions and new behaviors. Leaders practicing together in the leadership culture enlarge the mental and emotional space for change, allowing them to make unexpected and innovative decisions. The bigger the operational change, the more the cultural space needs to expand.

We call this the *inside-out* approach to transforming an organization. And it starts with you.

POWER OF CULTURE

Mike is a vice president at a prestigious financial organization. "A group of vice presidents were planning a special, all-day meeting at headquarters, bringing in VPs and directors from all our locations," Mike says. "We needed to use the largest conference room in the building and had to get special permission to do so."

Permission in this case was not simply an issue of scheduling. The large conference room was on the top floor of the building and was used almost exclusively by senior executives. The VP and director offices were on the floors below, with employees lower

Illustration by Bruce Flye

in the ranks filling the middle floors and the ground level occupied by administrative and support operations. The furnishings in the building, too, changed by floor. The executive level featured leather chairs, high-quality wood desks and tables, artwork, and attractive kitchen and washroom facilities. The lower floors were fitted with progressively less expensive furnishings.

"The night before the meeting, I was staying late to finalize a presentation," recalls Mike. "A couple of guys from our maintenance staff kept walking past my office with chairs from the meeting room down the hall. I didn't think much of it until the next morning when I arrived on the top floor for our big meeting. The maintenance staff had replaced all the leather chairs in the executive conference room with the fabric chairs from our floor."

The true power of culture is seen in the fact that no one had told the maintenance staff to trade out the chairs. There was no policy or precedent for this action. The maintenance crew made its own decision. It understood that certain chairs go with certain status levels, and it simply followed, without question, that cultural norm. The cultural value of authority and the trappings of status were so embedded in the organization that a group of lower-level VPs simply could not use the top executives' chairs.

For leaders at the financial organization, this incident revealed unchecked beliefs that were controlling the organization and preventing any meaningful change from taking place. Years of valuing hierarchy, status, authority, and control—even when those values were unstated—had led to assumptions and behaviors that were unnecessary, unhelpful, or at odds with stated goals. Although the executive team was both surprised and somewhat amused when it heard what had happened, it clearly saw that cultural beliefs drive decisions.

We use this illustration not because it is a big example of cultural decision making but rather because it is a small example. If cultural imperatives are so strong when it comes to furniture, imagine how powerful they must be in high-risk, complex, and changing situations.

Here are some questions to consider:

- What are the cultural imperatives in your organization?
- How do your leadership culture's beliefs and practices enhance or inhibit operational implementation of the business strategy?
- How intentional is your leadership culture in developing the organizational culture toward the organization's performance goals?

Any organizational culture holds tremendous power. Culture is the big elephant in the room when it comes to the imperative for change. Setting a significantly more complex direction in operations without developing a new culture in parallel can be folly.

Culture is simply a human system of closely held beliefs that require certain behaviors and exclude other behaviors. Mostly, it is a set of unwritten rules. When people describe "the way things are around here," they're talking about culture. It is how they have to operate to get things done.

DRIVING BEHAVIOR

Culture sets norms on everything in an organization: how to share bad news, whether to take risks, whether and how people are developed and promoted, how people interact with one another, how problems are solved, and so on. Culture may, for instance, dictate respect for hierarchy, with decision making that goes through clear channels. Operating outside that structure may be unacknowledged or flagged as renegade and unwelcome behavior. In another context, that same back channel or informal approach to getting things done may be the norm. Without knowing how to work in that structure, leaders will be ineffective.

Cultural beliefs drive behavior. Decisions are the go-betweens, interpreting inbound data and translating the cultural beliefs into action. But core beliefs are so strong that they drive decisions in subtle and automatic ways. The decision maker is often not even conscious of them.

Consider the hundreds of decisions—large and small—that are made in daily organizational life. People like to think that these choices are rational, but in fact they are mostly unguided by reason. Emotions and intuitions play a big part in decision making. However, although much of decision making is nonrational, it does have its own "logic."

That logic is this: the unconscious mind is always a half step ahead of the conscious mind. Many decisions are based on unexamined beliefs, thought patterns, habits, and assumptions. In other words, the inside drives the outside—not the other way around.

But culture produces more than a belief-based decision engine; it also creates a form of assurance. Culture creates a familiar space for getting things done, a sense of "rightness," and a means of survival. So why change it?

Organizational change begins when strategy is stuck. Something new must be done. Culture, then, will need to make a shift to accommodate the new thing: a shift in direction, market, customer, system, product, personnel, and so on. The organization needs to be filled with the cultural beliefs that will drive the decisions that will create needed changes in actions.

An organization needs all the help it can get to overcome the inertia of the status quo. When the organizational strategy runs counter to the beliefs about "how things are done around here," then the human system—the culture—will simply reject it. "Culture eats strategy for breakfast," one client told us. He meant that setting a significantly new organizational direction without developing a new culture is most often useless. That's why 66 percent to 75 percent of organizational change initiatives fail.

HIDDEN DIMENSIONS

Taking action is often the starting point, end point, and every place in between when it comes to organizational change. When faced with change, senior leaders tend to go on furious, extended sprees on management autopilot. Rolling up their sleeves and bracing themselves for the tough battle ahead, they focus on the technical systems and process changes required in the business operations. A bias for action becomes an obsession filled with activity and the appearance of progress. Many leaders will use language that tiptoes around culture—"innovation is our future," "in challenging times, we need to pull together," "people are our most important assets"—but then they quickly move beyond this lip service and on to the operations. It is as if they believe that when the job is done right by action alone, the culture will somehow naturally follow.

Even when senior leaders acknowledge the role of culture in their organization's success, few have a clear idea of how to change culture. They feel they have little time to focus on culture and little information about steps to take that will open the door to culture change. "We have gone as far as we can go with change management of the operations," one CEO told us. "Now we believe that the real change is in leadership and the culture, but we just don't know how to do that."

The way to successfully implement change in an organization is to give the hidden dimensions of change the same attention as the operational elements. If you change the beliefs, you change the culture. To *do* something different (an external outcome), the organization must *be* something different (an internal outcome).

The inside-out approach to culture change fits side by side with conventional outside-in operational strategies. When leaders examine beliefs and thinking, they increase awareness of why and how they make decisions. They gain new insight into what is working operationally and what isn't. Individuals, senior teams, and whole organizations can begin to consciously build a bridge between the hidden, internal drivers and the visible, external actions. By using reflective learning processes to factor in the power of culture, people are able to view a situation in a new way. This creates the space where genuine change occurs.

Culture change is about the interplay between individual growth and organizational development. Organizations, as well as people, vary in their level of readiness for culture change. (See "Five Factors for Organizational Readiness" on the following page.) Leaders cannot single-handedly reveal the hidden aspects of their leadership and organizational culture. They cannot manage and control culture or fix it and manipulate it the way one can a software system, a business plan, a floor layout, or a budget.

But make no mistake: if leaders expect culture change in others, they must change themselves first. Culture is not an object or a system "out there"; it is something internal, "in here." We often tell our clients, "You are *in* the culture and the culture is *in* you, and in a very real way you *are* the culture. You can't change the culture without changing yourself."

This is the pivot point on which all culture change sits. If senior leadership wants to keep the work of culture change at arm's length, the change won't take hold. Colleagues, direct reports, and employees throughout the organization will know that culture change is nothing but a catchphrase and will, in turn, learn to create the appearance of support without investing in change themselves.

To lead organizational change—both operationally and culturally—leaders must first conquer their own opposition to change. By changing themselves first, leaders start to provide themselves and others with an alternative system of beliefs and practices. To effect change, leaders must first invest in changing the leadership culture. In turn, leadership can and will change the organizational culture.

Leaders who buy into their personal role in changing culture will struggle, change beliefs, and likely evolve into different people and different leaders. When leaders engage collectively in this process, they learn to deal with change through public learning and by taking on risk and vulnerability. On the other side of the challenge, however, is the exhilaration of taking a risk that turns out

Five Factors for Organizational Readiness

Organizational culture change requires both individual development and collective development. Individual effort will have limited impact in the absence of five *organizational readiness factors*:

The executive team is engaged as both enabler and participant. The executive team understands that it cannot make change happen by itself. Yet it must lead the change, engage the organization, and participate in developing the change leadership capability.

Leadership development is part of the organization's cultural history. The organization has experience with and appreciation for leadership development as a means of building organizational capacity. The leadership culture has seen the effects of its previous leader development efforts.

A struggle to implement change efforts meets a realization that leadership culture is the missing piece. There is a compelling purpose for change. The executive team is clear about the need to get the operations right but seeks to balance them. There is high strategic intent to succeed through leadership's focused effort in culture change.

The executive team is willing to engage in emergent work. Organizational culture change is not a management program with a guaranteed deliverable; rather it is a leadership pathway that is constructed as the journey is made. The ability to tolerate uncertainty and ambiguity is key to success.

Cross-boundary work is deemed essential. Working across boundaries (such as functions, alliances, agencies, and suppliers) is recognized as critical.

well and the constructive, positive energy that comes from tapping into themselves and others as instruments of change.

THREE AREAS

What does it take to be a leader of change toward cultural transformation? We have identified three areas that create individual readiness and capacity for inside-out culture change.

Control Center

How important is it to you to manage and control the change process? How comfortable and open are you to the uncertain, unexpected, and unpredicted? The extent of the need to own or control change defines a leader's control center.

Control is usually a highly charged and emotional issue for leaders, who face internal pressure to perform. Even so, successful leaders of change move away from tightly held control and view themselves as instruments and strategic influencers of change. They distinguish between what is controllable and what needs to be addressed through an emergent process of influence and learning. They understand that leading change often involves relinquishing the personal need to control.

When a tightly held control center is challenged, leaders have a choice: hang on even tighter or let go. Letting go means behaving as if you don't have all the answers, listening more, and looking to see what's really going on at deeper levels. It involves struggles and new challenges. But letting go also holds opportunity. As leaders become more confident in others and in new leadership practices developing in the culture, new solutions and new options will emerge.

Giving up some of the need for control is a challenge, but it helps leaders develop tolerance for ambiguity and a facility for dealing with complexity. Leaders can begin to explore their control center by asking themselves the following key questions, both as an initial self-assessment and as an ongoing control center check during the course of everyday work.

- Where is my control center, and what are its symptoms?
- What role does control play in actually minimizing organizational risk versus just containing my anxiety?
- What function does control play in my decision-making process?
- What if I'm wrong? What if I don't have all the right ideas? What if there are multiple right answers?
- What is the real problem here?
- What role am I playing in the problem?
- What is the worst that can happen if I don't jump in and solve this?

Time Sense

Is everything urgent? Really? Have you considered that some things are too important to be urgent? Most leaders and organizations today face considerable external pressure to speed up their operations. In the rush to "get it done and get it done now," they circumvent the learning and leadership functions that will allow them to succeed at changing a culture.

Leaders alter their time sense by *slowing down to power up.* This is a process of slowing down and taking time out for learning. It involves asking questions, reflecting, and engaging in dialogue. Although it may look a lot like doing nothing, spontaneous, informal give-and-take is an important part of promoting the culture change agenda. Without deeply engaging key constituents and the workforce in active and applied learning, leading significant organizational change is impossible.

To better understand their own time sense, leaders can ask questions such as these:

- Am I confusing activity with meaningful action?
- What might happen if I take a slower approach and really engage others?

- Who or what is setting my pace?
- How do I respond to external demands?
- Is this really a fire I need to put out? Who actually started this fire?
- Why can't this wait?
- Whom haven't I heard from?
- What's missing?
- Do I need to give this more attention?

Intentionality

Intentionality is the inside-out interplay between the current state and the future focus. Intentional leaders become instruments of change. Leaders and organizations need to set their cultural intention as clearly as other goals and metrics. Intentionality is like an internal compass setting; it maintains the courage and commitment to hold true to the course.

Intentionality builds as insight and clarity develop. As the vitality of a leader's vision, aspirations, and conviction strengthens, connecting to his or her intentionality becomes second nature. As intentionality becomes embedded in the unconscious, more and more decisions are driven from the new belief structure—the one that supports the new direction.

The ongoing process of making the unconscious conscious hones intentionality. Intentionality is about building a bridge between beliefs and behaviors. Leaders can explore their motives and increase their intentionality by asking themselves questions such as these:

- Why change?
- Why am I leading change?
- Do I really mean to change myself and this organization, or am I just giving lip service to appearance and activities?

- What if acting on my intentions produces outcomes different from what I intended?
- Am I aware of my motives?
- What are my beliefs and assumptions about change and about this specific change?
- How do my decisions and behaviors reflect my beliefs?
- Are my decisions and behaviors supporting or contradicting what I say about culture?

GETTING STARTED

To change the organizational culture, all people systems and practices eventually need to be engaged in the transformation process. But to begin, senior leaders must acknowledge their place in the culture, engage fully in the work of advancing the leadership culture, and stand up first so that others can follow.

Ending the Board Game: New Leadership Solutions for Companies

Jay A. Conger

Events in corporate America have exposed some failings in the way most companies are led. When the CEO is also the chairman of the board, there is no effective system of checks and balances to ensure not only successful performance but also integrity. However, there are alternatives.

The accounting and fraud scandals in the first decade of the millennium at Enron, WorldCom, Global Crossing, Tyco, and other companies raise a critical question: why did their boards of directors fail to take a strong leadership role and preempt these disastrous outcomes? After all, a board has a legal responsibility for the management of its company. There are numerous reasons why the boards of these particular companies failed to take a proactive role, but one crucial contributor was the nature of leadership on corporate boards today.

Many current corporate governance policies and practices are intended to ensure a balance of power between the CEO and the directors, but reality usually gets in the way. Among the vast majority of U.S. companies, leadership is vested largely in the hands of a single individual—the CEO. But it's becoming increasingly clear that relying on one person to lead both a company and its board can be a serious mistake. To halt the procession of corporate scandals, leadership needs to be shared.

INSIDE KNOWLEDGE

If you look closely at today's boards, you'll see that in most cases the CEO is the unquestioned leader. This is largely because of the natural advantages of the CEO's position.

For one thing the CEO has far greater access than other directors to current, comprehensive information about the state of the company. The other directors usually have extremely limited knowledge of company affairs. Their enlightenment is restricted by the fact that they usually are company and even industry outsiders with a part-time role. Although their external perspective has some important advantages, it is a liability when it comes to cultivating knowledge and information about the company and its industry. Most directors are well aware of this gap in their understanding and, as a result, willingly concede authority to the CEO.

Directors also tend to see their primary role as serving the CEO; to them, providing oversight is a secondary role. Most directors are CEOs themselves, so they share an unwritten but binding etiquette that frowns on aggressively challenging a fellow CEO and on probing too deeply into the details of someone else's business. Many fear that they will end up micromanaging CEO responsibilities. All these factors encourage directors to defer to the leadership of the CEO.

As a result the CEO usually determines the agenda for meetings and controls the type and amount of information that directors receive. The CEO often is the one who selects board members and appoints the members of the board's various committees. These and other powers and prerogatives generally make the CEO the de facto leader of the board. The only exceptions—the only times when a board feels it must take the lead—typically come during the selection of a new CEO or during a change of company ownership.

DUAL TITLES

The CEO's effective leadership of the board is magnified and solidified in most companies by the fact that the CEO is the leader not only in essence but also in name—he or she is the board chairman. From a CEO's vantage point, there are clear positives to this dual leadership role.

- It centralizes board leadership and accountability in a single individual, so there is no question about who leads the board.
- It eliminates the possibility of a dysfunctional conflict or rivalry between the CEO and the board chairman, which might result in ineffectual compromises and drawn-out decision making.
- It avoids the potential problem of having two public spokespeople addressing the organization's stakeholders and possibly delivering conflicting messages.
- It achieves efficiency in that the board chairman is also the person who is most informed and knowledgeable about company affairs. The CEO doesn't have to spend a lot of time and energy on updating a board chairman on company and industry issues before each meeting.

For companies there may be another advantage—at least in the current environment—to combining the roles of CEO and board chairman. Research has shown that CEOs, almost without exception, strongly believe that they should also hold the chairmanship of the board. When it comes to recruiting the best CEO talent, companies whose policy is to hand the reins of the board to the CEO are therefore likely to have an advantage over companies that don't have this policy.

Superficially, at least, it appears that there are a number of advantages to having the CEO and the board chairman be one and the same. But there is a critical drawback to relying on this CEO model of board leadership—a drawback that has become painfully evident during the recent corporate scandals. Under the CEO model, too much leadership authority is concentrated in the hands of the CEO, and the company often has no effective system of checks and balances when it comes to leadership.

One way to balance power is to create another source of leadership, and organizations have at least three options available to achieve this: an independent, nonexecutive chairman (someone from outside the organization who has never held the CEO or other executive position in the company); a lead director; or strong, autonomous board committees.

SPLIT DECISION

The idea of a separate, nonexecutive chairmanship has been circulating for at least a decade. Few companies, however, have adopted this option—only about 10 percent of the largest firms in the United States have a chairman who is not also the CEO. This suggests fairly strong resistance to the concept among the top echelons of corporate America.

What are the arguments for having a separate, nonexecutive chairman? Perhaps the principal one is that it increases the ability of the board to monitor the CEO's performance. A board led by a fellow director will likely feel it has greater latitude to challenge the CEO and his or her actions when necessary. In addition, having a separate board chairman may enhance a company's standing among investment fund managers, who often assume that CEOs seek to serve themselves first and shareholders only secondarily. In the eyes of these fund managers, a separate, nonexecutive chairman with a mandate to elevate shareholder value is less likely to be compromised than a CEO-chairman.

There are a number of qualities and characteristics that a separate chairman should possess to be effective and successful. First, the chairman should not be a former CEO of the company. (A former CEO would likely have been involved in the selection and often the mentoring of the current CEO, so his or her objectivity could be compromised.) Second, the chairman should have the confidence and admiration of the directors, along with self-confidence and sufficient knowledge of the company and the industry to fit naturally into the leadership role. To gain this knowledge, the chairman must be dedicated to putting in the time and effort to closely follow the company and its industry.

This requirement means it's not a good idea for the outside chairman to be a board member or CEO of another company (although a recently retired CEO might fit into the role perfectly). Being a separate, nonexecutive chairman can be highly demanding—in large, diversified companies the chairman may need to spend seventy-five to a hundred days a year keeping abreast of the company if everything is going well, and even more if the company encounters a crisis.

Because the separate chairman will work closely with the CEO, it's important that the CEO be involved in the selection process. For this model of board leadership to function effectively, the chairman must feel that his or her allegiance is not solely to the CEO and must feel free and unafraid to challenge the CEO. At the same time, there should be strong positive chemistry between the two individuals—again because they will be working together so closely. However, the chemistry must not be so powerful that it could override the chairman's objective viewpoint. During the selection process, it's best if the chairman candidate and CEO decide for themselves whether chemistry exists between them. However, the scope of the potential chairman's ability to challenge the CEO is best determined by the sitting directors. In light of this, the best selection method is for the CEO to provide his or her input on each candidate on the roster submitted by the board nominating committee and then for the board to make the final choice.

Establishing from the start clear and negotiated expectations of the roles the separate chairman will assume is also critical to the success of this model of board leadership. Tasks and responsibilities to be placed under the purview of the chairman might include setting meeting agendas in consultation with the CEO; assigning tasks to board committees; facilitating full and candid deliberations of matters that come before the board; and annually reviewing the board's governance practices.

Despite the potential that this board leadership model holds for breaking up the concentration of authority and reducing the chances of scandal, it's unlikely to be widely adopted by U.S. companies. The primary stumbling block is CEOs themselves. As noted earlier, most CEOs are strongly biased toward having a single leader—themselves. They believe that sharing leadership of the company and the board is cumbersome and inefficient. In addition, candidates for the role of separate, nonexecutive board chairman face greater legal risks than other directors do—risks for which they might not be willing or able to get liability coverage. Moreover, they must be willing to make a much greater time investment than that required of a typical board member. For most people who would be considered qualified outside candidates, such an investment would be impractical.

There are strikes against the nonexecutive chairman form of board leadership, but companies looking to break away from the status quo have two other alternatives to consider.

PROCESS PILOT

A form of board leadership likely to be more palatable to many CEOs is having a lead director—an individual who does not assume the formal role of chairman but acts as the directors' representative to the CEO. Through this intermediary function the lead director can bring to the CEO sensitive issues or concerns that individual directors might not raise on their own or want discussed in a public forum. In this alternative the lead director *leads* not so much in the sense of influencing the board's stands on various issues as in the sense of piloting the boardroom process.

The lead director is both an ombudsman and a facilitator of the governance process. His or her role can include overseeing and preparing the agenda for board meetings, discussing controversial business issues one-on-one with the CEO, and conducting exit interviews with executives who are leaving the company to determine whether their resignations reflect problems in the organization or with the CEO's style and approach. In addition, lead directors might meet on occasion with major shareholders to determine their expectations and concerns. Such smaller meetings, without the presence of company management, could encourage more open, revealing, and helpful discussion than occurs at annual, public shareholder meetings.

What characteristics should be sought in a lead director? In addition to being from outside the organization, the ideal lead director should have significant executive experience, should be highly respected by other members of the board, should serve in another board leadership capacity (as chairman of a board committee, for example), and should possess the strength of personality and background to effectively challenge the CEO when warranted. The lead director should not be selected on the basis of seniority on the board; although boards are prone to honor an elder member with the lead directorship, this criterion is often unlikely to be a good indicator of an individual's ability to lead effectively in a changing business environment.

The lead director model of board leadership looks like an attractive alternative to leaving power solely in the hands of a CEO-chairman, yet less than one-third of the Fortune 1000 companies have opted for it. Many CEOs—and indeed, many board members—continue to believe that having a lead director merely gums up the works and is appropriate only in times of emergency. However, CEOs tend to be more amenable to the idea of the third option—giving board leadership to the board committees.

MAKING HEADWAY

Board leadership that is shared by the board committees has emerged as the most prevalent alternative to the CEO-chairman model. There are a number of reasons for this shift in power, but one of the most obvious is that CEOs, caught up in setting corporate strategy and overseeing day-to-day operations, realize that they have their hands full and don't have the time to be active members of each board committee. As a result, they often feel comfortable in assuming a consultative or advisory role and allowing the committees to lead themselves—and by extension to lead the board as a whole.

The growing use of board committee leadership has also been driven by the increased reliance on outside directors, who of course become committee members and chairmen.

With the proliferation of outside directors, the practice of CEOs' handpicking committee chairmen has largely been replaced by a system in which committees select their own chairmen.

In companies that have elected to turn to board leadership by committees—at least on a trial or experimental basis—committee members should take a number of steps to ensure that their panels not only retain their leadership but also enhance it. For outside directors to take full advantage of their relatively newfound majority status on boards and committees, they often need to develop action plans and positions that are independently produced rather than dictated or guided by the CEO and senior management. Board and committee meetings and other activities are generally the only opportunities the directors have to accomplish this. So it's important that some committee meetings be held without company executives present so the directors can discuss sensitive issues—such as those surrounding corporate performance and executive succession. These committee meetings also may be the only chance panel members have to arrive at strong positions that they believe are in the best interests of the company but may be contrary to the stated preferences of senior management.

It is critical that committees be able to meet on short notice when the members believe this is called for by an event such as a corporate crisis or rapidly developing change. It's also important for committees to ensure that they have the ability to seek and retain outside specialists who can make objective assessments of the company's operations—and that they can do so without the permission of senior management.

WHAT'S AHEAD

To date, strong leadership from board committees is the area in which the most progress has been made in achieving governance practices that provide more balance in corporate leadership. Considering the resistance to board leadership by a separate, nonexecutive chairman or a lead director, it's probably also the area in which the most progress will continue to be made for the foreseeable future.

But certain trade-offs involved in relying solely on board committee leadership may make it fall short of being the best option of the three. When leadership is splintered across a number of individuals, there is no single director who takes comprehensive responsibility for the board and for ensuring that its activities are well coordinated and meet high standards of governance. There may be no central ombudsman to give the full board a collective voice. In addition, because committees have a narrow focus, they can at best shape only portions of the overall agenda.

All these drawbacks suggest that committee leadership is only a partial approach to building a method of board governance that is truly effective and optimal for the well-being of companies. In the final analysis the practice of using empowered outside chairmen or lead directors should be the means of countervailing the corporate leadership practice of putting too much power in the hands of one person. In companies, as in governments, an effective system of checks and balances is critical to ensuring both successful performance and integrity.

Battles and Beliefs: Rethinking the Roles of Today's Leaders

Lee G. Bolman and Terrence E. Deal

The modern business environment is wild, messy, and unpredictable. That's why the two operating frameworks that leaders have typically relied on—the caregiver and the analyst—are no longer enough. Two additional frameworks—the wizard and the warrior—can help leaders make sense of the political and symbolic predicaments that organizations face daily.

Why do bad things keep happening to good managers? Their careers get stunted or fly off the rails. Well-deserved promotions are handed to someone else. A colleague flubs a project but succeeds in placing the blame on the manager. After a brutal day at work, one disillusioned manager said: "I thought I had covered all the bases, then realized that everyone else was playing football. I had a great strategy for the wrong game."

The problem is that managers usually rely on two operating frameworks—the caregiver and the analyst—that focus, respectively, on people and structure. Both outlooks are important and valuable because they help leaders become humane and sensible. But they work best in a rational world filled with reasonable people. Unfortunately, such an orderly world doesn't exist. The modern company is intrinsically wild, messy, and unpredictable.

Something more is needed: two additional frameworks can help leaders make sense of the political and symbolic predicaments that organizations face daily. These leadership roles decode a world dominated by passion and power. Sadly, this is the world in which business leaders are usually weakest.

Most managers avoid office politics because they view its dynamics as sordid or because they just don't like conflict. They fear the risk of losing control and losing out. They think politics would go away if the organization were just run properly. For many managers, understanding the elusive and mysterious

influence of symbols is even harder. Even though culture affects every decision a leader makes, executives discount cultural import as a fuzzy and flaky notion. They don't see it—or if they do, they don't get it. Great leadership cannot flourish without directly addressing political and cultural issues. Too many leaders don't even know which game they're playing. They try to play it safe and stay on the sidelines. That's why today's organizations need more wizards and warriors.

WORLD OF COMBAT

The wizard and the warrior occupy two separate but convergent worlds. The warrior's world is a place of combat, replete with allies and antagonists, courage and cowardice, honor and betrayal, strength and weakness. At times this world is dangerous and destructive—war really *is* hell. Most great warriors will agree that one of the noblest and most consistent human endeavors is the search for peace, for a way to avoid war's terrible costs. Yet conflict remains endemic. An organization that lacks warriors puts itself at great risk of being overrun by a group that does have them.

This is not to suggest that warrior leaders are always beneficial to an organization. Some become so obsessed with winning that they lose sight of the company's primary goals. Others are too myopic to see the big picture. An organization must look for a *principled* warrior to lead it. Through our research, we have found three general classifications of warrior leaders.

The Toxic Warrior

Leona Helmsley typifies the poisonous effect a warrior can unleash on an organization. Helmsley was placed in command of the lavish Helmsley Palace Hotel, where she became notorious as "the Queen of Mean." She was well known for throwing fits of rage and continually abusing employees. She posed as the keeper at the gate and demanded perfection from her staff. If perfection were not met—even regarding the smallest trifle—she would fire people on the spot. Her warrior persona was that of an iron fist. Eventually the disgruntlement in the ranks led to an inside tip regarding criminal financial dealings. Helmsley was later convicted of federal income tax evasion.

Leaders can take basic measures to avoid becoming toxic warriors. First, they should gain a realistic sense of self. Leaders need to request feedback from colleagues to stay tuned in to their own strengths and weaknesses. It's difficult for toxic warriors to notice their own faults. These leaders often isolate themselves, which only makes matters worse. Leaders should look for trusted counsel within the organization to help quell rash or misinformed decisions. Finally, it's important for leaders to experiment with their roles. If a leader is limited to a scorched-earth form of combat, it's very difficult to break his or her ineffective leadership patterns.

The Relentless Warrior

The leadership style of Bill Gates—a tech version of General George S. Patton—has been frank and often brutal. He attacked users over software piracy issues, writing blunt missives to publications, which quickly created many enemies in the fledgling geek community. He was famous for thwarting a rival's new product by announcing that a better Microsoft offering would debut sooner—even if that objective was wildly unrealistic.

Gates's relentless warrior mentality became fully transparent during Microsoft's prolonged battle against one of the biggest antitrust cases of the late twentieth century. After a federal court ruled against Microsoft, the mood at the company's headquarters was chaotic and confused. Senior executives thought it best to avoid a direct confrontation with the government and began soft-pedaling in the hope of deflecting the feds' wrath. Gates trashed the diplomatic approach. From his perspective the court's order threatened an unbending principle: Microsoft's right to design software as it saw fit.

Gates's tenacity and determination make him a relentless warrior. Relentless leaders produce boundless admiration from supporters and intense antipathy from enemies.

Their persistence and courage make them formidable foes. They excel when the objective is clear and they can advance against clearly defined adversaries. When situations become murky, many relentless leaders are dumbfounded. They also suffer from a constricted field of vision and are stubborn when presented with new perspectives. Like Gates, many relentless warriors become polarizing figures. This can lead to an insurmountable backlash. Although relentless warriors make many allies, they also make the same number of enemies.

The Principled Warrior

Principled warriors, although rare, are the leaders most likely to build enduring institutions. They are committed to a purpose. They recognize the reality of conflict but focus on achieving goals rather than destroying foes. This focus is what separates principled warriors from other warriors.

Nelson Mandela, like many principled warriors, did not glorify combat. As he faced a likely death sentence, Mandela told a South African court: "During my lifetime I have dedicated myself to the struggle of the African people. I have fought against white domination, and I have fought against black domination. I have cherished the ideal of a democratic and free society in which all persons live together in harmony and with equal opportunities. It is an ideal which I hope to live for and to achieve. But, if need be, it is an ideal for which I am prepared to die."

Mandela spent twenty-seven years in prison, continuously fighting against apartheid. Although he did not advocate violence, he clearly demonstrated that he would undertake whatever struggle the ultimate goal required. Principled warriors put conflict in perspective. They keep their eyes on the greater good because they do not relish conflict; they view it instead as a costly but sometimes necessary course of action. They put the cause ahead of themselves and will sacrifice to achieve it. It is the principled warrior's commitment to a coherent set of purposes and values that causes a lasting difference in an organization.

DEVELOPING HEART

The example of Nelson Mandela demonstrates that a leader doesn't have to like war to be a warrior. Warriors include doctors in war zones who risk life and limb to administer medical care and clergy members who battle to bring justice to their neglected communities. To be a warrior you need only have a cause for which you will give your all.

Of course, not everyone is a warrior. If you have little taste for conflict, face that reality directly, but also acknowledge it as a vulnerability. If your company faces real threats from real enemies, shying away from the battlefield will be costly if not catastrophic for you, your employees, and your purposes.

You can hope to be so lucky that a time of conflict never arises. You can hire a warrior who brings this skill set to your organization. Or you can develop a warrior's heart. Warrior skills can be taught and learned, but the heart of a warrior is more arduous to develop. For some, such as the toxic and relentless warriors, the warrior heart is inherent. The toxic and relentless warriors' innate passion for victory propels them eagerly into battle. For principled warriors the heart is found in a noble cause—one that can justify the costs of combat. For many leaders the principled warrior heart develops over time. Through experiences that test courage and strength during rigorous challenges with worthy competitors, a warrior's fortitude grows. These experiences materialize through many forms.

Military experience is a powerful way to test and develop oneself as a warrior. For some it's the best way. Athletics have served as influential formative training for many leaders. Of course, competition doesn't always have to be in the physical realm—it's important to hone your warrior heart in the intellectual and social arenas as well. One opportunity is running for office or participating in electoral campaigns, even if only at a neighborhood club. Other drills to nurture a warrior's heart include joining a debate team or learning the intricacies of bridge or Texas hold 'em. There are many paths, but all involve a conscious choice and willingness to enter competitive arenas, test capacities, and develop skills and courage.

Truly great leaders, however, cannot always rely on a warrior's ethos to push an organization forward. Fighting is not the solution to every problem. Leaders must have the ability to adapt to different situations, because an organization's challenges come mainly from inside rather than outside forces. In these circumstances a leader needs to build from the inside by summoning a corporate spirit that enchants both employees and customers.

SPINNING MAGIC

The wizard thrives in a realm of mystery, possibility, and magic. The wizard's strength doesn't come from conflicts and might but from wisdom and the ability to see below and beyond appearances. This type of leader brings unshakable faith that something fresh and better is really out there. The wizard uses icons, values, rituals, and stories to thread the day-to-day details of work into a momentous, symbolic tapestry. A company without wizards is sterile and often toxic; employees become individual mercenaries rather than forming a team bonded by shared spirit.

As with the warrior archetype, not all wizards are productive. Authenticity is crucial to the wizard's magic and the organization's well-being. Harmful or wannabe wizards cannot deliver the long-term successes that flow from the leadership of an authentic wizard.

The Harmful Wizard

At the heart of the Enron scandal was the harmful wizardry of the company's chief financial officer, Andrew Fastow. Through the use of a maze of off-balance-sheet special purpose entities (SPEs), Fastow created a fictional world in which Enron's reported profits kept soaring even as the company was hemorrhaging millions. When Fastow's tactics were uncovered in 2001, the edifice that he had built imploded and devastated thousands of Enron employees and investors.

Harmful wizards are both villains and victims. Fastow was a master of dark financial magic, but he was responding to pressure from his bosses, Kenneth Lay and Jeffrey Skilling, to generate the earnings needed to boost stock prices. Fastow's SPEs filled in the profit gap whenever Enron's operating units fell short. The harmful wizard flourishes in an environment that is akin to an ethical vacuum. Enron's culture nurtured a belief that its people were smarter than everyone else and could make their own rules. This environment gave Fastow the chance to practice his magic with little accountability.

It is important to remember that harmful wizards are never alone in their dealings. Fastow was abetted by a laundry list of co-conspirators, including accountants, auditors, bankers, lawyers, and his bosses. Without those allies, Fastow's dark wizardry would never have reached the heights it did.

The Wannabe Wizard

Wannabe wizards, like sorcerer's apprentices who unleash magic they cannot control, have aspirations that exceed their magic. Carly Fiorina, former CEO of Hewlett-Packard, was one such leader.

Upon her appointment, Fiorina tried to transform HP by dismantling rather than building on its powerful and deeply rooted culture. She produced a new mission statement, but it was spurned by many HP employees. Dockers were replaced by Armani suits, and divisions were created between executives and everyone else. She overestimated her own magic and underestimated the power of HP's values and practices.

This is a common mistake for wannabe wizards. Fiorina misread HP's symbolic code by superimposing images of herself standing next to HP's founders, William Hewlett and David Packard. The coup de grace was Fiorina's self-promotion. Her appointment was obviously newsworthy, and she took every media opportunity that was pitched. Her delight in the role of superstar CEO betrayed an HP core value—humility. Instead of building a new, reinvigorated culture, she only drained the remnants of the old one. Her actions, clear indications of a wannabe wizard, ultimately resulted in her ouster from HP in 2005.

The Authentic Wizard

David Neeleman, a former senior executive at Southwest Airlines, exemplifies the authentic wizard. He began with a dream. Neeleman imagined an airline dedicated to restoring humanity in air travel by combining low fares with high style. His wizardry gave birth to JetBlue, a high-performing enterprise in both profitability and customer satisfaction. Following the wizard's path, Neeleman began building his vision by enlisting a top-notch executive team, grabbing a few of his former colleagues from Southwest to infuse the start-up with true believers. To further enforce this dream, Neeleman and his associates set core values for every person at JetBlue. All these values focused on people: treat your people right, do the right thing, communicate with your team, encourage initiative and innovation, and inspire greatness in others.

Neeleman, ever the visionary, credits these early efforts and continued team-building functions as prime factors in JetBlue's success. The intangible "Kumbaya stuff" closely knits the company together. The result is a business-minded magic that rivets employees to the firm's nitty-gritty details honed for customer satisfaction.

Neeleman exemplifies the wise, passionate leader who recognizes the importance of symbols and encourages the link between words and deeds. This is the very essence of authentic wizardry.

FINDING A GUIDE

The majority of us wonder if we even have the capacity to become a wizard, as the role appears mysterious and alien. Whereas a warrior must overcome the fear of battle, wizards need to transcend fear of the irrational and the unknown. Wizards must be fully immersed in the subtler arts of magic, imagination, and creation.

If the wizard's path is foreign to your aspirations and identity, you can either accept your station or work to overcome your self-imposed obstacles. If you choose acceptance, focus on the other ways in which you can lead. You may be an adroit warrior.

You may also choose to ally yourself with a warrior. Oprah Winfrey was a magician who could elicit an unparalleled audience response. But the warrior role was harder for her to adopt. Early in Winfrey's career, she concluded that her agent was too nice, so she got a new one: a warrior named Jeffrey Jacobs, a lawyer with a blood-and-guts reputation. "I'd heard that Jeff is a piranha," Winfrey said. "I like that. Piranha is good." Jacobs, the warrior, worked a deal that allowed Winfrey, the wizard, to go nationwide.

How do you become a wizard? The answer is simple: start your journey, follow your bliss, and most important, find a mentor. Finding a wise magician to guide you is crucial. Such mentors can help you hone your spiritual center, which will be the foundation of your legacy. No wizard ever was created by perpetually falling into the mundane and performing the same tasks day after day.

Although some leaders find it easier to be a warrior than a wizard (and vice versa), it's best to keep both irons in the fire. By employing both the wizard and warrior dispositions, an individual can provide the political and symbolic superlatives often associated with effective leadership. The most influential leaders can switch between roles as each situation demands. It is a rare skill, but one that more leaders can develop.

Time magazine's list of the greatest leaders and revolutionaries of the twentieth century provides many examples. Leaders such as Margaret Thatcher and Mao Zedong were legendary warriors, well known for their steely resolve and willingness to fight. But Thatcher and Mao were also gifted wizards. The three U.S. presidents on *Time*'s list—Ronald Reagan, Franklin D. Roosevelt, and Theodore Roosevelt—all combined the warrior's courage and strength with the wizard's alluring magic and hot hope.

Though the paths taken by wizards and warriors are distinct, commonalities exist between the two. Both routes require self-knowledge as well as skill and discipline. Both the wizard and the warrior also benefit from teachers, masters of the art. These mentors, be they artisans of combat or magic, help others acquire skills. Through development and learning, evolving leaders deepen their overall understanding of the art and of themselves. It is through this method—in either discipline—that a future leader gains control over powers that could otherwise cause great damage if misdirected or misused.

Both wizards and warriors need passion and commitment to the path chosen, along with the determination to press forward—even when the path is hard and the destination is unclear. You just have to believe and have faith. The only way a leader can realize an organization's success is with bold steps into battles and beliefs.

Being Responsible: Boards Are Reexamining the Bottom Line

Andrew P. Kakabadse

More and more companies, especially in Europe, are shifting their myopic view of the financial bottom line to embrace an approach called *corporate social responsibility*, which proposes that companies' policies, practices, and decisions should take into account not only financial performance but also the social and environmental consequences of company activities. A recent study examined how boards of directors of companies around the world view CSR, which has gained such prominence that it is now firmly entrenched as a critical item on board agendas.

Since the dawn of the modern corporation, the standard modus operandi of companies throughout the world has been to focus almost exclusively on a single bottom line—*financial performance*. The overwhelming emphasis has been on profits, returns on investment, dividends to shareholders, and other such economic factors. In recent years, however, more and more companies—many of them based in Europe—have increasingly been shifting their attention to an approach called *corporate social responsibility*, which proposes that companies' policies, practices, and decisions should take into account not only financial performance but also the social and environmental consequences of company activities.

A number of developments have led to this shift in approach. Corporate wrongdoing—including the scandals perpetrated by top executives at Enron, WorldCom, Tyco, and other companies that led to these companies' demise—has certainly been one of the main ones. But other factors, such as corporate raiding and the escalation of CEO and other executive compensation even as stock values dropped, have also played roles in the emergence of corporate social responsibility (CSR) onto the global business scene.

Still, the move toward CSR continues to encounter resistance, as evidenced by the scene at a recent senior management team meeting of a company in the United States. When the senior vice president of human resources insisted that corporate social responsibility is here to stay and that the company should at least take a position on it to present to the media, he was met with an indifferent reaction from his fellow executives. So even though there is an increasing awareness of and sophistication about CSR, at many companies management remains reluctant to delve deeply into the topic.

In addition, CSR has arisen from an ethos of social obligation, a disposition that likely has grown from the culture of communal responsibility prevalent in Scandinavia, France, Germany, and parts of the Mediterranean area. In these regions both individuals and companies pay higher taxes than U.S. entities do, with the aim that governments can meet their responsibilities to their citizens. This in turn has created a perspective that companies are "owned" by the community, and politicians expect companies to embrace an array of social responsibilities that many U.S. companies would dismiss as not making economic sense. Molded into the essence of companies in Europe is an expectation that they will embrace CSR over and above economic rationalism.

DIFFERENT MEANINGS

At the same time, within Europe substantially different understandings of CSR exist. Its meaning varies according to the national and regional culture. In Scandinavia generally and also in some French companies, for instance, there tends to be a socially oriented view of responsibility to citizens and the community. To finance such responsibility to a broad spectrum of stakeholders, Scandinavians are required to pay high taxes; the more affluent pay rates of 70 percent or more. The rationale is that everyone throughout society will live better, especially the less fortunate. Sweden and Denmark are among the countries that provide the highest levels of health care irrespective of the ability to pay. In the United States, the United Kingdom, and Australia, such levels of health care are possible only to those who pay high rates for insurance or who are independently wealthy. In Scandinavia, CSR extends beyond corporate boundaries and involves a myriad of stakeholders, including government.

This community-oriented view of CSR holds less relevance in Germany. There and in other countries in continental Europe (including, to a certain extent, France), the focus is more on environmental sustainability, with the aim of leaving a pollution-free environment for future generations. Environmental concerns such as clean water and air and organic farming have taken center stage.

In addition, CSR has been leveraged by political parties, nongovernmental organizations, and pressure groups for political gain. Asserting that multinational corporations have shaped global politics for too long, many politicians in continental Europe (and some in the United Kingdom) are using CSR as a tool to attempt to reshape society. Thus the language of political legitimation has crept into the CSR lexicon. In the creation of a new world, CSR is viewed variously as a way to provide help to the less fortunate, a mechanism for social redistribution, a discipline for environmental protection, and a lever for gaining political advantage.

BOARD ISSUES

CSR has gained such prominence recently that it is now firmly entrenched as a critical item on the agendas of company boards of directors. Among the questions boards are contemplating are these:

- What relationship does the organization have with society and the environment, and what should that relationship optimally be?
- What are the roles and contributions of the organization in regard to society and the environment, and what should those roles and contributions optimally be?
- Is the government passing the buck for social and environmental concerns to the organization?
- Is the organization meeting CSR benchmarks, such as worker health benefits and family leave?

In Europe in particular these questions central to the CSR debate are under scrutiny from academics, the media, and the political elite. In fact the European Commission is extensively promoting a CSR awareness program aimed at organizations' top management teams.

To explore what is happening in the realm of CSR, a study by the Cranfield School of Management, an international business school based in the United Kingdom, looked at the adoption of CSR by boards of directors and top managers of companies in Australia, France, Germany, Great Britain, Ireland, Turkey, and the United States. Four key themes emerged.

Language

The lack of a single, universally accepted definition for the concept of CSR and the corresponding looseness of some terminology associated with CSR irritated the chairmen, CEOs, and board directors of companies in the United Kingdom, the United States, and Australia. *Vague*, *intangible*, and *ghastly* were some of the terms used to describe CSR. The commonly used CSR language substantially reduced any desire to learn any more about the subject; the subject was a turnoff for these individuals.

This was not the case in France and Germany. A substantial proportion of top managers in continental Europe were conversant with CSR language and displayed considerable interest in the topic. They were able to cite chapter and verse of particular CSR legislation and codes.

Said one French company president, "France is the first country in the world that has put the right to live in a healthy environment on the same legal footing as human rights." He then recited the details of the legislation in question.

Apparently, the use of CSR language powerfully determines the degree of interest in CSR.

Risk and Reputation

Another factor concerning language emerged from the Cranfield study. The attitude of U.S., U.K., and Australian board members toward CSR became more positive when the issue was positioned in terms of business. For many of these directors, CSR has no place in boardroom discussions and, by implication, little relevance to company strategy. The board's role, in their view, is to assess or determine strategy, particularly return on investment. However, when CSR initiatives are expressed in the language of risk and reputation, the attention span of directors increases and the possibility of approval is more likely.

"My role is to oversee the maximization of shareholder wealth," said the president, chairman, and CEO of a global logistics company based in the United States. "In order to make the case for intangible expenses with shareholder funds, concentrate on the bottom line and talk to me about cost effectiveness, profit optimization, and risk. Don't tell me about good ideas and what is right to do. That's my job."

Whether irritated with, dismissive of, or proactive about CSR, virtually all top managers agreed that not doing—or being perceived as not doing—something in regard to CSR could damage corporate reputation. But these managers disagreed on the degree of attention that should be given to CSR to avoid risking one's reputation. The research shows that CSR is viewed as something more than just charitable deeds, especially if lack of attention to CSR leads to the tarnishing of reputation. Most of the interviewees acknowledged that being recognized as a great company requires powerful engagement with significant stakeholders.

"We now have a responsibility committee, and I am the chair of that, examining the nonfinancial risks to the company," said the president, CEO, and chairman of a U.S. insurance company. "We know that being a responsible corporation adds a great deal to our reputation."

Corporations that minimized CSR stood in contrast to those that were active on the issue. However, members of CSR-motivated boards were irritated by other companies that adopted CSR as a tool for self-serving promotion.

"It is terrible what some companies are doing just because they look good while some of the good guys (like us), contributing through worthwhile projects, are being battered," said the president, CEO, and chairman of a U.S. pharmaceutical company. "The outside world needs to know what it takes to be responsible."

The Cranfield survey highlights the perception that attention to reputation has diverted investment of attention and resources away from CSR and toward public image. Virtually all the interviewees agreed that this trend is likely to continue into the future.

Spanning Boundaries

In some cases—although all too few—companies working toward CSR had made conscious attempts to attract independent outside directors from CSR-enlightened companies so that their CSR insights and enthusiasm could be introduced to their new companies. The spanning of boundaries—the transferring of knowledge and experience from one board to another—was realized through the addition of a board member with expertise in CSR. Whether the issue was health and safety, clean water, worker remuneration and job security, or charitable deeds, time was made available to capture and transfer the knowledge of the board member knowledgeable and experienced in CSR.

Follow-Through

When it comes to CSR application, how does a board know that its CSR program is on track? The disturbing finding is that most boards do not know. If there is no crisis, it is assumed that all is proceeding as intended.

One food manufacturing company known for its positive CSR stance was disappointed to discover that its CSR programs were not being implemented effectively. From the company's perspective, this was understandable. The company has seven divisions, one with more than eight thousand product lines. Policing such complexity is a difficult task, to say the least. Exercising too much control undermines responsiveness to volatile market shifts. However, allowing for greater discretion can induce inconsistency of practice and thus damage quality.

An investigation into one of the company's particularly profitable products, vanilla, highlighted top management's thoroughness of policy design and good intent. However, by the time intent was translated into reality at the level of the local vanilla bean farmers, curers, and buyers, the main focus was on costs. Costs determined profitability, and the easiest cost to control was CSR activities related to the farming and preparation of vanilla. The local buyers pressured the farmers and curers to reduce their costs, with the unfortunate consequence that all three groups existed just below the poverty line. The poor were unwittingly making the poor even poorer. The CSR program, despite so much support from top management, was unsuccessful at the level of the farmers, buyers, and curers.

Learning of this the company's top management was aghast. It stringently introduced control and measurement protocols throughout the vanilla supply chain, only to discover a dilemma—cost discipline was at odds with CSR attentiveness. Improving the social and living conditions among those in the supply chain would make the company's vanilla barely competitive in the open market; to fail to improve conditions would keep people at the poverty level.

The company's solution was to relocate the vanilla farms from Africa (Madagascar and Uganda) to India. India has less fertile soil and poorer growing conditions for vanilla, but it holds the cost advantage of collective farming, whereas Madagascar and Uganda have thousands of independent small operators who are unable to realize economies of scale. The net result was greater poverty in Madagascar and Uganda, greater levels of employment in India, and a more competitively priced vanilla product for the world market. However, disciplined follow-through at least forced a strategic choice that was manageable despite some unwelcome consequences.

VALUABLE LESSONS

What can companies and their boards of directors take away from the Cranfield study on CSR?

- Have a defensible CSR strategy that is executable given existing resources, needs, and challenges. All evidence points to the fact that CSR is here to stay.
- Be knowledgeable about CSR meanings and language. For some CSR denotes social care, for others environmental protection, for others philanthropy, and for still others health and safety. Sensitivity to language is particularly pertinent if one is to defend the adoption of CSR within a company when various other interest groups attempt to leverage the concept for their own political goals.
- Attract CSR skills to the board. Companies with CSR-experienced, independent, outside board directors are still a rarity. In today's global village, however, safeguarding a company's reputation may require appointing at least one board member who has a track record of making CSR work.
- To attract the attention of the board, determine and provide a strong business case for CSR. The clearer the reason for adopting CSR, the greater the likelihood of board approval

and of encouragement from lower-level management during the implementation phase.

- Be consistent in applying CSR. A big challenge for companies is following through on strategy into operations to make CSR work. There is little point in announcing a CSR program if the news media discover that it's being inconsistently applied.

Above all, ensure that the board as a whole cannot be labeled well intended but CSR-ineffective. Boards must be aware that in some parts of the world CSR is seen as a political issue. If the prevailing will of the board members is to comply with CSR, then the board should do so, clearly stating the CSR platform of the corporation. Competitive advantage is gained from what one does, not from what one promises.

Rising to the Challenge: How to Develop Responsible Leaders

Andrew Wilson

Today's companies recognize that they are actors in large, complex systems and that they need to interact in a web of relations with various groups of stakeholders. In particular, businesses are facing increasing pressures to make a positive contribution to society beyond the traditional economic benefits that derive from corporate activities. However, many organizations are struggling to define and develop the leadership skills and abilities necessary to translate the principles of corporate social responsibility into practice. A recent study provides some clarity.

Talk to any senior manager in a large company today, and you'll likely hear that the biggest challenge he or she faces is managing complexity. In the traditional hierarchical organization the role of leading people was relatively straightforward. Influence and authority came with position and status, the boundaries of decision making were prescribed by functional silos, and the business itself operated in a relatively stable and orderly system.

Today the picture is entirely different. Companies recognize that they are actors in large, complex systems and that they need to interact in a web of relations with various groups of stakeholders. Realizing corporate success requires a delicate balance of dialogue and interaction with groups and individuals both inside and outside the organization. Leadership is now about balancing competing demands and engaging people in collective goals.

Perhaps most important, businesses of all sizes, in all sectors, and in many different countries are facing increasing pressures to make a positive contribution to society beyond the traditional economic benefits that derive from corporate activities. Developing appropriate management behaviors for operating effectively in this new environment is at the heart of debates about the nature and character of corporate social responsibility (CSR). However, where many organizations struggle is in defining and developing the leadership skills and abilities necessary to translate the principles of CSR into practice.

A research study from the Ashridge Centre for Business and Society and the European Academy of Business in Society

set out to provide clarity in this nebulous area and resulted in the articulation of a set of *reflexive abilities* required for responsible leadership.

In essence the study involved two distinct but related strands of inquiry. The first comprised a large-scale questionnaire distributed to managers operating in public- and private-sector organizations across Europe. The questionnaire focused on the attitudes and beliefs that drive responsible management practice. More than a hundred senior managers responded to this questionnaire.

The second, qualitative approach comprised a series of in-depth interviews with senior managers in leading, European-based, multinational companies. For each interview the research team attempted to bring together senior representatives from functions including CSR, human resources, and operations. The interviews focused on how to equip managers with the knowledge, skills, and attitudes required to operate effectively in today's complex business environment. These in-depth interviews involved twenty-four senior managers in eleven leading multinational corporations: BP, Cargill, Dexia, Eni, IBM, Johnson & Johnson, Microsoft, Shell, Solvay, Suez, and Unilever.

CONSIDER THESE

When the wealth of qualitative information gathered from the interviews was combined with the quantitative data derived from the survey, it became clear that defining and describing behavior that leads to and supports CSR requires a consideration of leadership qualities, management skills, and reflexive abilities.

Leadership qualities. When defining responsible business behavior, the starting point is the leadership qualities found in individuals' personal attitudes and beliefs. These qualities are values driven and relate to the moral aspects of decision making—distinguishing between right and wrong and good and bad, for instance. As such, they comprise individual characteristics such as honesty and integrity. They are deep-seated personal qualities that change and develop only slowly and over time.

Management skills. Management skills can be seen as the antithesis of leadership qualities—they are amoral, normative, and entirely instrumental. They are the aspects of management practice that are the tangible manifestation of socially and environmentally responsible business behavior. They include expertise in areas such as stakeholder relations and building partnerships. Unlike leadership qualities, management skills are amenable to being taught and developed over the short term.

Reflexive abilities. The reflexive abilities identified through the research are a synthesis of leadership qualities and management skills. They are the core characteristics of responsible behavior and are made up of a mixture of skills, attitudes, and knowledge sets. Reflexive abilities can be considered the key competencies required to integrate social and environmental considerations into core business decision making.

REFLEX ACTION

Five interrelated reflexive abilities were identified by the research.

Systemic Thinking

Dealing with complexity requires the ability to think strategically, to understand the bigger picture, and to appreciate the diverse networks in which an organization operates. At its simplest, systemic thinking is the ability to understand the interdependency of systems across the business and between the business and society.

Interviewees suggested that systemic thinking requires a deep understanding of both internal organizational relations and external social, economic, environmental, and cultural dynamics. To be successful, managers are required to undertake a key strategic shift in the way they view the world—they need to recognize that their company is not operating in a closed system.

In addition, they are required to interpret the signals given by actors in the market and must be able to respond appropriately.

Several interviewees drew a distinction between systemic thinking and the appreciation of complexity required in such traditional management disciplines as finance and engineering. Traditional management disciplines often call for a form of analytical thinking that seeks to understand complex situations by breaking them down into their constituent parts and analyzing the impact of individual components on the problem being addressed.

In contrast, social and environmental complexity (an appreciation of which is at the heart of systemic thinking) is simply not amenable to this type of analysis. It requires a new form of complex reasoning, one that moves beyond the consideration of individual components to an analysis of the interrelations across the whole system in order to understand how things interact with one another at the broadest possible level.

Embracing Diversity

The second reflexive ability is embracing diversity. Clearly, at one level this ability is simply about building corporate teams that reflect the diversity of the societies in which they operate. Although this is considered necessary, it is not sufficient for managers to be truly responsive.

Diversity in its broader sense is seen as the answer to complexity. Interviewees were aware that heterogeneous groups (whether mixed in gender, race, culture, or some other aspect), thanks to their members' differences, are better able than homogeneous groups to appreciate the complexity of the situations in which they operate. It was suggested that the wrong way to deal with complexity is to deny its existence or to increase its amplitude by dealing with issues using homogeneous groups.

There was a strong agreement that individuals and organizations need to respect diversity by acknowledging it, building bridges across different groups, and seeking common ground without forcing consensus. In other words, respecting difference is vitally important in acknowledging diversity. Overall the message was that the business decision-making process needs to structure relations that will maximize the exchange of ideas and learning across different groups both inside and outside the company.

Balancing Local and Global Perspectives

The third reflexive ability concerns the capacity to see and appreciate the impact of local decisions on the global stage. The organizations involved in the research are largely decentralized companies that operate in many countries and deal with a wide diversity of cultures and values around the world. At the same time, they are often striving to operate according to one set of values and beliefs.

In itself this is simply a reiteration of the oft-repeated dilemma of a company trying to be both global and local. It raises issues of how to maintain a global framework of values and at the same time respect local diversity. It also relates to difficulties in ensuring consistent operational standards while encouraging innovation and entrepreneurship in operating units.

Most pertinent to the issues raised in this study, however, is that the interviewees believed the biggest challenge is understanding where the limits of corporate responsibility lie. Part of meeting this challenge is a willingness to take action on issues for which the company is considered accountable even though it has no direct responsibility as an individual organization. Examples of such issues include climate change, access to medicines, and social inequality.

Meaningful Dialogue

The fourth area of interest is the ability to maintain meaningful dialogue with others by listening, inquiring, and responding appropriately. One interviewee provided specific examples of how this approach has changed the decision-making process. He described it as moving from a process in which one "decides, announces the outcome, and defends the decision" to a process of "dialogue, deciding, and implementing." This simple description is a powerful shorthand portrayal of a much more comprehensive method of stakeholder engagement.

The value in developing new forms of meaningful dialogue is the opportunity they offer to explore assumptions, ideas, and beliefs that inform individual and organizational behaviors and actions. In this way companies and their stakeholders can begin to explore how cultural differences between groups can cause clashes—often without an appreciation of what is occurring.

One of the key advantages of building external connections and getting engagement from others is gaining an external perspective on the business. This does not, however, diminish the difficulties of deciding which issues are appropriate for the organization to address and which external viewpoints should legitimately be heard. Interviewees highlighted these decisions as a hugely important aspect of building meaningful dialogue; in understanding the pertinent issues at the intersection between business and society, leaders need to distinguish between the potential indirect impacts of the company and the core contribution it can make to society.

Emotional Awareness

The final area mentioned by many involved in the research was emotional awareness—described variously as empathy, perception, curiosity, and the ability to use the right-hand side of the brain in decision making. One interviewee described this simply as the ability to understand the broader implications of decisions and actions for others.

The capacity to identify the interrelationships between thoughts, behaviors, and emotions is considered vital to operating successfully in today's business environment. Interviewees observed that all too often reactions to business decisions are not based on rational analysis but on feelings and perceptions. When going through the decision-making process, managers frequently describe their thoughts on business issues in entirely rational terms—ignoring the fact that their viewpoints are not only the product of conscious intellect but are also colored by their feelings, emotions, and desires. Hence it is important for managers to have the ability and willingness to recognize that business decisions are not always driven by a process of economic rationality.

Another element of emotional awareness is a tolerance of unusual approaches. Integrating CSR into an organization requires managers to go beyond the well-known (and well-worn) analysis of business issues. To deal with uncertainty and complexity they need to adopt unorthodox approaches to addressing the competing demands that various stakeholder groups place on the business.

A final aspect of emotional awareness is related to the characteristics of managers themselves. Interviewees spoke of the need to develop and enhance personal qualities of reticence and sensitivity. This observation often revolved around the recognition that in today's rapidly changing business environment one must accept that it is not always possible to be in control or to have perfect knowledge of the outcomes of one's decisions. Although this was not put forward as a reason for abdicating responsibility, it was argued that successful managers must retain a sense of humility—a characteristic in sharp contrast to the model of heroic leadership.

THE IMPLICATIONS

As we consider these five reflexive abilities that represent the management skills and qualities required for responsible leadership, the question becomes: What are the implications for the way managers and leaders are developed?

It is clear that the managers who participated in this study feel that business schools can constructively participate in developing the reflexive abilities. However, at the same time the managers did identify some challenges.

First, it is clear that management development for corporate responsibility needs to address fundamental questions of how an individual views the world—how he or she ascribes value to certain types of management and corporate behavior.

Developing individuals' knowledge and skills will inform their worldviews and values to a certain extent. However, the reflexive abilities identified through this research describe more fundamental features of an individual's character and personality. If people are to question, explore, and make meaning out of the values and assumptions that inform their decision-making processes, they will require the support of a carefully structured process of analysis and reflection—something that is not necessarily compatible with much of the traditional content of management development programs in business schools.

Second, the experience of businesses involved in this research suggests that this process cannot necessarily be done in the traditional classroom environment. There is a strong need for greater use of experiential learning techniques—exposing people directly to different situations and giving them the opportunity to reflect and experiment with potential ways of dealing with these experiences.

Third, it is vitally important that a traditional Anglo-American or European business education should avoid what some describe as *cultural imperialism*—inadvertently promoting the social, political, and economic norms and values of the developed world. Interviewees argued strongly that responsible leadership requires an appreciation of cultural diversity. This view was extended by some to question the use of business models that focus exclusively on maximizing shareholder returns to the exclusion of other stakeholders.

The final challenge set down by the interviewed managers was one that is currently the subject of great debate in the academic community: to what extent should corporate responsibility be integrated into existing business disciplines rather than taught as a separate subject? Perhaps not surprisingly, the jury is still out on this issue.

Some interviewees were adamant that traditional management disciplines need to extend their scope to include issues of CSR. So, for example, finance and accounting should incorporate issues of transparency and accountability, marketing could encompass cause-related partnerships, and classes on organizational behavior might examine multiple styles of leadership and their various impacts on boardroom behavior.

Others argued that the issues are, by their very nature, multidisciplinary and so require treatment and consideration in their own right. If business school participants are to understand the changing relationship between business and society, they need to study this complex phenomenon from a systemic perspective—explicitly exploring the competing demands and interests of different stakeholder groups.

Fortunately, the purpose of this research was not to try to resolve this debate. However, it is interesting to note that the companies involved in the study have yet to reach a consensus; even within single companies CSR is both integrated into existing leadership development programs and taught as a stand-alone discipline for managers.

VALUABLE EXPERIENCE

It is clear that corporate practice in developing responsible business behavior is relatively well developed in the companies involved in the study. Although all these companies would be quick to point out that they still have a lot to learn, the evidence is that they have much experience from which business schools can benefit.

The research uncovered many examples of management development initiatives that are introducing people to topics and issues that make them question existing models of business behavior. Managers are being encouraged to analyze the potential future of their companies with a critical eye. They are addressing real-world issues and developing the capacity to innovate, to stretch, and to challenge conventional wisdom on how to deliver business success in a way that respects the society and environment in which they operate.

In short, the companies involved in the research are beginning to rise to the challenge of developing responsible leaders for tomorrow's business. Those of us who are involved in management training and leadership development can learn much from their experience.

Capital Ideas: Enhancing the Power of Human Assets

Gary Yukl and Richard Lepsinger

In today's rapidly changing and competitive business environment, organizations and their leaders must pay attention to an asset that is sometimes given short shrift—*human capital*, the skills and motivation of the organization's employees. Leaders at all levels can have a strong influence on human capital through a combination of relations-oriented behaviors and human resource management programs.

When most people think about organizational capital, they think about such things as production plants, equipment, property, and other tangible assets that contribute to yielding revenue and other desired results. But in today's increasingly volatile business environment, another form of capital may be more important for long-term performance. With global competition, shifting markets, and the emergence of new business models, organizations need to be more responsive to change, more flexible, and more resilient. To achieve these goals organizations need to be strong in the area of *human capital*—hiring, nurturing, and retaining skilled, talented people who are highly motivated to do their jobs well.

The eighteenth-century British economist Adam Smith described the concept of human capital, identifying it as one of four types of capital: useful machines and instruments of the trade; buildings as a means of procuring revenue; improvements of land; and finally human capital, which he saw as a combination of skills, dexterity, and judgment.

There is growing evidence that human capital has a significant impact on the financial performance of an organization. A study of three thousand companies, conducted by the National Center on the Educational Quality of the Workforce at the University of Pennsylvania, found that spending 10 percent of revenue on human capital increased productivity by nearly twice as much as spending the same amount on capital improvements.

Being proficient in managing human capital is especially important when the work is complex, when extensive training is needed for new employees or team members, and when it is difficult to recruit competent replacements for employees who leave.

Research on leadership and management makes it clear that leaders at all levels can have a strong influence on human capital. This influence can be achieved with an appropriate mix of relations-oriented behaviors and human resource management programs.

ACTIONS AND REACTIONS

Leadership behaviors that can be used to enhance employee skills, motivation, and cooperation include *supporting, recognizing, developing, consulting, empowering,* and *team building*. These relations-oriented behaviors are relevant for all leaders, but it is necessary to use them in ways that are appropriate for the leadership situation.

Supporting includes a variety of leadership behaviors that show consideration, acceptance, respect, and concern for the needs and feelings of others. Examples of supporting include listening carefully when someone is upset or has a problem, giving encouragement when a person has a difficult or stressful task or responsibility, being patient and helpful when giving complicated explanations or instructions, and offering to provide advice or assistance when someone needs help with a difficult task or problem.

More supporting is necessary when the work is repetitive and tedious, when there are interactions with demanding customers, when long hours must be worked to meet difficult deadlines, when employees have become frustrated and discouraged by temporary setbacks and lack of progress on major projects, when the work is dangerous and employees are worried about their safety, and when people are going through major transitions in their personal lives, such as changes involving a new baby, a divorce, or the death or serious illness of a family member.

Supportive leadership conveys positive regard for others and shows that the leader views them as worthy of respect and consideration. Supporting behaviors help to build and maintain effective interpersonal relationships and are strongly related to satisfaction with the leader. Effective leaders try to spend time with direct reports and other important colleagues to get to know them better and relate to them as individuals. In the process there are opportunities to build the mutual respect and trust that are the basis for a cooperative working relationship. The emotional ties created by supporting make it easier to gain the cooperation and support needed from colleagues to get the work done. It is more satisfying to work for or with someone who is friendly, cooperative, and supportive than with someone who is cold and impersonal—or worse, hostile, uncooperative, and lacking respect for others.

Supportive leadership is often demonstrated as part of a broader interaction, and it can take many forms. Consider these two examples. When a sales representative was concerned about getting credit for a sale he had helped to make in a region outside his own, his boss helped to persuade the manager of the other region to give the sales representative appropriate credit. And when an employee at an investment bank had a need to spend more time at home with her young children, her manager arranged for her to work from home two days a week.

Recognizing is giving praise and showing appreciation to others for effective performances, significant achievements, and special contributions. Examples of recognizing are giving awards and holding recognition ceremonies. Everyone from the clerk in the shipping department to the vice president of operations wants recognition for effective performance. Recognizing is very effective for building commitment, increasing job satisfaction, and improving working relationships, so it is surprising that it is one of the most underused leadership behaviors. Many leaders tend to notice and criticize ineffective behavior but fail to notice and praise effective behavior.

Recognition should be provided for contributions that are important for the success of the work unit and consistent with the values of the organization. These accomplishments may involve teamwork, customer service, open communication, respect for others, and initiative. People whose performance and achievements are highly visible often get more recognition, but it is equally important to recognize people whose contributions are less visible and whose performance is harder to measure. Recognition should be given to people in support functions as well as to people in line functions with easily quantifiable performance gauges such as production or sales.

Recognition should not be limited to successful efforts. Recognizing diligent even though unsuccessful efforts communicates to employees that the organization values risk taking, initiative, and experimenting with innovative ideas to improve work processes, products, and services. Another fallacy is to limit recognition to a few best performers. This can create extreme competition among people that in turn can produce such undesirable side effects as an unwillingness to help team members and resentment among people who performed well but received little or no recognition because someone else had a slightly better performance. It is better to give an award to everyone who exceeds a challenging performance standard than to recognize only the person with the best performance.

It is also better to recognize many winners than to recognize only a few. For people with only average accomplishments, some form of recognition for improvements in performance will encourage efforts to achieve higher performance. The leader should clearly communicate an expectation of continuing progress toward excellence, not an acceptance of average performance. Even when recognition is provided to many people, it is still possible to have different amounts of recognition for different levels of performance. Unless the people with the best performances receive greater recognition, their accomplishments will be unnecessarily diminished and the desired benefit from recognition may not be realized.

Developing includes several managerial practices that can increase relevant skills, help people adjust to their current jobs, and facilitate career advancement. Some examples of developing behavior are providing coaching and feedback, encouraging people to participate in relevant training programs, setting developmental goals for direct reports, making developmental assignments, promoting a person's reputation in the organization, and providing opportunities for people to demonstrate their skills and potential for advancement.

Coaching is one of the most effective ways for leaders to enhance competence, and it includes efforts to improve skills relevant for performing future jobs, not just skills necessary to perform a current job. Even a highly motivated person may not be able to improve performance or learn new skills without assistance, and coaching is one way to provide this help. Effective leaders help people assess their strengths and weaknesses, identify reasons for mistakes or problems, and evaluate whether improvement plans are feasible and appropriate. Asking probing questions is a good way to help a person identify key issues and explore options that are not obvious. Sometimes it is helpful to suggest specific things the person may want to consider when confronted with a difficult problem.

Career counseling can be used to increase the skills and self-confidence of direct reports and help them achieve their potential. To provide good advice, the leader must understand the person's background, interests, and career aspirations. Examples of career counseling include encouraging the person to set ambitious but realistic career goals, helping the person to identify career paths and promotion opportunities in the organization, and explaining to the person the advantages and pitfalls of various assignments or potential job changes. Often it is useful to share insights learned from experiencing problems or choices similar to those now faced by the person who is being advised. When appropriate, the leader can also suggest someone else in the organization or profession who can be trusted to provide good career advice.

A leader can facilitate career advancement for employees by helping them identify skills needed to prepare for a promotion or a career change, by providing information about opportunities for acquiring skills (for example, training programs, courses, and workshops), and by encouraging people to take advantage of these opportunities.

Attendance at training seminars and courses can be facilitated by providing financial compensation and rearranging an employee's schedule to allow time away from work. Another way to facilitate skill acquisition is to make developmental assignments that provide an opportunity to assume new responsibilities. It is important to provide opportunities to learn from experience in dealing with challenging assignments, but it is also essential for the person to experience progress and success in learning new skills rather than a series of repeated failures. Thus developmental assignments should be made carefully, and adequate support, encouragement, and coaching should be provided.

Consulting means involving people in decisions that will affect them; this behavior is sometimes called *participative leadership*. Consulting should be used with direct reports and colleagues when they have the relevant knowledge and information to develop strategies and plans and when the success of a decision or plan depends on their commitment to implement it successfully.

Consulting can take various forms that have different amounts of influence over the final decision. Some examples are asking for suggestions before making a decision, revising a tentative decision after listening to concerns expressed by others, and asking an individual or group to make a decision jointly with you. People can be invited to participate in any stage of the decision process—for instance, when diagnosing a problem to determine its cause, selecting decision criteria, identifying and evaluating alternatives, and developing action plans for implementing the decision.

People invited to participate in making a decision or planning an activity or change are more likely than nonparticipants are to understand the issues relevant to the ultimate decision and the reasons why a particular alternative was accepted or rejected. Participating in the process also gives people the opportunity to voice concerns about a proposal and to influence the development of a solution that deals with these concerns. People feel valued when they are involved and are more motivated to work toward accomplishing goals that are important to the organization and the work unit. These potential benefits are not automatic, however, and if consulting is not used skillfully for appropriate situations it can have negative consequences.

Leaders will elicit more candid reactions and helpful suggestions if they present a proposal as tentative and encourage people to improve on it, rather than asking people to react to an elaborate plan that appears complete. In the latter case, people tend to be inhibited about expressing concerns that appear to be criticisms of the plan. It is important to make a serious effort to use suggestions and to deal with concerns expressed by people who have been consulted. Many people focus quickly on the weaknesses of someone else's idea or suggestion without giving enough consideration to its strengths. It is helpful to make a conscious effort to find the positive aspects of an idea and mention them before mentioning negative aspects. An initial idea is usually incomplete but can be turned into a much better idea with a little conscious effort. Rather than automatically rejecting an idea that has obvious weaknesses, it is useful to discuss how the weaknesses could be overcome and to consider other, potentially better ideas that build on the original one.

Empowering is allowing a person to have substantial responsibility and discretion for meaningful and important tasks, providing the information and resources needed to make and implement decisions, and trusting the person to solve problems and make decisions without getting prior approval. An important aspect of empowering is delegation, which involves assigning new projects and responsibilities to individuals or a team and providing the authority, resources, direction, and support needed to achieve the expected results.

In today's organizations, leaders are neither able nor expected to do everything themselves. Substantial delegation is essential in fast-changing environments that require high initiative and quick responses from frontline employees. People are likely to have more commitment to implementing a decision when they feel they have ownership of the decision and are accountable for its consequences. Delegation can also result in better decisions when competent individuals or teams are closer than the leader to a problem and have more timely information about it. Delegation can provide more opportunities for people to learn new skills as they struggle with a challenging task that requires them to exercise initiative and problem solving. When a leader is overloaded with responsibilities, delegation is a good way to free up time to focus on key responsibilities.

Delegation involves giving people the discretion to determine how to do a task without interference, but it is only natural for a leader to be concerned about the quality of the output or the ability of the person or team to handle problems along the way. To achieve the potential benefits of delegation, it is necessary to find a good balance between autonomy and control. Monitoring too closely will send a message of a lack of trust in a person's ability, but abdicating all responsibility may contribute to failure and frustration for the person or team assigned to the task. The leader should explain clearly the amount of discretion to be allowed, which should reflect the skills and experience of the people who are empowered.

Team building increases team members' mutual trust, cooperation, and identification with the team or organization. Even a talented, well-organized team may fail to carry out its mission successfully if it lacks a high level of cooperation, cohesiveness, and mutual trust among team members. Cooperation is especially important when the group has tasks that require members to share information, equipment, and other resources; to help one another; and to work in close proximity for long periods of time under stressful conditions. A lack of trust and acceptance is especially likely to be a problem in newly formed teams and in teams whose members disagree sharply on work-related issues. It is particularly essential for leaders in these situations to use team-building practices and related behaviors to build mutual trust and cooperation.

Ceremonies and rituals can be used to increase identification with the team and to make membership in the team seem special. Initiation rituals may be used to induct new members into a group, and retirement rituals to celebrate the departure of outgoing members. Ceremonies to celebrate special achievements or mark anniversaries of special events in the history of the group are most useful when they emphasize the group's values and traditions. A symbol of group identity, such as a team name, slogan, logo, or insignia, can be an effective part of creating strong group identification, especially when team members agree to wear or display one or more symbols of membership.

A cohesive group is more likely to develop when team members get to know one another on a personal level and find it satisfying to interact socially. Periodic social activities such as dinners, lunches and parties, and outings (a sporting event or concert or a camping or rafting trip, for example) can be used to facilitate personal interactions. When team members work in the same facility, social interaction can be promoted by designating a room for informal meetings, lunch, and coffee breaks. The room can be decorated with symbols of the group's accomplishments, statements of its values, and charts showing progress in accomplishing group objectives.

COMBINING BEHAVIORS

Relations-oriented behaviors are most effective when used in complementary ways. Consistent use of supporting and recognizing, for instance, conveys the leader's respect and positive regard for people and improves interpersonal relations. Consulting, team building, empowering, and developing can be used together to improve decisions and build the skills, self-confidence, and commitment of direct reports. Developing more skills and self-confidence in people makes it more possible to involve them in making important decisions and to delegate important tasks to them. In turn, the performance of challenging tasks and assignments provides an opportunity for people to further refine their skills as they learn from experience. Team building to increase mutual trust and cooperation makes it more feasible to empower the team to determine for itself how to solve problems and accomplish shared goals.

HR PROGRAMS

There are many types of human resource management programs that can be used to improve human relations and resources, including programs for recruiting, selection, employee orientation, training, mentoring, compensation and benefits, talent management, succession planning, recognition, empowerment, and employee stock ownership. When appropriately designed, these programs can improve employee satisfaction, motivation, creativity, and commitment to the organization. Top managers have more influence over these programs than do middle- and lower-level managers, but the success of the programs depends on the support and cooperation of these other managers.

Human resource management programs can be expensive, and it is the responsibility of top management to determine which programs are cost effective, mutually compatible, and relevant for the organization's competitive strategy and external challenges. Even costly programs can be worthwhile for organizations when they provide offsetting benefits and are compatible with the strategy and challenges. For example, discount retailer Costco makes significant financial commitments to providing generous pay, excellent health benefits, and a good retirement plan, but as a result the company has some of the most loyal and productive employees in the industry. The cost of compensation and benefits is higher than at competing firms, but this cost is more than offset by the savings realized from lower turnover costs, lower employee theft, and higher employee productivity.

Relations-oriented behaviors and human resource management programs can be complementary ways for leaders to influence human capital. The relations-oriented behaviors can also facilitate the implementation and successful use of new programs.

For example, a new training program is more likely to be successful when managers encourage direct reports to attend the program and provide them with opportunities to use newly learned skills on the job.

Management programs can enhance the effects of direct leadership behaviors. For example, a program that provides rewards for innovative ideas can facilitate the efforts of managers to encourage their people to be more creative. Management programs can also serve as substitutes for some types of direct behaviors. For example, company-wide training programs for generic skills that are relevant for many employees can reduce the amount of training that individual managers need to provide to their immediate subordinates.

To achieve the maximum potential benefits from human capital, leaders need to find an appropriate combination of behaviors and programs for their current situation. It is also essential for leaders at each level of the organization to coordinate their efforts to enhance human capital. Finally, it is important for top executives to understand that enhancement of human capital includes developing not only lower-level employees but also the future leaders of the organization.

Good Choices: Making Better Decisions by Knowing How Best to Decide

Christopher Musselwhite

Effective decision makers know that deciding what's best and knowing how best to decide are two very different skills. A leader's mastery of the difference between these two capabilities has major implications for both the decision maker and those affected by the decisions.

Making good decisions is a primary responsibility and challenge of leadership. Every day, individuals and organizations face a constantly changing landscape of dangers and opportunities. To some degree every decision directs strategies, commits resources, sets current courses of action, and creates future opportunities and challenges.

Research shows that organizations with above-average decision-making practices achieve a substantially greater financial return on sales and return on investment. Add to this the reality that today's leaders must make decisions in dynamic environments characterized by changing circumstances and complex situations—all of which are further complicated by competing individual interests, incomplete or questionable information, personal biases, and in most cases limited time.

A recent high-profile decision exemplifying this importance and complexity is the highly debated American Recovery and Reinvestment Act of 2009, the economic stimulus package signed into law by President Obama on February 17 of that year.

Under pressure to act as the economy continued to tank, Congress drafted and enacted this complex piece of legislation in less than a month, establishing a controversial package that would distribute nearly $800 billion of taxpayer funds.

This example suggests the degree to which the decision-making process is more complex today than ever before, the quality of decisions more important, and the development of decision-making competency among leaders more critical to organizational performance and sustainability.

Regardless of the complexity of the decision-making environment, there is strong evidence that many leaders demonstrate personal preferences in decision-making styles. A key characteristic

of these preferences is the degree of input the decision maker solicits when making a decision. The good news is that leaders can improve the effectiveness of their decision making by using a process that has been proven to help them recognize when they need to adapt their personal decision-making style to bring about the best outcome.

When this skill of knowing how best to decide is developed, leaders avoid defaulting to familiar but limiting decision-making preferences and instead are able to choose the style that will produce the optimum outcome in each situation.

LESSONS OF EXPERIENCE

Effective leaders know the value of experience in learning how to make good decisions and are open to learning from both others' successes and mistakes and their own.

Researchers have observed certain attributes and behaviors in leaders who are consistently associated with high-quality and viable decision making:

- Flexibility and risk taking
- Honesty and trust
- Openness to new ideas and feedback
- Willingness to challenge the status quo and to voice and hear unpopular truths
- Reliance on accurate information
- Consideration of the far-ranging consequences of a decision
- Consideration of those who must accept and implement the decision

Note that these attributes and behaviors affect the decision-making process. Effective decision makers know that deciding what's best and knowing how best to decide are two very different skills. Mastery of the difference between these two capabilities has major implications for both the decision maker and those affected by the decisions. It also affects the way leaders go about developing their decision-making ability.

The first skill—deciding what's best—can be developed over time through education and experience. The latter skill—knowing how best to decide—can be taught directly and applied immediately.

The intangible aspects of decision making make it challenging to learn and develop. In the effort to use experience and resources to learn how best to decide, it helps to gain a better understanding of the decision-making process and what can go wrong.

A common phrase heard in leadership circles is that "decision making is an art." This supports the belief that the decision-making process is highly personal and intuitive. Decision making is indeed something people do naturally, minute by minute, and it is influenced by such individual factors as logic, emotions, culture, and values.

As is the case with most skills, some people are naturally better decision makers than others. However, research supports the nurture-over-nature argument in this instance, demonstrating that decision-making effectiveness is not correlated with personality preferences or gender. These findings support the belief that all decision makers are susceptible to common decision-making traps and that being able to choose the most appropriate decision-making style is a learned capability.

HURDLES AHEAD

Leaders who draw on experience to improve their decision making have probably catalogued the many pitfalls and barriers they encounter when making and implementing decisions. These barriers to good decision making can be grouped into four categories: inadequate problem identification, interpersonal barriers, analytical barriers, and failures in learning.

Inadequate Problem Identification

Most people have experienced this dilemma—you work diligently to solve a problem only to discover well down the road that you are working on the wrong problem. No amount of manipulating or reframing will result in the outcomes you originally hoped for. Inadequate problem identification can lead to weak problem analysis, a focus on inappropriate data, incorrect identification of stakeholders, over- or underestimating the scope and range of the problem, and failure to consider the full range of consequences. All this results in effort spent on the wrong problem, which wastes time, energy, and resources.

One way to improve problem identification is by asking good questions. For example, let's say the problem you face is to rid your house of mice. If you ask, Why do I want to solve this problem? you could answer that the reason is to ensure the health of your family. If you go further and ask, Why do I want to improve the health of my family? then the answer might be to ensure your family's happiness. Asking *why* you want to solve a problem broadens the focus and will affect the way you define the problem and consequently how the decision-making process is framed.

In contrast, asking, What's stopping me from solving this problem? narrows the focus. You might answer that you lack an effective device to catch mice, which then leads to the conclusion that you need to build a better mousetrap. Identifying what's stopping you from solving the problem as well as why you want to solve the problem improves your understanding of the problem and enables you to identify the most appropriate frame for making a decision.

Interpersonal Barriers

Interpersonal barriers to decision making include overconfidence, assigning blame, excluding important stakeholders, and groupthink.

- Overconfidence is confidence not balanced by humility, and it can lead to illusions of invulnerability and inappropriate risk taking among leaders because they mistakenly believe they have more control over events than they really do.

- Assigning blame is the tendency of people to affix fault instead of fixing the problem. Finger pointing inhibits trust, rapport, appropriate risk taking, and collaboration.
- Excluding important stakeholders can occur because of stereotyping and believing that one group is more qualified than others. This can blind leaders to both faults and opportunities, resulting in practices such as in-group favoritism, which bestows benefits on unqualified individuals simply because of their association with power holders.
- Groupthink is a phenomenon in which people, to avoid disharmony or disapproval, go along with what they think the leader and key stakeholders have already decided. This practice can lead to extremely adverse consequences.

Analytical Barriers

Analytical barriers include seeing what you expect to see, analysis paralysis, and choosing on the fly.

- Seeing what you expect to see is a form of information bias that results in leaders accepting evidence that aligns with what they already believe to be true and discounting evidence to the contrary.
- Analysis paralysis occurs when so much differing information is available that it virtually paralyzes leaders, leaving them unable to discern which information is useful and which is merely noise.
- Choosing on the fly is the practice of analyzing options quickly when under pressure or when the decision is assumed (perhaps incorrectly) to be of low importance. This can result in not analyzing enough options or not analyzing options well, even with accurate and relevant information available.

Failures in Learning

Failures in learning that create barriers to good decision making include not reflecting on experience, revising history, and going along with a converging culture.

- Not reflecting on experience is a habit that causes leaders to fail to reflect on prior decisions and their outcomes and to miss out on the learning that can come from analyzing what made a project successful or what made it fail, determining what lessons need to be noted, and assessing what can be improved in the future.
- Revising history causes leaders to inaccurately remember their original assumptions or, worse, to rationalize a failure rather than learn from it.
- Going along with a converging culture means not recognizing an organization's tendency toward becoming more like it already is. This results, for example, in hiring people who resemble current employees, thus limiting the organization's capacity to view itself objectively. A converging culture screens out possible alternatives and often constrains creativity and innovation.

FINDING A PROCESS

Awareness of these barriers can help leaders avoid potential pitfalls and improve decision-making quality. However, cultivating and practicing an effective process for deciding how to decide, one that is applicable in real time, is the most effective deterrent.

Process Step 1: Choose to Decide or to Delegate

In any situation requiring action, the first decision a leader must make is whether to decide or delegate. This choice can be driven by several considerations, such as workload, urgency, degree of crisis, and magnitude of importance.

One of the most important considerations for effective leaders is whether the situation presents an opportunity for developing the leadership skills of someone for whom they are responsible. Developing others is a critical responsibility of leadership. Plus, if good decision-making practices at the leadership level directly correlate to better financial performance, consider the exponential benefit when good decision making is practiced across the organization.

Delegating the right and responsibility to decide an issue is an action that experienced leaders don't take lightly. Delegating decisions to others frees leaders to focus on issues requiring their personal attention. However, even though the responsibility can be passed on, the accountability for performance remains with the leader.

A leader can delegate decision making to an individual or to a team of stakeholders whose interests may include the use of their resources and time, participation in implementation, and the impact of potential outcomes.

Process Step 2: Select a Decision-Making Style

The single biggest complaint I hear about ineffective decision makers is that they are either too inclusive or not inclusive enough in their decision making. Research reveals degree of inclusion as the critical element by which to measure decision-making effectiveness. The work in the 1970s of industrial and organizational psychologists Victor Vroom and Philip Yetton identified degrees of inclusion in a decision-making process that formed a continuum from an autocratic to a consensual approach.

This work has been refined over the years by CCL and by Discovery Learning, which has analyzed input from more than 40,000 managers. This analysis identified five distinct decision-making preferences:

Directing. The leader decides alone with no input.

Fact-finding. The leader gathers some information and decides but doesn't share the problem or solicit suggestions.

Investigating. The leader shares the problem with a select group of stakeholders, solicits their input, and then decides.

Collaborating. The leader shares the problem with all key stakeholders, solicits their input, and then decides.

Teaming. The leader engages all key stakeholders in a consensual decision.

Decisions made in the directing, or highly autocratic, style when stakeholders would have preferred a more inclusive style can have a damping effect on the commitment of stakeholders to implement the decision. Similarly, leaders who require unnecessary and inappropriate participation from others waste people's time and call into question their own capability to decide appropriately. When Captain Chesley B. "Sully" Sullenberger decided to land US Airways Flight 1549 in the Hudson River, the passengers (stakeholders) depended on quick decisions based on his experience, knowledge, and training. The last thing the stakeholders wanted in this situation was for the leader to ask for their input. Leaders who learn to appropriately balance the inclusion of others to secure their commitment but not waste their time will dramatically improve the effectiveness of their decision-making process.

Two decades of data suggest that many managers prefer one of these decision-making styles to all the others, regardless of the specific problem or circumstance. The data also strongly suggest that effective decision makers comfortably use all five styles, from directing to teaming, based on the situation. Having learned to identify key decision factors that point to the style appropriate to any given situation, these effective leaders know when each style is indicated and adapt to that style, regardless of personal preference.

FIVE FACTORS

The appropriate degree of inclusion can be determined by considering five key factors. When each of these factors is fully considered, the style of decision making that will produce the best outcome becomes clearer. The five factors are

Problem clarity. The degree of understanding about the nature and scope of the problem.

Information. The facts and knowledge needed to make the best decision.

Level of commitment. The degree of buy-in and support needed to implement the decision.

Goal agreement. The degree to which stakeholders have common or competing goals among themselves and with the organization.

Time. This factor has two dimensions. The first is the degree of urgency surrounding the decision; the second is the time and effort others must make to participate in the decision-making process.

When these five factors are carefully considered, several positive outcomes can occur. First, the ability to make accurate, quality decisions in a timely manner is enhanced. Second, the risk of being caught by decision-making traps is reduced. And third, obstacles to decision implementation—such as lack of commitment, lack of understanding, resistance or possibly malicious compliance, and long-term damage to relationships between decision makers and stakeholders and among stakeholders—can be eliminated.

The practice of integrating knowledge of the five decision-making styles with consideration of each of the five key factors has been proven to enhance decision-making capability by helping leaders gain a better understanding of the decision-making process, identify which of the five decision-making styles they are most comfortable with and are most likely to default to, and learn how to adapt their decision-making style to produce the most effective outcome.

PROVEN MODEL

Increasingly challenged to reduce the risk from poor decisions and increase positive results from good decisions, leaders must learn how to choose the best way to decide in any given situation. Leaders' failure to understand the barriers they face and to use the appropriate decision-making style can lead to hit-or-miss outcomes.

In contrast, the practice of integrating the five recognized decision-making styles and the five key factors that affect good decision making is the basis for a research-based model proven to help leaders move themselves and their organizations toward more effective outcomes. Leaders using this model will

- Enhance their ability to produce acceptable, quality decisions.
- Reduce the risk of being caught in decision-making traps.
- Eliminate by-products of ineffective decision making.
- Make a positive difference in the organization's bottom line.

With these advantages, there is no question that investing in the development of better decision-making capabilities across the organization will pay off.

ABOUT THE CONTRIBUTORS

Katherine Beatty is director, global portfolio management, at CCL's campus in Colorado Springs.

Michael Beer is chairman and cofounder of TruePoint, a management consulting firm that works with senior executives to transform their companies into high-performing, people-centric businesses. He is the Cahners-Rabb professor of business administration emeritus at Harvard Business School and author or co-author of ten books.

Lee G. Bolman holds the Marion Block Missouri chair in leadership at the University of Missouri–Kansas City's Henry W. Bloch School of Business and Public Administration.

Frank P. Bordonaro, a consultant in corporate learning based in Wilton, Connecticut, formerly was chief learning officer at Prudential Financial and McDonnell Douglas.

Jay A. Conger is the Henry Kravis research professor of leadership studies at Claremont McKenna College, a senior research scientist at the Center for Effective Organizations at the University of Southern California, and visiting professor of organizational behavior at the London Business School.

Terrence E. Deal retired as the Irving R. Melbo professor of education at the University of Southern California's Rossier School of Education.

Shane Douthitt is a managing partner and executive consultant with Strategic Management Decisions, which helps organizations develop human capital strategies based on analytics linking people to critical business outcomes.

Wilfred H. Drath is a former senior fellow and group director of the Leadership for Complex Challenges practice area at CCL.

Magnus Finnström is an associate director at TruePoint, a management consulting firm that works with senior executives to transform their companies into high-performing, people-centric businesses. He is based in the firm's Stockholm office.

William A. Gentry is a senior research associate at CCL.

Richard L. Hughes, a former director of CCL's research and innovation work in the area of groups, teams, and organizations, is transformation chair at the U.S. Air Force Academy.

Andrew P. Kakabadse is a professor of international management development at the Cranfield School of Management in the United Kingdom.

Richard Lepsinger is president of OnPoint Consulting, an organizational and leadership development firm.

John B. McGuire is a senior enterprise associate at CCL's campus in Colorado Springs.

Scott Mondore is a managing partner and executive consultant with Strategic Management Decisions, which helps organizations develop human capital strategies based on analytics linking people to critical business outcomes.

Christopher Musselwhite is president and CEO of Discovery Learning, a company that specializes in executive education and organizational leadership development.

Charles J. Palus is a senior enterprise associate at CCL.

Laura Quinn is a portfolio manager at CCL's campus in Colorado Springs.

Gary Rhodes is an honorary senior fellow and adjunct faculty member at CCL.

Günter K. Stahl is a professor of international management at the Vienna University of Economics and Business and a visiting professor of organizational behavior at INSEAD, an international business school with campuses in Fontainebleau, France, and Singapore.

Andrew Wilson is director of research and development at Ashridge, an international business school based in the United Kingdom, and director of the Ashridge Centre for Business and Society.

Gary Yukl is a professor of management at the University at Albany, State University of New York.

Ordering Information

To get more information, to order other CCL Press publications, or to find out about bulk-order discounts, please contact us by phone at 336-545-2810 or visit our online bookstore at www.ccl.org/publications.

CPSIA information can be obtained
at www.ICGtesting.com
Printed in the USA
FSOW04n0105061016
25803FS

9 781604 911121

The Nelig Stones

SHARON SKINNER

Brick Cave Media
brickcavebooks.com
2013

ISBN-13 978-1-938190-13-1
ISBN-10 1938190130

Printed in the United States of America.

The characters and events in this book are fictitious. Any similarity to real persons, living or dead, is coincidental and not intended by the author.

Cover Illustration by Keith Decesare
Chapter Illustrations by Keith Decesare

Brick Cave Media
brickcavebooks.com
2013

Dedication

To my beautiful, amazing stepdaughters,
Harmony and Aura.
You've taught me more than you will
ever know, especially about
mother-daughter relationships.
Thank you.

Acknowledgements

This book was written with the support of my amazing editor, Anne Lind, who read uncountable drafts and made immeasurable contributions to the final manuscript. Thanks to her, it is so much better than it might have been.

Thanks are also due to the many beta readers along the way and to my incredible publisher, whose unwavering faith in my creative abilities helps keep me writing.

By Sharon Skinner

In Case You Didn't Hear Me the First Time
The Healer's Legacy

*Mirabella and the Faded Phantom**

Also available from brickcavebooks.com
* Forthcoming

The Nelig Stones

SHARON SKINNER

Cameron — May you always find the magic inside you! Sharon Skinner

Brick Cave Media
brickcavebooks.com
2013

CHAPTER ONE

Stupid earrings! Stefani thought. It wasn't like they were diamonds or anything. *And I didn't lose them on purpose. I only wanted to borrow them.*

She sighed. She should never have taken her mother's earrings without asking. But lately it seemed like she couldn't ask her anything without getting some long lecture about rules and responsibility.

She pushed the thought to the back of her mind and gazed at the shimmering desert. Heat rose in blurry waves as the Phoenix valley baked its way toward the predicted high of 112 degrees. That's Fahrenheit, Stefani thought. Scientists should always be specific about measurements. *Anyway, no matter how you add it up, it's hot.*

She took out her bandanna and wiped the sweat from her forehead and gazed at the cloudless sky. At least the temperature was lower inside Hole-in-the-Rock. Stefani leaned against the wall of the rock formation and ran her fingers across its smooth surface. There was nothing better than spending time at Papago Park, exploring the large millions-of-years-old formations, hunting for rocks and taking field notes.

And, best of all, get away from her mother.

She hoisted her backpack and stepped through the stone arch and into the shady, open-air cavern overlooking the park.

She rubbed her thumb across the surface of the plain, black stone she'd just picked up on the trail. Finding it here didn't make sense. It was completely out of place geologically. She rotated it in her fingers, trying to decide what it was. She'd have to look it up in her rocks and minerals guide later. She slipped the stone into her backpack with the others she'd collected, then climbed back down to the main trail.

She took out her cell phone and checked the time. The next connecting bus would stop at the zoo in twenty minutes, plenty of time for her to get down to the bus stop, but her feet refused to head toward the parking lot.

She kicked at a stone. It skittered along the ground, leaving a puff of dust and a slither of gravel in its wake until it came to rest at the base of the formation. She stopped and stared. “What jerks!” Someone had sprayed graffiti on the side of the rocks near the opening of Hole-in-the-Rock.

She hurried over to inspect it closer. The writing was too small for graffiti and it didn’t resemble anything she’d seen painted on the walls of buildings. It was more like symbols than writing. It actually looked a lot like the Native American pictographs they’d been studying in school, or the symbols the ancient Egyptians had carved into the walls of their tombs and cities.

How weird. She’d been coming here forever and never noticed anything like this before.

CHAPTER TWO

Robbie stepped back and stomped on the end of his skateboard, flipping it up and over. He reached out to catch it, but his fingertips only grazed the smooth edge and the board clattered to the pavement. He glanced around to see if anyone had seen his not-so-smooth move. Then he bent down, picked up the board and placed it right side up on the hot sidewalk.

Whenever Robbie's mother worked part-time at her job in the zoo's gift shop, she let him spend time skateboarding nearby in Papago Park. He wasn't very good yet, but the bike path was usually deserted at this time of day. Robbie hated to have an audience when he made mistakes.

It was bad enough he never got any taller, no matter how much he ate, but then this year he'd had to start wearing glasses, too. All the other boys in the sixth grade were bigger and some went out of their way to pick on him. His dad told him not to worry. He'd had the same problem at Robbie's age and now he was over six feet tall. But that didn't help much, especially when it was Brad Taylor doing the bullying. Brad was even bigger than the rest of the guys at school, and right now Robbie was his favorite target.

Robbie set his board down and tried the trick again. This time he nearly caught the board, juggling it with his hand a moment when he heard a familiar voice.

"Hey, wimp!"

Robbie cringed and the skateboard thudded to the ground.

"Nice trick." Brad pumped his thick legs, propelling himself from the parking lot, his cheeks red from heat and exertion.

"Oh, no," Robbie groaned. Not Bulldozer Brad.

"Who said you could skateboard in my park?" Brad asked, closing in. "Nice board." He eyed Robbie's skateboard like it was a double cheeseburger with fries.

Robbie's heart pounded and his hands shook. He was no match for Brad in a fight. The only edge he had on Brad was speed. Brad was big, but he was also the slowest runner in the class.

Now! Go, now!

Robbie grabbed his board and made a break toward the big rock formation at the west end of the park. He dashed up the trail, searching for a place to hide or some tourists to use as a barrier.

"Come back here, nerd," Brad shouted, huffing and puffing as he lurched up the trail.

Robbie raced on, glancing back for signs of Brad. He zipped around the corner and saw the girl too late.

"Hey! Watch out!" she yelled, putting out a hand to ward him off.

He skidded into her, knocking her against the rock.

Robbie fell backward and hit the ground in a cloud of dust.

The sky dimmed and the air grew cold as a dark cloud passed overhead, blocking the sun. The ground shuddered.

Earthquake! Stefani thought. But we don't have earthquakes in Arizona, do we?

Then, as quickly as it had disappeared, the sun was back and everything looked normal again.

Until Stefani saw the forest. Tall trees filled her view. She must have hit her head when that kid knocked her into the rock. She closed her eyes, squeezing them shut, then opened them again.

KAD

The forest was still there.

CHAPTER THREE

R-i-i-i-i-p. Greenback's talon sliced through the paper like a dagger, separating the book's pages from the binding. He leaned in to inspect his work. It was almost impossible to tell that any of the pages had been removed. And since no one in the castle could read but him, the missing text would go unnoticed.

He closed the book, sighing and patting the tattered cover before setting the tome aside. A shame to mar such an ancient volume, he thought, but as Mother used to say, a dragon can't grow without shedding a few scales.

He threw a quick glance over his shoulder. It wouldn't do to have Ashkell discover what he was up to.

His employer might be the densest dragon

Greenback had ever known, but Ashkell was also twice his size. "Being the runt of the clutch was more than difficult," Greenback muttered, "but it did teach me to use my wits." He rolled the loose pages inside a sheet of parchment, tied it with a loop of twine and hid it in a pile of scrolls. "That should keep His Royal Pain-ness from finding them."

A tingle buzzed inside his head and his scales quivered. Greenback tensed, sniffing the air with flared nostrils. Something powerful stirred the land, but what? And where? Outside his study the sky turned gloomy, and the castle trembled, sending the pile of scrolls rolling off the shelf and onto the floor. He held up his claws, reaching toward the cause of the disturbance, but before his magic could show him anything, the tremor stopped and the sky brightened.

He sensed—nothing.

The book lay on the table where he had left it. He eyed it with suspicion, then dismissed the idea. He was certain the book itself held no power. Only the words were important, and he had not spoken them aloud.

Not yet.

He retrieved the scattered scrolls, picking them up and dusting them off.

"Greenback!"

He started at the sound of his bellowed name echoing along the stone passageway. What did Ashkell want now?

"Greenback, you lizard's spawn, where are

you?"

"Coming, Sire," he called, shoving the last of the scrolls onto the shelf. He growled in frustration and stomped out of his study and down the hall to Ashkell's audience chamber.

CHAPTER FOUR

Robbie jumped up. "I'm really sorry," he said, brushing the dirt off his pants. The girl shook her head, blinked and stared. Her eyes had a far-off look. She must still be dazed from when he crashed into her. "Are you okay?" he asked.

"F—f–forest," she said. Her face was pale.

"Oh, my name's Robbie," he said, extending his hand. "Nice to meet you, Forest."

"No!" She stared past him and pointed. "My name is Stefani and *that* is a forest!"

Robbie turned and his mouth fell open. Tall oak trees, lush and green, stood where the dry desert should have been. Strange birds warbled from the nearest branches.

Robbie glanced back down the path he'd just run up. Was he dreaming? Maybe he'd been knocked unconscious. There was no sign of Brad. No tourists. Not even a path. Just trees.

A cool breeze puffed across the back of his neck, drying the sweat and sending a shiver up his scalp. He jerked back around and stared at Stefani.

She was slim and lanky, taller than Robbie by a couple of inches, with tangley red-blond hair. Her nose and cheeks were reddened from the sun, and her green eyes filled with fear.

Maybe he should say something. He opened his mouth to speak, but she spun away and made a frenzied examination of the rock.

"I know I saw them," Stefani mumbled, pushing down her panic. She needed to focus, to figure out what was happening. A good scientist would consider the facts, not become emotional. "They were right here. I'm sure!"

"What were?" Robbie asked.

"The symbols," she said.

"Symbols? What symbols?"

"The ones I was studying when you came zooming around the corner and knocked me sideways," she snapped. "I know they're here somewhere." She peered at the rock face, running her fingers over the surface and pushing aside leafy plant tendrils that hadn't been there a few minutes ago.

Robbie took off his glasses, cleaned them,

and put them back on. "Are you crazy? We go from a desert to a forest in the blink of an eye, and you're worried about some kind of dumb marks on a rock?" His voice broke and the last syllable came out as a squeak.

She frowned. "I'm just trying to gather all the facts. Observe things in a scientific manner." She gestured at their surroundings.

Robbie snorted and rolled his eyes. Scientific manner? Who did she think she was, Albert Einstein? "And what does your scientific observation," he made air quotes with his fingers, "tell you?"

Stefani opened her mouth and closed it again. She wanted to tell him off, but he was right. She had no answer. She might be dreaming, except things were too real. And they wouldn't both be having the same dream. Maybe she was hallucinating. Maybe Robbie wasn't even real.

Didn't scientists look first for the most obvious answer? And the most obvious answer was that they weren't in Arizona anymore. But that was impossible. Only they were someplace she'd never been before. Other than her and this Robbie kid, there were no people in sight. No cars. No roads. And, it appeared, no way home.

Just for a moment, Stefani pictured her mother worrying about her, crying even. *As if.* She pushed the picture away.

Out over the forest, a large dark form soared across the sky, circled above the trees, then sped off at an incredible speed, growing smaller and smaller as it disappeared into the distance. It was as big as an airplane, but no airplane Stefani had ever seen could flap its wings. Her skin prickled and the flow of blood in her head sounded like a rushing river. She sat down with her back to the rock face, took a deep breath, and reviewed the facts the way her grandfather had taught her.

"I don't know what's happened to us," she said, "but I know my name is Stefani, and it's obvious we aren't in Phoenix anymore." As she spoke, she looked up at Robbie. Brown eyes blinked at her from behind a pair of wire-framed glasses. His toast-colored hair stuck out in every direction. He seemed to be about her age. Although, he was a couple of inches shorter than her.

He glanced around. "I can see that," he said, "But what do you think has happened to us?" He sounded worried.

"I don't know. Everything is different right now except for you, me, and Hole-in-the-Rock." She leaned back against the stone. The hard surface helped to anchor her swirling senses and clear her mind. "Except that Hole-in-the-Rock is covered in all these vines. And the writing is gone."

"What writing?"

"The symbols I saw on the rock right here." She pointed. "I was trying to see what they were when you ran into me. Why were you running so fast, anyway?"

Robbie stared at his feet and shifted his

weight. "No reason," he said, his face turning red.

Stefani squinted up at him, wondering what he was hiding. Well, it couldn't be that important.

She rose to her feet and brushed her dusty hands on her pant legs, then stepped through the small arched entryway of Hole-in-the-Rock. She stood on the ledge and stared out. Thick forest stared back from where the zoo and the rest of the park should have been, too.

Robbie came up and stood beside her, chewing on his bottom lip. "It looks like the Rim."

"Do you mean Mo-go-yon?" She pronounced it using her best Spanish class accent, even though she'd never been to that high mountainous region of Arizona.

"No, I mean Muggy-own. That's how the people who live there pronounce it. I used to go camping there with my dad on weekends before he started his new job. Now he's gone most of the time."

Stefani huffed out her breath. "I don't see how that helps," she said. "Let's just list the facts." She leaned out and surveyed the land in all directions. "The desert is gone. And there are no parking lots or sidewalks. It's not Arizona, that's for sure. At least, not the Arizona we know." She paused for a moment before continuing. "We know where we aren't, but not where we are." She slid off her backpack, opened it and pulled out her cell phone. "No signal, of course. How about you?"

Robbie shoved his hands in his pockets. "No phone."

Stefani shook her head. What kind of kid didn't have a phone? "Whatever." She rummaged in her backpack again and pulled out her compass. She held it flat in her hand and watched as the dial wiggled, swinging back and forth before it stopped. "Hmm, here's something besides us and Hole-in-the-Rock that isn't different."

"What?" Robbie asked.

"North is still north," Stefani said in triumph.

Outside the cave, loose rocks tumbled down the hillside with a clatter and hiss. Stefani and Robbie froze and stared at each other. Except for the animals in the zoo, there weren't any dangerous creatures around Papago Park.

Only this wasn't Papago Park, and any animals here weren't likely to be living in a nice safe zoo.

Footsteps crunched in the dirt outside the entryway. Behind them loomed the huge opening with a sheer drop down the side of the cliff. The small opening they had entered through was the only way out. Stefani's feet turned icy. A shiver crept up her legs and settled in her stomach. She glanced at Robbie. His eyes shone dark in his suddenly pale face.

A shadow fell across the entryway.

CHAPTER FIVE

Long fingers reached inside the cavern. Sharp nails gripped the edge of the opening. Stefani bit her lip to keep from screaming. A round head with pointed ears followed the hands inside. Huge eyes peered at them through the shadows.

Stealthily, the strange creature crept forward. It was short, about the size of a first-grader, with stubby legs and big feet. She glanced over at Robbie—he stood frozen in place, eyes open wide.

The creature crouched low and peered around. It had pale green skin, and wore a dark green shirt and baggy brown pants. A large sack was slung over one shoulder. Squatting on its haunches, the strange being swung its head up and eyed them each in turn.

"Hullo," it said in low voice.

Robbie and Stefani stared, mouths open.

"Hul—lo," it said louder, pausing between syllables. It stood up and took a tentative step forward, keeping its gaze fixed on them. "I—am—Gam—dol—of—the—Glim—mer—ing," it said, pointing to itself with a slender finger.

"Um, er, uh," Robbie stammered.

"Gam—dol," it repeated, tapping its chest.

"I'm Stefani and this is Robbie," Stefani finally managed.

The creature stepped back, startled. Then it smiled, its big eyes glittering in the gloom. "You speak as me," it said in a rush. "How do you know my tongue? Are there others with you? I have not seen any like you before. Is your dwellplace far? Which way do you travel?" His head bobbed up and down as he spoke.

"Dwellplace?" Robbie tried to keep his voice from shaking.

"Yes," Gamdol said. "Dwellplace. The place of your people. Do you not have a dwellplace?"

"We have homes," Stefani blurted, "but we're not really sure which way they are." She knew she wasn't supposed to talk with strangers, but the little fellow appeared harmless enough and things were all mixed up right now. Maybe this glimmery person could tell them where they were. "We're sort of lost," she said.

"Lost?" repeated Gamdol. "Have you asked Aurien the way? Have you seen Aurien? Aurien is wise. Aurien will know the way," he chattered.

"Aurien knows many things."

"Who is Aurien?" Stefani asked.

"Who is Aurien? Who is Aurien?" Gamdol replied. He tilted his head back in surprise. "Aurien is wise," he said with certainty. "Aurien knows many, many things. Gamdol knows Aurien. Gamdol will take Staff-awni and Row-bi to Aurien."

He hopped around the cavern, waving his arms. Then he headed out through the entryway, gesturing for them to follow.

Stefani shrugged. "What do you think?"

Robbie crossed his arms and glared at her. "What do I think? I think we shouldn't even be talking to this Gamdol character. We don't know anything about him, or where he's planning to take us. What do you think I think?"

"I think you sound like my mother," Stefani snapped. "This little green guy seems harmless enough, and friendly, too. And he seems to know his way around. Think about it. At least now we have someone who knows where he is."

"Just because he knows where he is, doesn't mean we can trust him," Robbie said.

"We can't just stay here."

"Why not? Maybe if we do stay here, whatever happened to us will unhappen."

"Unhappen? That's not even a word," Stefani said. "I think that if this Aurien person can help us, we should go and talk to him. Besides, we have no idea what else might be lurking in these woods. Would you rather wait around for something less friendly to come along?"

"I guess not." Robbie frowned. "But I'm keeping a close eye on him."

Stefani pulled her backpack onto her shoulders and left the cavern.

Robbie followed slowly. Down the hill, Gamdol jogged toward the forest, Stefani hurrying after him.

Robbie hesitated, taking one more look around. In the distance, a gray mountain peak stabbed into the sky. Robbie stared at the dark mountain for a moment. Something about it didn't seem right. Of course, nothing was right about this place.

Stefani and Gamdol were almost out of sight. Robbie kicked at the dirt, then hustled after them.

CHAPTER SIX

In the shadow of the dark mountain, a greasy stream flowed past the walls of a crumbling castle. Inside the walls, in a dimly lit room, a black dragon sat back on his haunches. His dark scales glistened in the flickering firelight as he poked a scaly finger through the door of a small metal cage, attempting to coax out a trembling bluebird. The tiny bird shrieked and flapped its fragile wings, beating against the sides of the cage.

The black dragon slammed the cage door shut in frustration and spun about. He glared down at the pale-green dragon cowering before him. The bluebird sank onto its perch with a shuddery chirp.

A small fire smoldered in the pit in the center of the chamber, its feeble blaze failing to drive the cold and damp from the room. The large dragon flexed his claws, knuckles popping. "Worthless advisors are easily replaced, Greenback," he snarled. Black smoke rose from his wide nostrils.

The smaller dragon raised his eyes to regard the huge form before him. Ashkell was large even for a dragon and he had a horrible temper. His heavy black scales rippled in anger and the razor-sharp edges of his long curved claws glinted like knives in the weak firelight.

Greenback chose not to test his prowess against someone twice his size and strength. He knew his limitations. He remained silent, waiting for the other dragon to speak.

"I am tired of lurking at the edge of the land while my saintly brother lives in splendor in my rightful place," Ashkell bellowed. "I should be ruling now, not Emris. It isn't right that he sits on the throne in my place! You will find a way for me to be rid of him soon or I will be rid of you!"

"Yes, Your Greatness." Greenback bowed low. Ashkell meant what he said, and Greenback hadn't spent these many years bowing and scraping to gain the bigger dragon's favor just to lose his position now. Not when he was so close to achieving his goal. "As a matter of fact, Sire, I believe I have found a solution," he said.

"What is it?" Ashkell asked with a snarl. Interest glistened in his eyes.

"Well, Your Scaliness," Greenback said, narrowing his eyes to slits, "I have been investigating the powers of the land, and my extensive research has uncovered the secrets of the Nelig Stones." He paused, awaiting Ashkell's reaction.

"Nelig Stones?" Ashkell clenched his fists and rose up on his hind legs to tower over his advisor. Smoke wreathed about his head and sparks flew from his mouth. "Is that what you've been squandering your time on? Foolishness and lizard's tales?"

"Wait, Your High-and-Mighty-ness. A moment, please," whined Greenback. He crouched low in submission, hunching his shoulders and turning his head to the side, poised to ward off a blow. "There is often truth in hatchlings' tales," he said. He squeezed his eyes shut and braced himself in expectation of the punishment he was certain would come. When nothing happened, he opened one eye, and then the other. "And there is still much magic in the land," he added when the bigger dragon remained silent.

Ashkell stood over him, his fists still clenched, but his brow was furrowed in thought. "Magic," he muttered. His eyes glinted and his fists began to uncurl.

Greenback seized the opening. "Yes, Your Immeasurableness. The magic of the land is still strong in Anoria. I believe the Nelig Stones are the key for tapping into that power. He who controls the stones, controls the land." He paused for a moment, then lowered his voice. "He who controls the land, rules it."

Ashkell ran a talon along the side of his chin. "Yessss," the word came out in a hiss. "If I can cut the ties between my brother and the land, I will be in complete control. I will rule everything!" As he spoke, his voice grew to a loud roar and flecks of gray-green spittle sprayed from his mouth. "The kingdom will be mine!" He leaned his head back and laughed, then swung around to glare at Greenback once more.

Greenback turned away to hide his fear and loathing of Ashkell. He shuffled over to the side of the room where a stack of ancient leather-bound books lay on a narrow shelf. He stroked the covers of the books, running his claws gently along the spines, then picked up an especially tattered tome. "Ahh," he said, and it came out like a sigh. He cleared his throat before continuing. "Ah, yes. Here it is, Sire." He opened the book, gently turning the pages with a single claw. "It took a long time to decipher the text. It is written in the ancient tongue and phrased in the form of riddles. But I have puzzled them out," his voiced dropped to a whisper, "and I now know where at least one of the stones of power lies hidden."

"Quit muttering, Greenback," Ashkell ordered.

"Yes, of course, my Lord," Greenback

responded in a loud voice. "I was just saying that I have found the key that will unlock the riddles of Igrok, the Nelig troll, last of his kind and guardian of the Nelig Stones. You see, Sire, the stones were not destroyed as most believe. Igrok could not bring himself to do it. Not after he'd mined them, set them and infused them with his own power. No, he could not destroy his creations. So, he hid them instead—fool that he was—believing they would never be found again. And he was almost right. Few there are who would seek them." His voice dropped to a whisper once more. "Fewer still are those who have the knowledge to find them." Or to use them, he mused.

"You're muttering again," Ashkell growled. He glowered at Greenback, eyeing him with suspicion. "If the stones exist as you say, then tell me where they are. At once," he commanded.

"I am afraid, Sire," Greenback said agreeably, "that it isn't quite that simple. I have managed to divine the approximate location of one of the stones already, but it will take time to retrieve it. And it will take more time to decipher the rest of the riddles and find the other stones. But we are close, my Lord, very close." He clutched the book to his chest, bowing before the other dragon.

"How much time?" Ashkell curled his lip in a wicked sneer.

"I will know better, Sire, once we have the first stone. Be assured, Your Immensity, success is very near. Your ascension to your rightful place is only a matter of time." Greenback gave him a syrupy smile.

Ashkell whirled about and began pacing back and forth, his pounding footsteps echoing off the stone walls. "I have waited too long already. I am tired of waiting." He continued pacing. "Anoria belongs to me. Along with everything in it!" He stopped in front of Greenback and shouted. "You had better bring me that stone soon! Or you will suffer the consequences."

The heat of Ashkell's flame singed Greenback's snout and his foul breath made the smaller dragon want to sneeze. Greenback knew only too well what horrible consequences Ashkell could inflict. He'd seen enough to know that failure would mean terrible pain, and probable death. He licked his lips with his narrow tongue. "Yes, Sire. I serve only you. All that you deserve, I shall work to attain for you," he said in his most flattering voice. "I will seek the stone and bring it to you myself."

"I want it here in my claws before the rising of the next full moon."

"But Sire! That is no more than a week's time. A week is hardly—"

"A week is all you have, Greenback." The finality of Ashkell's words rang through the room.

"Yes, Your Stupendousness." Greenback's jaw was tight with anger, yet his voice dripped with sweetness and cordiality. "As you command. I shall have it for you within the week."

"See that you do!" Ashkell roared. He wheeled about and raised his powerful tail, lashing it down on the stone floor and narrowly missing Greenback's snout. Then he stalked out of the room.

"Oh, I shall," Greenback whispered to the quivering bluebird after Ashkell was gone. "You are not alone in your impatience. There are others who long for a change of rulership in the land. Not all, however, wish for the same change." A wicked smile spread across his muzzle and his voice trailed off in a hissing laugh like a sizzling volcanic vent.

CHAPTER SEVEN

Stefani shifted the weight of her backpack and checked her watch. They had been walking through the forest for over an hour, but she couldn't tell how far they had traveled. Ancient trees reached heavy branches in all directions, blocking out the sunlight and catching at Stefani's hair as she hurried after Gamdol.

Robbie hadn't said much, but Stefani had asked their guide a ton of questions. Gamdol answered most of them, but he didn't seem to understand the most important one. Where were they? It wasn't that he hadn't tried to answer. In fact, he kept insisting they were in a place called the Forest of Light. But when she asked him what state or country it was, he didn't seem to understand.

"Aurien's country," he told her several times.

"But who is the president or the governor?" Stefani finally asked in frustration.

"Gov-er-nor? What is a gov-er-nor?" he asked, stretching the word out and pronouncing each syllable the way someone learning to read sounded out a new word.

"The person in charge," she said.

"In charge?"

"Yes, you know, the boss, the ruler, the—"

"Ah!" he cut her off, "You mean High King. High King Emris. Emris is ruler. Yes. High King Emris."

"I suppose so," she said.

"Yes, yes, good King Emris is ruler and protector of all lands of Anoria. King Emris is this governor you speak of," he chattered. He seemed delighted to finally have come up with an answer that satisfied her.

"Do you really have a king?" Robbie asked, showing interest for the first time since they had left Hole-In-The-Rock.

"Oh, yes. Good King Emris. High King Emris," Gamdol went on.

Their path led over gnarled roots and under sweeping branches and wound between the trees. As they traveled, Gamdol talked of his home. "Glimmering dwellplace is where all Gamdol's family stays. Not far. Two days from

Great Rock," he told them. "Great Rock. Where Gamdol finds you!"

He told them about his people, the Glimmering. He talked about his family and friends, and how on certain nights of the year the whole village would celebrate together, sitting around the fire, late into the night.

"Gamdol ventures to prepare for his Second Cycle ritual. All young Glimmering spend time alone, traveling. Learning to take care. Learning to protect. Learning strengths and weaknesses." He puffed out his chest. "No other Glimmering has found any like you while venturing."

As far as Stefani could make out, the Second Cycle ritual was some sort of a becoming-an-adult celebration.

Gamdol told Robbie that after he completed the requirements, he would be tested. "When I pass the test, I will gain my staff. I will earn my Staff of Cycles. I will notch my staff well. Notch it for deeds of bravery. For deeds of honor."

"I went to Harold Siemen's Bar Mitzvah," Robbie said. "It was kind of cool, everybody celebrating his thirteenth birthday like that. But his folks don't really treat him like an adult. I mean, he got a really cool cell phone, but he still has to go to school and do chores and stuff."

"Well, maybe they ought to," Stefani said. "I think if my mother treated me more like an adult, I'd be a lot more responsible."

"I don't know about that," Robbie said. "My parents say it works the other way around. First you act responsibly, then you get treated more like an adult."

"That's typical," Stefani said with a huff.

Something zipped out from the trees to their left and stopped in midair before them. Stefani let out a startled shriek. Gamdol stopped, but showed no sign of surprise at the sight of the six-inch tall, winged person hovering in the air.

"Halt!" The flying person raised his arm, palm out as if to bar their way. "Who dares trespass in the realm of Lightwings?" he demanded.

"What are Lightwings?" Stefani asked.

"Will it sting us?" Robbie asked. "I'm allergic to bees."

"I am Gamdol of the Glimmering and we do not trespass," Gamdol said. "Glimmering have long had freedom of travel through Lightwood and to the farthest parts of the Forest of Light. Glimmering do not trespass here."

"Glimmering perhaps, but not strangers. Not these!" The Lightwing thrust his sharp-pointed sword in the direction of Robbie and Stefani. "These beings are trespassers in the domain of the Lightwing faeries. As such, they must answer to the Queen." Stefani watched the small being in fascination. He wore armor that looked like it was made from leather and polished bits of acorn shells all laced together with fine cord. His hand clasped a miniature sword. Transparent wings whirred, as he barred their way.

I've never heard of soldier faeries before, Stefani mused, then stopped herself. Scientists don't believe in faeries! She stared hard at the little flying soldier.

"These travelers are with Glimmering," Gamdol replied. "A Glimmering is their guide. They have passage with Glimmering."

"That is for Queen Karissa to decide," said the soldier faerie.

What a jerk, Stefani thought. She reached out to swat him away like a fat June bug. But he slashed out at her with his tiny sword.

The sharp blade pricked her finger and drew blood. "Ouch! That stung." Stefani stuck her finger in her mouth.

"We go to Aurien. Seek Aurien for answers," said Gamdol. "We do not disturb the Lightwings."

"That, too, is for the Queen to decide," said the faerie, giving them all a stern look. As he spoke, more faeries emerged from the shadows of the trees. There were fifteen or twenty of them, all dressed like the first one, and all carrying the same sharp-bladed weapons. Swords drawn, they circled the three travelers, like a swarm of unfriendly hornets.

"We will see Queen Karissa then," Gamdol said. "Queen Karissa will be just."

The dour Lightwing took the lead. Gamdol, Stefani and Robbie followed with the rest of the faerie soldiers close behind. They had walked for about half an hour, Stefani nursing her sore finger the whole way, when the Lightwing leader whirled around and shouted, "Halt!" He left his soldiers on guard and sped away.

A waterfall ran down a low hill and splashed over quartz-streaked rocks and formed a shallow rivulet. Stefani started toward the inviting water, but a stout faerie flew into her path. His hand rested on the pommel of his sword. He shook his head and frowned. Stefani frowned back, annoyed. "Don't get your wings in a twist," she said, but she stayed where she was.

After a few minutes the Lightwing leader returned. He gestured for them to follow, and led the way through a thicket of trees. They stopped in a clearing by a sparkling pond. "We will wait here and you may slake your thirst," he told them.

"Can we have some water?" Robbie asked.

"That's what he just said." Stefani rolled her eyes. Robbie gave her a sour look, then he knelt by the pond, cupping his hands and drinking noisily.

"You could have washed first," Stefani grumbled. "Don't you know about germs?" She reached into the water and grabbed a handful of sand from the edge of the pond, scrubbing her hands with it, careful not to rub sand into her sore finger before drinking from her cupped hands. She made a point not to slurp. Then she filled her water bottle and tucked it back in her pack. Gamdol watched her intently. Then, he squatted beside the water and followed her example, thoroughly scrubbing his green hands before taking a drink.

The troop of faeries remained on guard along the edges of the glade, hovering a uniform distance above the ground. Their fluttering wings filled the meadow with a low hum that sounded like a room full of murmuring children.

"Gamdol," whispered Stefani, "who are these Lightwings?"

"Lightwings are the most fierce faeries in the Forest of Light, but Glimmering have been allies with them for many years. As for Queen Karissa," he said in a hushed voice and without his usual chattiness. "I have never seen her. This is my first time out venturing. But I have heard of her beauty. And her pride."

"I've never met a queen before," said Robbie.

"Neither have I. Do you have a queen?" Stefani asked Gamdol.

"The Glimmering have no queen," he replied. "We are guided by our elders. They make counsel together. They are our governors," he said with a smile.

A loud buzzing noise filled the clearing. Gamdol stood, motioning for Robbie and Stefani to do the same. Stefani got up, brushing dirt and leaves from her jeans. She frowned, noticing a dark stain on her left pant leg. One more thing for her mother to be mad about. She groaned. Robbie elbowed her in the side and she snapped at him. "Wha—"

"Shhhhhh," Gamdol shook his head and pointed with his chin across the clearing. Stefani started to say something, but his wide eyes and serious face stopped her. She turned her attention to the far side of the glade. A large group of Lightwings darted out of the trees and flew toward them.

The faeries swooped down and landed in front of Stefani and the others. The faeries paused for a moment, then spread out into the grove. A glittering faerie woman stood alone in the center of the clearing. She wore a gown adorned with butterfly wings and a crown of gold inlaid with gems. She eyed the three strangers in front of her, a severe expression on her petite face.

Gamdol bowed to the little queen.

"I am Karissa," the queen said, her voice shrill and haughty. "And you have trespassed in my realm. Who sent you to spy on my people?"

"Noble Karissa," Gamdol said, taking on that formal tone again. "I am Gamdol of the Glimmering. Since the dark times my people have had leave to travel in Lightwing lands. I guide two lost ones. We seek aid from Aurien the Wise, to find the path back to their dwellplace."

"Who are these so-called lost ones? Where do they come from? Why do they come spying on the Lightwings?" Queen Karissa demanded.

"But we're not spies," Stefani exclaimed. "We're from Arizona and we don't know how we got here. Gamdol told us this Aurien person could help us and he was taking us to see him when your soldiers stopped us for no reason." An angry murmur rose up among the gathered faeries.

"Silence," the queen said. "I was not speaking to you. I was speaking to the

Glimmering. You are a stranger here, but that is no excuse for rudeness."

Stefani flushed. Hot words pushed their way into her mouth, but it wouldn't do to cause more trouble. She chewed her tongue to keep from speaking.

Gamdol bowed once more to the Lightwing ruler, and went down on one knee. "Queen Karissa," he said, "all in the Forest of Light know of your fair and just dealing with my people. As Glimmering, I ask only for leave to guide these travelers to Aurien's Glen. Will you grant your permission?"

"Your friends are bold, Gamdol of the Glimmering, and though I do not detect evil in them, still I do not trust the safety of my people to the words of strangers. You may continue your journey to seek advice from Aurien the Wise, but the captain of my royal guard and his best lieutenants will accompany you." She eyed Stefani and Robbie. "If there is harm in you, Aurien will know."

"I thank you for wisdom and fairness, good Karissa," Gamdol said. He bowed his head. "And my friends thank you." He nudged Robbie, who bent forward at the waist. Stefani felt awkward, thinking that maybe she should curtsey instead of bowing. But when she tried it, she teetered and lost her balance.

Robbie put out a hand to help steady her, as tittering laughter spread among the gathering. Queen Karissa swiveled around and glowered at the ring of Lightwings. The laughter died.

"You will camp here tonight and take your leave in the morning. Tomorrow, my soldiers will guide you to Aurien's Glen. My subjects will make you welcome until then."

The queen gestured to her subjects and they erupted in flight like a swarm of startled butterflies. Groups of four and five Lightwings hefted baskets the size of cereal bowls filled with fruit, berries, and some kind of cakes drenched with honey.

Robbie and Stefani stuffed themselves, but Gamdol sniffed at the cakes and other food, refusing them with a polite nod. Queen Karissa spoke to one of her attendants and a special tray of odd-shaped nuts and bright green berries was placed before Gamdol. The Glimmering smiled and thanked the queen. He ate hungrily, smacking his lips and licking his thin fingers.

"I admire your courage and your desire to be heard," Queen Karissa told Stefani. "But you should remember that it is often better to do things as they are done, rather than how we would like them to be done."

Stefani pretended to inspect her fingernails. The queen's advice sounded a lot like something her mother would say. She wondered for a moment if her mother was worried about her, and then she remembered their last argument. Her jaw tightened. Why should she be trying to get back home at all? This new land might be better than home. Or would be if they didn't have to put up with Queen Karissa and her stab-happy soldiers.

Robbie yawned without bothering to cover his mouth. It made Stefani yawn, too.

They fell asleep with Lightwing soldiers standing guard over them.

Morning came with the songs of birds. Stefani sat up, opened her eyes, squished them shut, then opened them again. Robbie snored a few feet away. So much for wishing it was all a dream. She brushed stray leaves out of her hair with her fingers.

She stood up and stretched, then walked to the shallow pool, and knelt at the edge. The freezing water stung her face and she quickly rubbed herself dry with her bandanna. Standing, she surveyed the glade. There were uniformed faeries stationed every few feet along the edge of the open space. They didn't move, but she could tell they were watching her. She went back and nudged Robbie with the toe of her shoe. "Hey, wake up."

Robbie rolled over and squinted up at her. "Oh," he said. "I was hoping I would wake up in my own bed."

"Well, you didn't." She glanced around. "I could sure use a bathroom."

"Plenty of bushes, but you're not going to find a human-sized outhouse anywhere around here." Robbie scratched his head, mussing up his already bedraggled hair. "What's for breakfast?" he asked. "I'm starving."

"How should I know? I haven't seen anyone except the soldiers. I was just wondering where Gamdol went."

Robbie sat up straight. "You mean he took off? I knew it. I knew we should have stayed where we were. I told you not to trust—"

"Oh, be quiet," she shot back. "What other choice did we have?"

He glared at her. "Now what are we going to do? Those faeries are small, but there are a lot of them. And those swords they're carrying are really sharp."

"Like I don't know that." Stefani held out her sore finger. "Ow!" Something hard struck her on the head and bounced to the ground at her feet. A large brown nut rolled to a stop and Robbie picked it up. Branches rustled above them and Gamdol stuck his head out of the thick leaves.

"Sorries," he said. "Want some?" He hung upside down from a branch and extended an arm toward Stefani, offering her a handful of nuts.

Stefani rubbed her head as Robbie lifted the nut to his nose and sniffed. He jerked his head back. "It smells weird," he said.

Gamdol swung down out of the tree, landing lightly on his feet. He knelt beside Robbie, put the nuts on the ground, picked up a rock and slammed it down on them with a whack. Then he separated the dark green nut pieces from the brown shells.

Robbie pinched his nose closed with his fingers. "Ew! Are those rotten? Thanks for the offer, but no thanks."

"Best when picked late," said Gamdol, stuffing a handful of nutmeats into his mouth.

"Mmmmm . . ."

"You sure eat some weird stuff," Robbie said.

"Weird? What is weird?"

"You know, different. Unusual. Strange."

"And you eat smellies," Gamdol said, making a face and swinging back up into the tree to pick more nuts.

While the Lightwings set out fruit and cakes for the morning meal, Stefani snagged some tissues from her backpack and managed to find a private spot not too far away.

After breakfast, the travelers were each given a full water skin. Gamdol added a large number of the nuts he had gathered into the sack slung across his chest. "Not venturing," he said, grinning. "Not venturing anymore. Now questing." He smiled.

Robbie stuffed what he could into his pockets, wishing he had a pack like Stefani's, or even a bag like Gamdol's.

Stefani emptied out her pack and refilled it, carefully stacking everything to make room for plenty of the honey cakes. The whole situation is so strange, she thought, stuffing the rocks she'd collected into the front pockets of her jeans. It was like they were in some sort of weird movie or something.

Queen Karissa flew up onto a low tree branch. "I wish you safe and swift journey," she said. "Travel in the Forest of Light is not too difficult," she said. "But there are dangers. My guards will protect you as well as guide you, but you must follow their orders." She paused for a moment and regarded Stefani before continuing. "Try to remember, it is often what we give that brings us the most in return. And sometimes we must choose to serve the needs of others and sacrifice our own desires."

Stefani pursed her lips at the queen's words. "Bossy little thing," she mumbled as the queen rose into the air and flew away.

The Lightwing Captain and two of his soldiers buzzed past her. "Follow me," he ordered.

Stefani adjusted her pack. No problem, she thought, the sooner we get to this Aurien's place, the better.

CHAPTER EIGHT

Ashkell snorted, sparks flying from his nostrils. Based on the insignificant rock in his claw, his servants had been wasting precious time.

He stood at the window, dangling an ovoid stone on a gold chain, holding it up to the wan morning light. The milk-white stone was no bigger than a bird's egg, wrapped at both ends with a few bits of gold. His agents had hunted long and hard to find this tiny bauble.

"Tell me, Greenback. What power is this puny trinket supposed to hold?" he demanded, eyeing the stone closely. "You told me these stones held vast power. I see nothing powerful here."

Greenback made a clawing gesture at the bigger dragon's back, careful not to let Ashkell see him. "Why, Your Tremendousness," he replied, with as much respect as he could force into his voice. "It is known as the Moonstone. The books and scrolls I have studied say that it sings when touched by moonlight." He kept to himself the fact that the stone could also control the rivers, lakes and seas of Anoria. Let the imbecile think that all the stone does is sing, he thought. He eyed the bigger dragon, careful not to betray his true feelings.

"A singing rock! What kind of fool do you take me for?" Ashkell rounded on Greenback. His nostrils flared. The powerful claw that held the Moonstone clenched in rage.

"It is true, Your Expansiveness. The stone does sing. It sings quite clearly in the moonlight. I heard it myself, just last night." Greenback's words tumbled from his lips. Then he stopped, lowered his eyes and cringed, bracing himself for the blow he knew was coming.

"What? How dare you!" Ashkell bellowed. He swung a large claw downward, and struck Greenback across the face.

Greenback rolled his head to lessen the impact as heavy scales bit into his cheek. Thick blood trickled down his chin. He gritted his teeth in pain and anger, but stood still. Because of their difference in size, brute force would not serve him against Ashkell. He had to use his superior intellect to accomplish his goals. And he still needed the help of Ashkell's underlings to find the other stones.

Ashkell continued to rage. "You should have informed me the moment you had the stone in your possession." He raised a foreleg to strike again.

Greenback quailed. "I wanted to be certain it was real." He tried to keep the fear and hatred out of his voice, but his words rushed out in a nervous squeal. "I didn't want to waste your time," he said, trying to placate the angry dragon. "I wanted to be sure that the stone Longscar had brought back was indeed one of the stones of power. So I took it out into the courtyard last night when the moon was high. And it did sing, Your Behemoth-ness. Truly." He bowed and scraped before Ashkell.

"Even if it does sing, what good is it?" Ashkell growled, as Greenback stooped before him in fear. "Do you think a singing rock will drive my valiant brother from the throne?" He hissed the words, shoving the stone in Greenback's direction.

Greenback's eyes followed the violent arc the stone made in the air. "No, Your Vastness, of course not," he forced his voice to remain calm. "Each stone alone holds only minor magic. It is only when all are together that they will release the powerful magic that controls the land." He watched the stone swing back and forth. The full power of the Moonstone could not be released without the other Nelig Stones, but Ashkell's careless handling of it might set off any number of calamities.

"That is part of their secret," he continued, "and the reason they were hidden far from each other when the ancient Nelig troll was dying." Greenback paused. The idea of wielding such immense power made him shiver with excitement. Ashkell eyed him suspiciously and he quickly continued. "Because of this power, he hid them apart, spreading them across the land before breathing his last."

"If I must have them all together, why have you not brought them all to me?" Ashkell growled.

"But Your Mammoth-ness," Greenback whined. "I have yet to decipher the whereabouts of the others. I brought you this one in less time than you had given me. And now you have proof of their existence and their power." Ashkell, you are an idiot, he thought. You have no idea what real power is.

"Proof?" Ashkell said. "A singing stone? One that you alone have heard? This is not proof." He started to fling the stone in Greenback's face, but stopped himself. What if Greenback spoke truth for once in his lying life? Ashkell would hold the power of all Anoria in his claws. Not only would he have the throne, but none would oppose him. Even Aurien would be powerless against him. "This had better not be some sort of trickery to delay your fate," he warned Greenback, "or you will wish you had never been hatched."

"Trick?" Greenback acted shocked. "Why, I would never attempt to trick you, Your Ponderousness," he said in a sugary voice. "I can show you the passages in the book that tell of the Moonstone and its companions." He couldn't resist reminding Ashkell, who had never learned to read, that he needed Greenback to find the Nelig Stones.

"Why would I want to see it?" Ashkell asked, trying to sound uninterested. "It is just an old book."

"Precisely. A very old book indeed. The Ancient Book of Dark Truths. And listed in it are descriptions of four of the stones and their powers." Greenback thought wistfully about the pages he'd torn out. The pages that described the methods for using the stones.

"And where are these other stones?" Ashkell's eyes narrowed in suspicion.

"That is a puzzle I have yet to work out, Greenback replied. "But I will. I will. I have never failed you, yet. Have I?"

"Not yet." Ashkell fumed.

"On my word, my Lord, everything is as I have said," Greenback continued, wiping the dried blood from his face. "The stones exist. Their power is real. We need only to find them and bring them together, and all of Anoria will be ours." A low growl escaped from Ashkell's throat. "I mean yours, of course," Greenback corrected himself. "Once you hold the stones, you will control the elemental powers of the land. You will be able to destroy it with a single word. And your brother, my Lord, who has sworn to protect the land at all costs, will have to step down from the throne. Then you may rule in his place."

"It is not his place!" stormed the huge dragon. "It is mine! Mine by rights! And I will claim it!" He turned to glare out of the window. "Do you hear that, Emris?" he called out, shaking his fist in the direction of Dragon's Tor. "Anoria is mine!"

He glared over his shoulder at Greenback. "Call my commanders. Tell them to prepare my troops. And you, Greenback, had better find those stones and bring them to me soon," he ordered, turning back to the window. "I will have my throne!"

"Yes, my Lord." Greenback bowed, backing out of the room. "As you command." He all but spit the last words into the room before making a hurried retreat down the hall.

CHAPTER NINE

"My feet hurt," Stefani grumbled. "Why couldn't there be a bus or a light rail or something." The Lightwings flew ahead, guiding the way along the twisting path. "Must be nice to be able to fly." She shifted her pack, testing the weight of it. Her stomach gurgled. Lunch seemed like years ago. "How much farther?" she asked.

Neither Robbie nor Gamdol responded. They walked on, deep in conversation. "Do you have any brothers or sisters?" Robbie asked.

Stefani glared at them. For someone who didn't want to go anywhere with the Glimmering in the first place, Robbie sure had gotten chummy with the little green guy.

"It's been three days since we left Arizona," Robbie said. "My mom's got to be completely panicked by now. And I suppose my dad had to come home from his business trip." He shook his head as he trudged alongside Gamdol. "He's got to be flaming mad."

Stefani rolled her eyes. What a worrywart. First he doesn't trust Gamdol, then he doesn't want to leave Hole-in-the–Rock, and now he was moaning how his parents were going to be mad at him. She snorted. *If I were his parents, I'd sure be glad to be rid of him for a while.*

She kicked at the dirt and felt her cheeks grow hot. It wasn't really Robbie's parents she was thinking about. It was her mother. *I bet she's glad I'm not around to mess up.* For some reason, she felt like she might cry. She hurried to catch up to Gamdol and Robbie.

"My people do not worry for me," Gamdol puffed out his chest. "All Glimmering go venturing during the last seasons before our Second Cycle feast. I am the youngest to go this season and my huts are proud."

As they travelled, the forest got darker and the path narrowed, winding through overgrown trees. The air grew heavy and silent and the ground squished underfoot. A sour smell rose from the path with every step.

"These trees are from the dark times," Gamdol told them. "From the time before Aurien. Before Aurien claimed the forest. Made it light.

The Forest of Light."

The Lightwing commander flew back to them. "It is becoming too dark to travel. We must stop for the night. There is a clearing not far from here that will make a good camp." He spun around in midair and flew into the gloom ahead.

Great! Another awesome night camping out with no facilities. Stefani glared around at the tangled woods. And what was the deal with this little I'm-totally-in-charge-of-everything guy? He sure wasn't like any of the faeries Stefani had ever read about. Apparently, none of those authors ever met a Lightwing. She watched the Lightwings zip ahead, tiny swords glinting, and noticed for the first time that one of the Lieutenants was a female. Not that you could tell by her uniform. All the soldier faeries dressed alike.

"Oof!" She tripped on a gnarled root and skidded to her knees, scraping her palms and tearing a huge hole in her jeans. Her hands stung and blood oozed from her left knee. She started to call out for the others to wait, but they had disappeared around a bend in the trail. Great. *Thanks for nothing!* Angry tears welled up and she bit the inside of her cheek to keep them from falling.

Stefani picked herself up She shrugged her pack into position and marched forward, determined not to let anyone see her cry. Rounding the bend, she saw the others in the gloom up ahead. She hurried to catch up.

"We will stop here," the Lightwing leader said as Stefani reached them. "My lieutenants and I will stand watch." With a quick nod, he zipped out of sight. Stefani took off her pack and threw it on the ground at her feet. She wondered if all the Lightwings were as crabby as this one.

"Gamdol," she hissed. "Why are the Lightwings so mean?"

"Mean?" he repeated.

"Yes," she said. "Mean. Stabbing people. Giving commands. Not listening. The way Queen Karissa wouldn't listen to me. You would think we were some kind of evil monsters or something."

"The Lightwing soldiers do the queen's bidding," he replied. "It is their duty to protect their people."

Stefani frowned. That wasn't what she meant at all, but she was too tired to make him understand. She shoved her pack over with her foot and plopped down beside it, gingerly examining her knee. She dribbled water over it to wash the dirt away. The bleeding had stopped, but it still stung.

Overhead, the gnarled branches of a rough-barked tree reached down like bony fingers, and the sour stench of the forest floor stung her nostrils. "I don't like it here," she grumbled, but Robbie and Gamdol hardly glanced at her as they opened their packs and dug inside for something to eat.

Stefani shivered in the chilly evening air. She pulled her arms inside her t-shirt and curled around her backpack.

She found herself inside a blurry dream where she tried to find her way through a hazy tunnel. Only, something held her back. No matter how hard she struggled, she couldn't move. She wrestled against the pull of something and . . .

She opened her eyes. It was dark. Too dark to see. She tried to get up and found that part of her dream was true. Something held her tight. Her head was pressed against the ground and her arms and legs were bound together.

"Hey!" she shouted. "Someone help! Where is everyone?"

"Over here!" Robbie gasped. "I can't get up. Something's squeezing me!"

"Tanglevines," Gamdol said from somewhere off to their right. "Do not struggle. They tighten. They grab more."

"Then how do we get out?" Stefani felt panic taking over. The vines scraped her legs, coiling around her and pinning her to the ground. Deep breath, she thought. Deep and slow. But her chest heaved and the curling vines twisted around her, constricting. "I can't breathe!"

"Stay calm," the female Lightwing flitted near her ear. "We will cut you loose." With her sword, she began hacking at the vines that surrounded Stefani. With each stroke of her blade, the vines jerked back, loosening their grip.

The other Lightwings hacked at the plants that pinned Robbie and Gamdol. Dim light filtered through the branches overhead, and a quick movement caught Stefani's attention. "Watch out!" she yelled. The faerie flitted sideways as the end of a vine whipped past.

Another tendril lashed out, knocking her aside, but she winged back to slice again and again at the writhing greenery that held Stefani captive.

The Lightwings continued hacking and dodging as the vines thrashed and whipped through the air. Finally, the vines slackened their grip, and Stefani, Robbie and Gamdol leaped free. They grabbed their belongings and ran.

Once they had put some distance between themselves and the tanglevines, they stopped to check that everyone was all right.

"That was close," Stefani said, examining the itchy red spots on her arms. She didn't know what hurt worse, her knee or the fresh scrapes from the tanglevines.

"It sure was. Thank you for rescuing us," Robbie said to the Lightwings, still panting from their escape. "You know," he continued, examining several fresh rips in his shirt, "we don't even know your names."

"You are welcome," said the faerie Captain. "As for our names, I am Captain Kelin Graystar." He bent at the waist as he hovered before them. "These are Lieutenants Katar Stormlight and Tamel Brightsword." The two lieutenants saluted in turn. "As members of Queen Karissa's royal guard, we have sworn to see you safe to the Glen of Aurien." His tone was proud and stern, but Robbie saw him smile.

"Oh, sure," Stefani said. "Thanks a lot. Of course, if you'd been watching out like you're supposed to, we wouldn't have needed rescuing in the first place."

Gamdol rubbed his ankle where one of the

tanglevines had raised a nasty welt. He shook his head at Stefani. "It honors us to have such an escort," he said. "We are grateful, very grateful," he added with a nod of his head.

"Come," said Kelin, taking command once more. "We must move on."

CHAPTER TEN

Stefani could still feel the grip of the tanglevines where they had raised red welts and left scratches on her skin. Gamdol walked with a limp and Robbie kept glancing back over his shoulder, as if he thought the vines might somehow be chasing them.

Maybe next time they'll listen to me, Stefani thought angrily. She couldn't explain how, but she had known there was something wrong with the place where they'd camped.

At dusk, they stopped near a shallow stream. Gamdol sniffed the water and nodded. "Good.

Clean." he said. They drank deep, then filled their water containers before settling down for the evening meal.

Her hunger satisfied, Stefani used her bandanna as a washcloth, scrubbing her face and neck and rinsing the cloth in the fresh water. Then she folded the bandanna into a square, dipped it in the stream and held it against the sores on her arms and the scab on her knee. The burning subsided beneath the cool compress. It felt so good that she took off her shoes and socks and dangled her feet in the stream.

"Hey, whatcha doin'?" Robbie asked.

Couldn't he leave her alone? "I'm cooling off my feet, what does it look like?" she said in a sour voice.

"You don't have to bite my head off," he said, sitting down a few feet away and taking off his ratty sneakers.

"What do you think you're doing?"

"Looks good. I think I'll soak mine, too." He pulled off his socks, tossing them on the grass, and plopped his feet into the stream with a splash.

"Ew!" said Stefani, turning up her nose. "What a stink."

"You're not so flowery yourself."

"You could at least put your nasty old socks on your other side."

"Oh, excu-use me." He rolled his eyes, but picked up his socks and tossed them off to the other side. "You know," he said. "You're not the only one stuck in this place, trying to get home. It wouldn't kill you to be nice. Especially to the people who are trying to help us."

"Oh, great. Now you want to be my mother, too?"

"You sure have some kind of problem with your mom."

"You don't know what you're talking about."

"Really? So, why is it that everything seems to be about her? I mean, you bring her up every time anyone says anything you don't like. Seems to me, there's something in that."

"You know," Stefani said with a huff, "no one invited you to sit here."

"It's a free country."

"Yeah, right," she said. "About as free as ol' Queen Karissa lets it be." She pulled her feet out of the stream and shoved them into her socks and shoes. "She thinks she's the boss of everything."

Robbie shrugged, splashing his feet in the water as Stefani stomped off.

After the close call with the tanglevines, the Lightwings kept watch in shifts, one patrolling the surrounding area while another guarded the camp.

That night, Gamdol showed Robbie and Stefani how to cut the broad leaves from the plants that grew along the edge of stream and use them to make soft beds. The night was warm, the air fragrant with the smell of fresh grass and flowers, and they slept with no disturbance.

Stefani awoke as the sun slanted through the leafy branches, casting its rays across her face. She stretched and yawned, then sat up and gazed around. For the first time since they'd found themselves in this strange world, Stefani noticed how green and beautiful it was. She sighed. If it weren't for the bruises and sore spots from the tanglevines, she might think she was dreaming. She headed for the stream to wash her face, but before she'd taken two steps, the female Lightwing, the one named Tamel, flew up beside her.

"I will accompany you."

"I can take care of myself," Stefani said in a curt tone.

"That may be," Tamel said. "I will accompany you, nonetheless."

Stefani shrugged. "Have it your way."

She hovered while Stefani knelt down and dipped her bandanna into the water. This time she washed her ears, too. Then she scooped up some water and rinsed out her mouth, swished and swallowed. "I wish I had my toothbrush."

In a flash of movement, Tamel flew over to a bushy hedge, picked several large leaves and zipped back over to Stefani.

"Chew these," she said, holding up the leaves.

Stefani eyed the faerie with suspicion, but took the leaves. She sniffed them. They smelled sweet and sort of minty. She nibbled one. A minty taste burst over her tongue. "Not bad," she said, stuffing the entire leaf into her mouth.

"Way better than toothpaste." She chewed and swallowed. "Thanks."

"You are welcome." Tamel smiled.

Stefani thought about apologizing to the Lightwing for her grumpy behavior, but just then Robbie strolled up.

"What's that?" he asked around a wide-mouthed yawn.

"Toothpaste. Well, more or less," Stefani said. She started to tell Robbie to cover his mouth, but instead she handed one of the leaves to him. "It's all natural. And you could use some."

Robbie rolled his eyes, but popped the leaf into his mouth and chewed.

"Wow. That's great," Robbie said. "Where'd you get it?"

"From Lieutenant Tamel. She got it from that bush over there." Stefani pointed to the hedge. "Can we take some with us?" she asked the Lightwing, who still hovered nearby. "I mean, will they stay fresh?"

"For a few days," she said. "But they can be used dried, as well. Though they are not as fragrant or as easy to chew."

As they gathered handfuls of the minty leaves, Gamdol strolled over. "Eesh," he said. "Why do you want those smellies?"

"They're like toothpaste," Robbie said. "They make your breath nice. Here, try one." He offered a leaf to Gamdol.

"No. No. Smelly." He waved his hand back and forth in front of his face. "Glimmering never eat smellies." He went back to where they had slept, picked up the bedding and carried it to the edge of the stream. Then he said some strange-sounding words and tossed the plants into the water. Squatting down, he scooped up some mud from the riverbank, then rinsed his hands in the water. Holding his hand above his head, he dropped something wriggling into his mouth. Digging into the mud once more, he pulled up another handful of the wriggly things. "Breakfast?" he asked, extending a muddy hand toward Robbie and Stefani.

"I think I'll stick to what we have," Robbie said, looking almost as green as Gamdol.

"We don't have much left," Stefani said. "And the bread is stale." Her cheerfulness at the discovery of the toothpaste leaves dimmed as she realized they were running out of food. She wasn't ready to eat worms with Gamdol. "How much farther do we have to go?"

"Not much, not much," Gamdol said. "Maybe one day's journey."

They ate a small ration before setting out again. They didn't stop until the sun was high overhead. While they rested, Gamdol disappeared for a short time. When he returned, he offered to share the handful of tiny yellow berries he'd brought back. They tasted bitter to Stefani and Robbie, and the Lightwings refused to touch them, but Gamdol once again smacked his lips as he ate.

As they traveled, the forest thinned out. The setting sun shone brightly through leaves and branches, causing the ground to sparkle with light that danced between the shadows. The air smelled fresher and bore the scent of flowers.

Kelin flew ahead of the rest of the group and waited in a patch of sunlight at what turned out to be the edge of the forest. The travelers stepped out of the trees into a sunny meadow.

A stream splashed its way across the center of the glen between green banks dotted with colorful flowers. Beside the stream grew a huge oak tree with heavy branches. Near it, a wooden bridge spanned the brook.

The sunlight was dazzling and Stefani blinked and blinked again as a handsome unicorn crossed over the bridge and walked toward them. He was pure white, his coat and mane brilliant in the sunlight. His hooves and horn swirled with iridescent color. He strode across the meadow, stood before them and bowed low, touching the tip of his majestic horn to the ground.

"Welcome to my home," he said, raising his head. "I am Aurien. I have been expecting you. Please, come and refresh yourselves."

Stefani gasped. A creature from her imagination had just spoken to her. She stared in astonishment, and Robbie looked like a sleepwalker, while everyone else casually followed the unicorn across the clearing. It was several seconds before Stefani realized she'd been standing with her mouth gaping. She hurried to catch up, following Aurien and the others over the bridge where they sat in the cool shade of the oak.

Aurien clicked his hooves and shook his gleaming mane, and little brown-skinned people, half the size of Gamdol and dressed in green tunics, jumped down from the branches. They scampered up and down the tree, setting out a meal of fruits and nuts, singing and laughing while they worked.

"Now, tell me why you have come to see me," Aurien said.

Stefani looked over at Robbie who seemed to be as stunned as she was, but Gamdol acted like meeting an imaginary creature was nothing out of the ordinary. He stood and spoke in a solemn voice. "Wise Aurien, I have brought these lost ones to you. They seek the path to their dwellplace."

"These young ones are more lost than you know, young Glimmering. They have come from another world, far from Anoria." Aurien turned his gaze on Stefani and Robbie. "There is a way for you to return to your world. But only if you have the courage." He paused, eyeing each of them in turn. When he continued, his voice was hushed, as if he was telling them a dire secret. "In this land, there exist five stones of power that hold the key to the Gate of Worlds. They are called the Nelig Stones and they have been lost for many lifetimes. However, if you are able to find the stones and bring them together, it will be possible to open the Gate and return to your home."

"But are the stones not a story?" Gamdol

asked. "A sleeptime tale for little ones?"

"No, my fine Glimmering, they are not," Aurien said. "There is more truth in stories than you know."

"But if they've been lost for so long, how are we supposed to find them?" Stefani asked, finally getting up the courage to speak.

"The legends themselves give clues to the hiding places of the stones," Aurien replied. "And you will have help should you take up this quest."

"Are you coming with us?" Stefani asked hopefully.

"That I cannot do, my young friend. My power does not extend beyond the borders of the Forest of Light. The help I speak of comes from Laurel Silverbark. It is her aid you must seek. She is wise and well versed in all the lore and history of Anoria. She will help control the magic of the stones until they are brought to safety at the seat of power on Dragon's Tor."

Kelin frowned. "I have heard, oh Wise One, that the one you speak of is a powerful witch," he said.

Aurien laughed. Stefani liked his laugh. Bright and tinkling, like wind chimes in a cool breeze. She really wished he could come with them.

"Ah, Captain," Aurien said. "One cannot believe everything one hears. Laurel is no witch. She is the finest Treemage that ever sprouted in Anoria."

"Treemage?" Robbie said. "What's that?"

Aurien laughed again. “Why, an earth sorceress, of course.”

CHAPTER ELEVEN

Before she'd landed in Anoria, Stefani would have laughed at the idea of magic rocks, but now the idea fascinated her. "Please, tell us more about the stones," she pleaded.

"Long ago, a race of mighty trolls walked this land. The Nelig trolls were wise in the secrets of magic and power, but as their race grew old, much of their knowledge was forgotten and the trolls began to disappear," Aurien said.

"Igrok was the last of that race to walk these lands. Because he had no friends or family, he came to care most for the earth and its treasures, especially the ores and precious stones. These he gathered and wrought into the finest gems of beauty. He cut and polished each stone to reveal its secret heart and set it in the finest gold and silver. Of these gems, five he loved best. What magic he remembered he set into the stones, and revealed their true natures."

Aurien's words cast a spell over Stefani. "What do they look like?" She asked.

"It is said that the stones themselves are small enough to fit into the palm of your hand. Each has its own particular magic connected to one of the world's elements, but together they unleash an awesome power. Beyond this meager information there is little more that I know. Except that they are dangerous."

"Dangerous?" Robbie had been pulling up blades of grass as he listened to Aurien speak, but now he sat up straight and attentive.

Dangerous? Stefani thought. They sound wonderful. Visions of glittering gems sparkled in her mind.

"With great power there is always danger," Aurien tilted his head to one side and eyed Robbie. "Particularly when that power is not fully understood."

At Aurien's last statement, a shiver surged through Robbie. "Can't someone else go look for them? Someone who understands these things? Someone like this Laurel Silverbark?"

"Perhaps," Aurien replied. "But since it is you and your friend who have need of this power, do you not think it is your task to seek it? Of course, you may choose not to—that is your right, and it might be safer for all if the stones remain hidden. But if you wish to use their power to return home, then it is up to you to find them."

"Where should we search for such magnificent gems, such powerful stones?" Gamdol asked. "They must be well hidden, very well hidden, not to be found for so many, many seasons."

"That is why you will need the aid of Laurel Silverbark," Aurien answered. "She has knowledge that will aid you in your quest."

Quest. The word hung in the air like a glittering gem.

Night had fallen as they spoke and stars now filled the sky filled. Stefani gazed up at the twinkling spots of colored light. Even the stars were strange here, brighter than back home in Arizona and more colorful. Would the Nelig Stones sparkle this brightly when she held them in her hand? She was so distracted by the images in her head she was startled when Robbie touched her on the shoulder.

"Everyone's going to bed now," he said.

Stefani lay down with her back against a large tree root that curved around her like a hug. That night, she dreamed that she'd lost something important, but she had no idea what it was.

CHAPTER TWELVE

Morning arrived bright and crisp. Droplets of dew sparkled on the meadow. Stefani stretched and yawned, breathing in the cool air.

Robbie and Gamdol were already helping themselves to breakfast. "You'd better get cleaned up before we eat everything," Robbie told Stefani between mouthfuls. He pointed upstream.

His hair was wet and he wore a fresh shirt, pale green with long sleeves. The hem of the shirt hung below his waist and was cinched with a brown sash. Instead of his jeans and sneakers he wore loose brown pants over leather boots.

Stefani headed in the direction he'd pointed. A hedge grew beside the stream, and on the other side lay a sandy beach beside a deep pool. A pile of fresh clothes lay atop a flat stone.

Stefani looked back. The thick hedge gave her complete privacy. She crouched at the edge of the pool and trailed her fingers along the surface, sending ripples spiraling outward. The water was cool but not icy. She glimpsed around once more to be sure no one was in view, then undressed and eased into the water. It felt good to get clean.

After bathing, she put on the tunic, pants and boots that had been left for her, tying the sash about her waist as Robbie had. She combed her fingers through her hair, to get out the tangles, but it was no use She finally gave up, rolled up her old clothes and carried them back to the tree.

Robbie glanced up. "Nice outfit," he nodded at her new clothes. "Lucky for you, there's still some food left."

While she ate, Stefani watched the little brown people gather supplies. Packs were filled and long cloaks added to the pile of provisions.

Finally, Aurien called them together. "This day I have heard news that concerns me," he said. "There are unusual disturbances in the land and you must be wary on your journey. I have asked your Lightwing guards to accompany you on your quest and they have agreed."

Kelin nodded. "Which path shall we take?"

he asked, with his usual grim air.

"You should travel east to Crystal Lake. The fishing village of Windrow lies on the southern shore. When you arrive, seek out Master Ketch.

He is a friend and will make arrangements for the next part of your journey to the edge of the Lower Hills where you will find Laurel Silverbark." Aurien turned to Stefani. "Take this to her for me," he said. "It is a token that I have sent you."

He lowered his head. On the tip of his horn was a shiny silver ring. Carefully, Stefani slid the ring from his horn and held it in the palm of her hand, admiring the way it caught the morning light. She lifted the ring, intending to place it on her finger, but stopped, remembering her mother's earrings. What if she lost the ring, too?

Aurien gazed into her eyes. "I have faith that my trust in you is well placed," he said.

Stefani tucked the ring into her pocket.

"I wish you good venture, my friends," Aurien said as they picked up their packs and supplies.

Stefani followed the others across the meadow. When she reached the edge of the forest she stopped and gazed back. Aurien watched from the shade of the giant oak. She reached into her pocket and touched the silver ring, then turned and ran after the others.

CHAPTER THIRTEEN

Crystal Lake was large, the opposite shore a dark smudge. The setting sun felt warm on Stefani's back. It had taken a long day of trudging through forest and fen to reach the lake.

After they set up camp, Stefani searched the edge of the water for a place to soak her aching feet. She found a large boulder that jutted out over the water, but when she stuck her toes into the lake, she jerked them back out with a sharp intake of breath. The water was icy. So much for that idea, she thought, and limped back to sit beside the fire.

"Where did you go?" Robbie asked.

"Just a little way along the water," she said. "Why? What do you care?"

"Just curious. See anything interesting?"

"Not really," she paused and Robbie watched her, as if he expected her to say something more. "If you must know, I was trying to find a place to wash up, but the water's freezing." Just the memory of the icy water made her shiver.

"Cold. Cold. Crystal Lake is always cold," Gamdol chattered, peering around at the trees and brush nearby. "Yummies!" He dashed over to a patch of leafy plants and grabbed handfuls of sickly blue flowers, stuffing them into his mouth. He made noises of delight as he chewed.

Robbie walked over and pulled a few leaves off the plant and sniffed them. Although most of the things Gamdol liked smelled and tasted disgusting, these didn't seem too bad. "Hey," he said, putting one of the leaves into his mouth, "this stuff is pretty good."

"Perhaps," Tamel called as she flew over to take the first watch. "But I would not eat of it. It does not agree well with most stomachs." Robbie saw she was serious, spit the leaf out onto the ground, and wiped his mouth on his sleeve.

"Ew, that's disgusting," Stefani said.

"What? It's not like we have napkins and stuff out here." Robbie gestured around them. Gamdol smiled and continued to eat happily.

Around the campfire that night, Kelin told them the stories he'd heard about the Treemage,

Laurel Silverbark.

"Her kind are dabblers in the dark arts, he said, his voice flat. "My great-great-grandmother told us of a time when the Treemages came seeking knowledge of the dark lore from any who had heard even faint whisperings of it."

"But Aurien said we should trust her," Robbie said, "and I thought everyone trusted Aurien."

"It is not that I do not believe in the wisdom of Aurien," Kelin said, "but even the noble and wise may be deceived. I will do as Aurien says, but I will be watching for signs of trouble."

When they awoke the next morning, a cloud of mist blanketed the water.

After breakfast they packed their gear and set off, winding their way along the rim of the lake. The bright sun burned away the mist and made them all sweat. They arrived at the edge of the Windrow fishing village just as the last rays of the sun brushed the surface of the lake and sent flashes of color bouncing off the water.

The settlement was quiet except for the sound of the water lapping at the shore. Light showed through the shutters of the fisher folk's homes, and the smell of cooking wafted on the evening air. Stefani sniffed, hungrily inhaling the pleasant aroma. After the long afternoon's hike, the scent of frying fish made her mouth water.

Following Aurien's instructions, they made their way past the main dock and knocked on the door of the house at the center of the village. A weathered old man wearing a plain cotton shirt, breeches and a dark vest answered. He held a pipe carved in the shape of a leaping fish. His gaze fixed on each of them in turn, settling finally on Stefani.

"How can I a-help you?" he asked. His deep voice rasped as if he was used to yelling orders in a storm.

"Excuse me, sir," Stefani said in her most polite voice. "We're looking for a man named Ketch. We were told he is the Master Fisherman of this village."

"Aye, a-that he is," said the old man, eyeing them with curiosity, "but what would you a-want with him?"

"We were told he could help us on our journey," Stefani answered.

"And who would have a-told you that?"

"Aurien did," Robbie blurted.

"Aurien? Well why didn't you a-say so?" the old man chuckled. "A-come on in," he said, opening the door to reveal a cozy room with a fireplace at one end. Rows of shelves filled with all sorts of fishing equipment covered an entire wall. An odd assortment of items hung from pegs on the other walls. The old man took down chairs for his visitors, placing them around the table where an oil lantern burned with a bright light. The Lightwings made a quick survey of the room before taking watchful positions on the fireplace mantle

When everyone was settled, the old man leaned back and lit his pipe with a glowing stick he'd pulled from the fire.

"And a-how is my old friend Aurien?" he asked. "Seems ages since we've a-seen one another."

"He's fine, I guess," Stefani said, suddenly unsure if she should trust this stranger. "He sent us to ask if Master Ketch could help us."

"A-well, of course he a-can," chortled the wiry old man. "Anything for good old Aurien." He stopped short when he saw them staring at him, then laughed again, louder. "Oh my, I am a-sorry," he said. After catching his breath, he flourished his pipe with a quaint bow of his head. "I a-forgot my manners. Master Ketch, at your a-service."

"Oh, I uh-see," Stefani said. Robbie nudged with his elbow. "I mean, I see," she corrected herself and bit the inside of her cheek, waiting for Master Ketch's reaction. The fisherman's eyes only twinkled in the lamplight, the same way her grandfather's did when something amused him.

Over the fire the teakettle began to whistle. Master Ketch got up and poured tea while they spoke of their quest and the warnings Aurien had given them. The old man listened, becoming thoughtful. He puffed on his pipe for a moment before he spoke.

"Well, a-since you're in such a hurry," he said, "the quickest way to a-get where you need to a-go is to a-follow the river down to the point just before the gorge. Yes." He rubbed his chin whiskers in thought. "We'll a-speak to Finn first thing in the morning. He's the best a-steersman and a-guide in the village and I'd a-trust him with my life."

Just then, Stefani's stomach let out a loud growl. Master Ketch glanced over at her and smiled. She winced. "A-by the way," Master Ketch said, "have you a-eaten supper, yet? I've still a-got some fish stew in the pot, and you're a-welcome to it."

The stew tasted wonderful. They all ate with gusto, wiping the last of the stew from their bowls with thick slices of brown bread that Master Ketch cut from a fat loaf. Even Gamdol had a large helping.

When they finished eating, Master Ketch pulled some blankets out of an old chest and, after hanging the chairs back on the wall, they curled up on the floor before the fire. Master Ketch had gone to his own bed and Stefani heard his deep snoring from the next room. She lay awake for a while, watching the embers glowing in the fireplace before falling asleep. Suddenly, she was running from something huge and dark that she couldn't quite make out. All she could do was keep running.

She woke with a start and found Master Ketch stirring the coals to stoke up the morning fire. It was dark outside and she wondered what time it was.

"It will a-be dawn soon," Master Ketch rasped, as though he'd read her mind. He hung the teakettle over the fire. "Time to a-be up and about our business. I'll just a-be over to Finn's place for a bit, and I'll a-be back to stir up some morning feed. A-keep an eye on the kettle for me, eh?" Stefani thought he winked at her, but it was too dark to be certain. He went out the door with quiet steps, and she stood and stretched before rousing the others.

The sky had turned a rosy pink and the kettle had just begun to whistle when Master Ketch returned with a tall man.

"This is Finn," Master Ketch said. "He's agreed to a-guide you downriver. He won't a-go farther than Wayfarer Landing, but it'll a-get you a fair bit on your way."

While he talked, Master Ketch prepared a hearty breakfast of fishcakes and fried potatoes. Finn nodded once in a while to show he was listening, but few words passed his lips. When they finished eating, they agreed to meet at the village docks, and Finn left to prepare his boat for the journey.

Master Ketch handed Robbie a worn but sturdy knapsack. He took a coil of rope down from a wall peg and handed it to Stefani along with a bundle of food and several loaves of fresh bread. Then he helped them roll and tie their blankets with twine.

Down on the docks, they found Finn standing next to a small but sturdy looking boat. Around them the village fisherman made ready for the day, unfurling their sails to catch the morning breeze.

"Stow yer gear in the bow with the extra paddles." Finn pointed to the front of the boat. Stefani clambered aboard, but Gamdol stood still, staring wide-eyed. He cast fearful eyes toward the craft bobbing on the wide lake before him.

"Come on, Gamdol." Robbie swung his pack over the side of the boat. "What's wrong?"

"There's, there's too much, too much." Gamdol's face showed terror and his breath came in gasps.

Robbie felt bad for the Glimmering. Fear was something he understood only too well. "Isn't there some other way we can get there?" he asked Master Ketch.

"There's no time." The old man shook his head. "From what you've a-told me, you've good reason to a-hurry. Even if there were a way to a-go around the lake and down to the gorge without a-traveling by water, it would a-take weeks longer. No, I'm afraid your journey from here must a-be by boat."

"Oh, come on, Gamdol," Stefani said. "There's nothing to be afraid of." She shoved her pack into the bow and sat down. Robbie climbed aboard, followed by the three Lightwings, who zipped up into the rigging. Gamdol stared at them as if they'd all lost their minds. He didn't move. They tried everything they could think of to reassure him, but he refused to budge. Finn shook his head and began to untie the boat.

"Come on, Gamdol," Robbie pleaded, "we don't want to leave without you. Please come with us." He held out his hands to help the Glimmering aboard.

Gamdol forced himself to take a step forward, inching toward the boat. When he reached the edge of the dock he squeezed his eyes shut and, feeling his way like a blind person, stepped into the craft. The boat rocked and he stiffened, but Robbie helped him on board and onto a seat in the center of the skiff. Gamdol kept his eyes scrunched tight and gripped the edge of the narrow seat.

Master Ketch tossed the last of the mooring lines on board and Finn cast off, steering the boat away from the dock and out onto the wide lake. Stefani waved farewell to Master Ketch, who stood on the dock and waved back. The sails caught a gust and they skimmed across the water toward the mouth of the river and into the unknown.

CHAPTER FOURTEEN

They floated swiftly on the shimmering water, the tree-crowded bank rushing past. Gamdol anchored himself in the center of the craft, eyes squeezed shut. Nothing Robbie said seemed to help. Tense and afraid, the Glimmering refused to budge or even open his eyes.

The boat swayed on the water and, although the Lightwings all turned as green as Gamdol, they showed no fear.

Stefani stared at the river that carried them further and further from Hole-in-the-Rock. There was no going back now. She stuck her elbows on her knees and propped her head in her hands. It was as if they'd had no control over anything that had happened to them since they'd found themselves in this strange land. Sort of like Alice in Wonderland, when she went down the rabbit hole. Only this was real, not a dream you could just wake up from.

Stefani felt sad and tired. She glanced around at the others. Despite their discomfort, the Lightwings stood straight and stiff, keeping watch. Kelin perched on a roll of rope in the bow facing forward while Tamel and Katar stood on the seat on either side of Gamdol, who still trembled and shook.

"It's only water. It won't hurt you." Robbie told the Glimmering.

"There's too much!" Gamdol squeaked from between gritted teeth. "Too much!" He gripped the seat so tight his knuckles turned white.

"Don't you know how to swim?" Robbie asked. He'd always thought that swimming was something everyone could do. But here was his new friend, frightened to death of being in a boat.

"Swim?" Gamdol screaked.

"Yeah," Robbie said. "You know, the backstroke, the crawl . . . swim."

"What does this mean, swim?" Gamdol asked, his voice less tense as his curiosity got the better of him. He opened one eye to peek at Robbie.

"Well, you get in the water and you move

your arms . . . "

"Get in?" Gamdol cut him off before he could finish. "Get in the water? This big water? Get in?"

"Yeah," Robbie said, "like a bathtub, only bigger. Don't you ever take baths? Wash yourself?"

"Washing is done at the edge of a small stream," Gamdol said, opening his other eye and giving Robbie a severe look.

"Gee, I always have to take baths at home," Robbie said. "Except in the summer when I get to go swimming."

"Boys." Stefani rolled her eyes.

"What?" Robbie turned toward her.

"You'd think bathing was some kind of torture," she said, with a snort.

"That's not it," he said, frowning. "It's just that there are always lots of better things to do when I'm home." The way he said the word "home" sounded sad. Stefani started to say something, but he looked away, and she decided to keep her comment to herself. She didn't really want to hear again how great his home was anyway.

Gamdol slowly relaxed as Robbie talked about swimming and how much fun it was. He still gripped the seat with both hands, but before long, he was peering around as they floated steadily downriver.

They ate in the boat, still moving on the swift current. Gamdol refused food of any kind. Not even the sour-smelling nuts he seemed to love could tempt him. A breeze sprang up behind them, and Finn raised the small boat's sails. The little craft skimmed along, sails billowing.

Toward evening Finn guided the shallow craft to a sandy cove on the right bank where they camped for the night.

Once ashore, Robbie stood in front of Gamdol and raised his hand in the air. "High five," he said.

"Five what?" Gamdol asked.

Robbie laughed. "High five," he said. "To celebrate how great you handled being in the boat."

Gamdol looked confused. "To celebrate?"

"Yeah. Like this." Robbie raised Gamdol's hand in the air and then slapped his own hand against it. Gamdol looked at his hand and the corners of his mouth quirked up in a quizzical smile.

Just after dawn, they started off again. Gamdol still eyed the craft with suspicion, but this time he boarded the boat without being coaxed.

Stefani's thoughts drifted to the time she and her mother had gone paddle-boating. She'd been seven and her feet hardly reached the paddles. Her mother had encouraged her, telling her she could do anything she wanted, if she just put her mind to it and tried hard enough. For a while they had gone in circles, laughing and splashing the water with their hands, but after a bit she got the hang of it and they paddled all the way around the small lake. She wondered what had changed to make things between them so different. *Why does it seem like everything I do is wrong, now?* she thought.

She was wondering if it was too late to fix things between her and her mother when a shadow passed overhead. She started to say something, but when she looked again, whatever had been there was gone. It must have been a bird or a cloud.

The sails caught a good wind and the shore flew by. "We're nearing our landing," Finn said, easing them away from the center of the river, toward the left bank. But as they drew near the shore, something huge flapped up over the trees and dove at them. It was big and dark, and looked like a giant worm with wings. It swooped down, spewing stinking flames from its mouth. With a scream, Stefani ducked, crouching low in the boat.

"What's that?" Robbie yelped.

"Fireworm!" Gamdol shrieked, sliding back to the center of the seat and grabbing on with both hands. Finn struggled with the tiller, trying to keep them near the shore, but the giant reptile flew between them and the land.

They suddenly picked up speed.

"Rapids!" Finn shouted. "Robbie, pull that line free and drop the sail."

A massive bluff rose straight up from the water on the opposite shore. There was no way to land the boat. The Fireworm flew back and forth, belching fire. Clouds of black smoke streamed from its nostrils along with a smell like burnt food.

"Paddle!" Finn hollered.

Stefani reached beneath the seat, grabbed one of the oars and passed it to Robbie. Then she reached back and grabbed the other one. Together, they back-paddled as fast as they could. At first, the boat appeared to slow with their efforts, but before long they were once more picking up speed.

The river narrowed. Both banks grew steeper, rising into towering cliffs. Then, the Fireworm stopped its attack, veering away and disappearing as suddenly as it had appeared. Finn kept a firm grip on the tiller, watching the rapids ahead. Gamdol gripped the seat, trembling, while Robbie and Stefani struggled with the oars. The Lightwings clung to the rigging.

The water surged, growing rough and wild. The boat pitched, nearly tossing them overboard. They stopped rowing and clung to the sides. Gamdol squeezed his eyes shut tighter than before, making a low groaning noise in his throat. The sound of rushing water filled the air and the little boat plunged up and down propelled on the sloshing currents.

Finn struggled to keep the front of the boat pointed forward, but the white water rocked the small craft, spinning it around and around. Water sloshed over the sides, and Stefani stiffened with fear.

Suddenly, the boat heaved high into the air and slammed back down onto the water, tipping at a crazy angle. With a horrified shriek, Gamdol flew over the side.

"Gamdol!" Robbie leaped forward, making a grab for the Glimmering, who disappeared beneath the frothing water.

CHAPTER FIFTEEN

"Hang on!" Robbie shouted, clutching at his friend while holding on to the seat with his other hand. His glasses slipped off his face and fell into the bottom of the skiff. Stefani slid closer to try to help, but before she could do anything, the three Lightwings flew in. They each grabbed a handful of Gamdol's jacket and heaved as Robbie hauled.

Gamdol grabbed the side with his free hand and pulled. Together, they hefted him back into the boat. He lay on the bottom panting and gasping as the rapids pounded the tiny craft, jarring and shaking its passengers.

Stefani dropped the paddle inside the boat and reached down to snatch up Robbie's glasses. She held onto them with one hand and clutched at the side of the boat with the other. Water sloshed over Gamdol. He squeaked in fear and squeezed his eyes shut again.

"Bail!" Finn shouted. He strained at the tiller, guiding the careening boat around the huge rocks that jutted out of the river.

Robbie grabbed two wooden containers that floated in the bottom of the boat. Together, he and Stefani scooped up water and dumped it over the side. But angry waves crashed over them and the little boat filled faster than they could bail.

By the time the roaring of the river began to subside and the tiny craft stopped bouncing and tilting like an out-of-control carnival ride, Stefani's arms ached. Gradually, the river widened and the boat slowed. The riverbank sloped down, tall cliffs giving way to narrow beaches.

Finn's face was red and his muscles taut. Leaning all of his weight against the tiller, he brought the craft over to the left shore. Wearily, they climbed out of the battered boat and flopped down onto dry land. Coughing and groaning, Gamdol crawled as far from the water as he could and collapsed, shaking and shuddering.

Stefani caught her breath and sat up. The sun beat down on the weary travelers as they lay recovering from the shock of their narrow escape. White puffs of cloud drifted across the bright blue sky, but the Fireworm was nowhere in sight.

"Where are my glasses?" Robbie said.

"Here they are, Robbie. They didn't even break." Stefani held them out, her voice quavering. Water drops still speckled the lenses. "What you did was really brave," she added.

Gamdol whimpered, his hands clutching handfuls of the sandy soil.

"Thanks." Robbie took his glasses. He tried to clean them on his shirt, but couldn't find a dry spot.

Finally, he shrugged and put them on. Water dripped from his hair and ran across the lenses.

"Well, you were right about one thing." He got to his feet. "There are more dangerous things out here than a Glimmering." He glanced at Gamdol, who was lying face down in the sand.

"Hey, Gamdol," he said. "When I told you about swimming, I didn't think you'd go and try it right away."

Gamdol spun over and sat up. "Wh-what?" he sputtered. "Swimming? I wasn't—"

Robbie chuckled. "I'm only kidding," he said, offering a hand to help the Glimmering up. "I'm really glad you're all right. You are all right, aren't you?"

Gamdol hesitated before taking Robbie's hand. "Yes. Yes. I am. All right," he said, standing. "Safe, thanks to you and our brave guides." He gestured toward Tamel and the others. "I am owing to all of you."

"Don't worry about it," Robbie replied. "That's what friends are for. We may not have chosen to be here, but we can still work together to get through this." He wandered over to stand beside Finn, who was surveying the damaged boat.

Gamdol followed him over and lifted up his hand, palm outward. "High five?'"

"Absolutely," Robbie said, raising his hand in the air.

Gamdol's lips curved up in a smile and he slapped his hand against Robbie's.

Tightness gripped Stefani's throat. She felt like she might cry. That's stupid, she thought. It isn't like we're really friends.

"Mister Finn says the boat is in pretty bad shape." Robbie walked back to where Stefani sat. "We won't be able to use it. He says it was never meant to come down the rapids. We were supposed to go through the woods upriver. That way we could go around some big, old swamp. Now I guess we're going to have to go through the middle of it."

Stefani glanced quickly to where Gamdol sat on an old tree stump. He stared out at the river. "Gamdol," she asked in a soft voice, "do you know where we are?"

Gamdol shook his head, then rose and retrieved his waterlogged pack. He opened the pack and took out the map Aurien had given him, carefully unfolded the wet document and peered at it.

"We are near to the end of the river. It widens out just beyond here and becomes a part of the Sestol Swamp. The dwellplace of the Treemage is on the other side."

"Is it far?" Robbie asked.

"A few days journey only," the Glimmering replied, refolding the map. "I thank you again for my life, Robbie."

"I can't really take credit," Robbie said, his neck and face reddening. "It just sort of happened. Besides, I'm not sure what I would've done if Kelin and the others hadn't been there to help."

"It was a brave act," Gamdol said firmly, "and I am grateful."

"I'm just glad you're okay," Robbie said.

Once more, Stefani felt tears trying to sneak out. She forced herself to smile, stood up and began sorting through their packs. She kept her face averted as she worked. "The fruit is bruised and the bread is all mushy." She wiped her hands on her jeans.

"We could make a fire to dry things faster," Robbie suggested.

Finn shook his head and frowned. "Could be dangerous."

The Lightwings returned and reported no sign of the Fireworm. "Nor any other danger that we can see," Katar said. "But I would not stay close to the river. The Fireworm may decide to return. And it might not come alone."

"Shouldn't we get moving then?" Stefani

asked, still jittery from their close call with a dragon. Gamdol could call it whatever he liked, but that fire-breathing thing was no worm.

They quickly repacked and made their way through a sloping forest where cicadas buzzed and gray-green leaves drooped from pale-limbed trees. Stefani found herself looking up at the sky every few minutes, expecting to be attacked from above.

Finn traveled with them in silence and camped with them that night, but on the following morning he took his leave. "I wish I could help more," he told them, "but I must return to my family. 'Tis nearing end of season and we've much work." Before he disappeared into the trees he stopped, turned back and tipped his hat.

They soon found themselves on the edge of a gray, dismal swamp. Nothing moved, not even the air, which had become thick and sticky. It felt like a steamy shower in a grungy locker room.

"It looks kind of creepy," Robbie said.

Stefani wrinkled up her nose. "It doesn't smell so great, either."

Even Gamdol, who seemed fond of things that smelled perfectly horrible, hesitated on the edge of the cheerless marsh, a look of distaste smeared across his normally cheerful face. He reached out one foot and tested it on the boggy land. "Not nice," he said, with a grimace. "Not nice."

"Not nice?" Stefani asked. "Like as in the old

part of the forest where those tangly-vines trapped us? Because that was so much fun," she grumbled.

Gamdol tilted his head and thought about it. After a while he pointed at the swamp. "Not the same. No. Not the same. But not nice." He frowned. "Too much water. Too much mud."

"Too much yuck, if you ask me." Stefani crossed her arms. "Why do we have to go through that?" She jutted her chin in the direction of the swamp. "There ought to be another way."

"Not according to the map." Robbie's shoulders slumped as he contemplated the parchment.

"If this is the way we must travel," Kelin said. "Then to tarry here is pointless."

"Easy for you to say," Stefani grumbled. "You can just fly right over all the nasty muck, while the rest of us have to sludge through it." She wished she had a pair of those rubber pants her grandfather fished in.

"True," Kelin said. "But we will also be able to fly ahead and find the best path through the bog, which will make your trek easier."

Stefani still wasn't happy about having to slog through a muddy swamp. It just wasn't fair.

The Lightwings took to the air and zigzagged above the swamp, searching for the best way to cross. "This way," Kelin called.

Stefani stepped out onto the marsh and sank down several inches. "Hey! I thought you checked this out."

"This is the best path," Kelin told her. "The ground is even less solid to either side."

"Sure it is." How could they tell from up in the air? She took two steps to the left and sank up to her calves, cold mud oozing inside her boots. "Must be nice to have wings," she grumbled. It was all she could do not to cry.

CHAPTER SIXTEEN

Ashkell stood in the center of the high tower room, dangling a gleaming blue jewel before his face. "I suppose this bauble dances while the other one sings," he said with a sneer.

"No, Your Enormousness," responded Greenback. "This is the Skystone. It has the power to control the weather. It can cause great winds to blow, and it can stop or start rain anywhere in Anoria."

"Oh?" Ashkell became interested. "And how does it do that?"

"It's actually a rather simple spell, My Lord,"

replied the other dragon with a superior air. “Shall I demonstrate?”

“Do it!” Ashkell commanded, thrusting the jewel in Greenback’s direction.

“As you command, Sire.” Greenback took the Skystone. It shimmered in the light, swinging on its braided chain of white and yellow gold. It glowed with an inner light as he carried it to the nearest window mumbling arcane words of ancient enchantment. With a flick of his claw he set the jewel spinning on its chain and puffed on it as it twirled. His smoky breath turned the crystal a darker blue, wreathing it in a gray cloud as it spun. The cloud twirled about the stone as it picked up speed, spinning faster and faster at the end of its chain.

The sky outside the tower grew dark. Thick clouds crowded in and covered the sun. Gentle rain fell from the sullen sky. “What good is all this feeble magic?” demanded Ashkell. “I want power!” His nostrils flared and black smoke curled about his huge head.

Greenback cast a sly glance at Ashkell’s angry face, then turned toward the window and blew with all his might on the twirling jewel. The Skystone darkened until it looked more like an ugly bruise than a gemstone. The sky turned black. Thunder rumbled and lightning flashed and the rain became a torrent.

Ashkell rushed to the window, eyes wide in astonishment. “There may be some meager power in these trinkets, after all,” he said, turning toward his advisor. “Perhaps, you’re not completely worthless."

"Thank you, Your Massiveness." Greenback curled his lip. He blew gently on the Skystone, reciting the spell of abeyance, and strong winds pushed the storm away from the castle, sending it roiling into the distance.

"From now on I shall keep the stones locked in my consulting chamber," Ashkell said, snatching the glittering Skystone from Greenback's claw. "Bring me the others as soon as they are found."

"Ah, that brings us to another point of business," Greenback said, his eyes greedily following the gleaming stone. He licked his lips. "One of our scouts has returned with disturbing news."

"What is it?" Ashkell lashed his tail. "Has my brother discovered our plans?"

"No, Your Full-sizedness, it isn't about your brother, although I did take the liberty of sending out a troop of Fireworms to divert his attention. In fact, they should be laying waste to a very fertile area of farmland right about now. Emris won't have time to think about us for a while. No, it's something else."

"Spit it out, Greenback!" Smoke poured from Ashkell's nostrils.

"There are rumors that others are searching for the Nelig Stones."

"Who are they?" Ashkell demanded. His eyes blazed with fiery rage. "Why haven't you stopped them?"

"Please, Your Extensiveness. I am certain

there is nothing to worry about. True, one of our spies has reported a small group of motley travelers. However, they are clearly weak and harmless. After all, it is only a Glimmering, three Lightwings, and two young humans."

"I don't care what they are. Have them destroyed immediately."

"The fact is, Your Direness, that the scout was able to force them into the rapids of Derole where they are certain to have perished. But even if they have managed to survive they cannot possibly stand in our way. Remember, we have The Ancient Book of Dark Truths. They do not. And because of my skillful reading of the ancient text, we already have two of the five stones in our possession. It is only a matter of time before we—uh—I mean you—will control all the lands of Anoria." Greenback bowed low as he finished speaking.

"Then, why do you bother me with such petty things?" Ashkell said. "Just make sure they do not interfere with our plans. That is after all your job, Greenback. See to it!"

Outside the window, water dripped from the eaves landing in loud splats on the paving stones below. Greenback envisioned the power that would be his once he possessed all five Nelig Stones. "Of course, Your Spaciousness. I am yours to command," he said, barely able to keep from sneering. "I will see to it immediately." He nodded his head before leaving the room.

Greenback tromped down the long corridor, grumbling to himself. He didn't like leaving the stones with Ashkell, but for the moment he didn't have much choice in the matter. He would have to find a way to get Ashkell to give the stones back to him at the proper time. The idiot! He had no knowledge of how much power the stones contained, much less any understanding of how to use them. No matter. When the time came, he would be the one to control Anoria. Not that bag of soot and smoke or his weakling brother. No. The right to rule belongs to the powerful, he thought, and with the Nelig Stones and my knowledge of the dark arts, I, Lord Greenback, will be all-powerful!

In the meantime he had work to do. He would send out spies to watch for the Glimmering and the others. If they did survive the river, they might prove useful. They might even lead his spies to one of the missing stones. He contemplated the possibility before lapsing into his usual daydreaming about how he would deal with Ashkell, and everyone else who had ever treated him badly, once he took power. He grinned. The tortures he devised were never pleasant, but he always found them amusing.

SEVENTEEN

The swamp went on forever. Twisting trees hung with dripping moss and strange misshapen plants grew in clumps. The Lightwings continued to scout the way, warning them of dead ends and muck-filled ponds, but more than once, ground that had appeared solid from the air became soggy and sank beneath their weight. They were forced to retrace their steps so many times Stefani lost count. Even with Gamdol's map and Stefani's compass, they found themselves going in circles that drew them deeper into the murky swamp.

Pesky insects buzzed near their ears and swarmed their faces, biting them and getting in their eyes and noses. “Some insect repellent would be nice.” Stefani swatted at the annoying bugs. "You don't happen to have any plants to keep these things from eating us, do you?"

Tamel shook her head. The Lightwings pulled out their swords and slashed at the bugs to drive them off. But for every insect slain, it seemed two more attacked, and the three little soldiers finally gave up.

The swamp smelled like old mildewed clothes. Stefani tried to breathe through her mouth, but ended up tasting the smell, which was even worse.

They tramped all day, stopping only once to grab a quick bite. "Yuck. Everything tastes swampy." Stefani waved her hand over her food to keep the bugs off, but she was sure she'd already eaten a ton of the nasty things. "How long are we going to have to be here?"

"Difficult to tell. Our path does not go straight," Gamdol said, slapping his neck and wiping away several squished bugs.

"Duh." Stefani tossed her food on the ground and jumped up. "My boots are full of grossness and my feet are all shriveled up from being wet." She suddenly longed to be back home in her nice dry room. "Let's get out of this place."

"Yeah," Robbie said. "If these bugs don't stop biting me soon, I'm gonna bite them back."

Late in the day a low mist began to rise. By evening the thick fog made it impossible to travel. In the eerie gloom they settled on a soggy patch of ground and set up camp. They spoke in hushed voices. Gamdol tried to start a fire, but the sorry twigs and branches they'd been able to find were so wet they refused to burn. They ate a cold, cheerless dinner and went to bed early, waiting for the dismal night to pass.

A drizzling rain woke them early. Before long, the rain grew into a dripping shower that turned the already mucky swamp into a sloshing ocean of slime.

"Who ordered the rain?" Robbie asked, wiping water out of his eyes.

"Seems like the bugs don't like it any more than we do," Stefani said.

"Oh, like that makes it okay," Robbie grumped.

With a crack of thunder, sheets of rain poured from the sky. The wind blustered and buffeted the Lightwings until they were forced to ride on the packs and shoulders of their companions. Kelin sat hunched on Stefani's pack. Even over the noise of the storm, she could hear the Lightwing Captain's teeth grinding in frustration. I guess it must suck to be so small, Stefani thought, even if you can fly.

A shout from behind made her spin around. Through the torrent she could just make out Robbie, arms pin-wheeling, and Gamdol trying to grab onto him. Something was wrong. Robbie looked shorter than Gamdol. Stefani tried to run, but the gloppy swamp sucked at her feet and she could only slog slowly back to Robbie and Gamdol. By the time she arrived, Robbie had sunk up to his waist in a gooey pit.

"Stay back!" Gamdol warned. "Hungry sand!" He lay on his stomach, arms stretched out toward Robbie, but even the Glimmering's long fingers couldn't reach. Robbie struggled to grab Gamdol's hands, but the more he moved the lower he sank.

"What can we do?" Stefani cried.

"Vines!" Gamdol hollered, "or a long branch."

"Over there," Kelin hollered in her ear, "to your left."

"Hurry! I'm sinking!" Robbie yelled.

He was up to his neck in thick watery sand. He had his chin stuck up in the air to keep his face out of the muck, but the pouring rain filled his mouth. He gagged and coughed as he sank.

Stefani felt a surge of panic. Her hands shook as she dug inside her pack and finally pulled out the length of rope Master Ketch had given her. Dropping her pack on the ground, she grabbed one end of the rope and tossed the coil across to Gamdol. "Robbie, grab the middle of the rope. Gamdol, grab the end. Together we can pull him up."

Robbie took a big breath, and his head sank under the viscous sand. Stefani stifled a gasp and held tight to her end of the rope. She stared at the still surface of the quicksand, holding her breath.

With a loud slurp, Robbie's hands thrust out of the muck and he grabbed the rope, wrapping it around his wrists.

"Pull!" Stefani shouted, gripping the end of the rope and stepping back from the murky pit. She pulled and pulled, and Gamdol strained at his end, but it wasn't enough. Robbie slipped further under, dragging the center of the rope with him.

"No!" Stefani screamed. She threw every bit of her fear and panic into pulling. Her muscles burned with the effort and the wet rope tried to slip out of her hands, but she wound it around her fists and strained. Tears of frustration and anger mixed with the pouring rain.

Then, slowly, inch-by-inch, Robbie began to emerge. First his elbows. Then the top of his head. Soon his face was free and he gasped, spitting out muck. They dragged him all the way out onto the soggy ground, where he lay panting and coughing. The rain still drove down in torrents, but it wasn't enough to wash away the sticky ooze that clung to every inch of him.

"Here. You can wipe your face with this." Stefani handed him her bandanna.

"Thanks," he said, still gasping. "Thank you both."

They staggered over to an old gnarled tree and collapsed beside it. The tree provided some protection from the angry wind, but its thin, twisted branches did nothing to guard them from the pouring rain. The Lightwings were nearly washed away until Gamdol used his bag to shelter them.

They huddled in silence, still shaky from their experience. The cruel weather seemed like it would never end. Their food was completely soggy and none of them could stand the thought of eating it. Stefani reached into her backpack and scooped out a gooshy mass of what had once been bread and dumped it on the ground, shaking her hand to get the last of it off her fingers, rinsing her hands in the torrential rain.

They hunched together until the howling wind finally died down. Once on the move again, they went more cautiously. No one wanted to discover another pit of slimy quicksand.

Finally, just as they arrived at the edge of the murky swampland, the rain slowed to a drizzle. Terra firma. Stefani stepped forward and felt a new appreciation for the scientific name for the earth.

Before them, meadowland sloped upward into rolling hills. Behind, the ugly clouds that had followed them seemed to be stuck over the vicious swamp.

As the final rays of daylight pierced the clouds, a patch of blue opened up ahead. A rainbow appeared, flashed brightly, then faded. “The bright arch is a good omen,” Gamdol said.

Robbie sneezed.

“Ugh! The rainbow might be a good omen,” Stefani grumbled, “but that sure isn’t.”

They made camp in a copse of trees beneath a roof of thick leaves and branches where the sheltered ground was delightfully dry. Gamdol gathered dry kindling and started a cheerful blaze, and they sat by the fire drying their clothes and blankets.

Once dry, their spirits rose considerably, and talk turned to their upcoming meeting with Laurel Silverbark and what she might be like. None of them had ever seen a Treemage.

Gamdol was excited about meeting a sorceress. "Earth magic is very powerful, very special to Glimmering," he said, his normal chattiness returning. "Any being with earth-lore is wise and powerful. Very special. Very important."

But the Lightwings were still unhappy. Kelin frowned. "I go uneasy, and not unwary, to this meeting."

CHAPTER EIGHTEEN

Stefani woke to the twitter and chirrup of birdsong. She sat up and rubbed her eyes. A feeling of relief filled her. It had been days since they had seen or heard any creatures other than hungry insects. Although still chilly, the cool morning air felt refreshing rather than biting and the rays of the rising sun warmed her.

Stefani stretched, reveling in the feel of dry clothes after spending so much time cold and wet. She scratched an itch on her left elbow, then another on her right shoulder. Her body suddenly felt like one great big itch and she realized she was covered in angry red insect bites. She rubbed at them, trying not to scratch. Oh great. Just what she needed.

Robbie sneezed and sniffed loudly, then dragged his sleeve across his face.

"Ew, gross!" Stefani said.

"I can't help it." Robbie sniffled again. "It's not like I have a box of tissue in my back pocket."

As usual, Kelin, Katar and Tamel were already awake and on guard. Tamel's left eye was dark and puffy where one of the nasty bugs had bitten her.

"Um, Tamel," Stefani said, "you don't happen to know where we can get some leaves that will stop this itching, do you?" She rubbed at a large mass of red bumps on the back of her hand.

"Sadly, I do not." She hovered in the air and surveyed the area around them. "This is not my forest, and I do not have knowledge of the green-life here."

Gamdol pulled out his map, unrolling the damp parchment with care. While the others huddled over the map, Stefani wandered a little way off, breathing in the fresh air and trying not to scratch. A short distance from the grove, she picked up a large gray stone to examine.

Something rustled nearby and she spun in the direction of the sound. She could have sworn one of the saplings had moved. She stared at the small tree and jumped back when it moved again. Her heart pummeled her ribs and she gripped the rock, thinking she might be able to use it as a weapon.

The tree moved closer. "Don't be frightened, Stefani," it said in a voice as gentle and quiet as the rustling of leaves.

"How do you know my name?" Stefani asked, still clutching the rock in her trembling fist.

"I know many things." Soft green eyes gazed out from beneath a cluster of dark foliage. "I know who you are and where you came from. I even know that you seek the Treemage known as Laurel Silverbark, who lives in these woods."

"How do you know that?" Stefani's voice quavered.

"Because, child, I am the one you seek," it said, extending its thin woody arms outward with open palms. "I am Laurel Silverbark."

"How do I know you're who you say you are?"

"Open your heart," the creature said, "and you will know the truth."

Stefani peered at the strange being before her. Something in the creature's manner reminded her of her mother. Not the nagging mother that Stefani could no longer seem to get along with, but the warm hot-cocoa making mom who used to take her shopping and roller skating and out for ice cream. The fear drained out of her and a peaceful feeling rose up through her feet and rushed to the top of her head. She relaxed, opened her fingers, and let the rock fall to the ground.

As the figure drew nearer, Stefani saw that what had appeared to be a tree was actually a slender woman with silver-gray skin. The

Treemage wore a long green robe streaked with brown that shimmered as she moved, so that she appeared to be walking through shifting light and shadow. Instead of hair she had a full head of rich leaves that fell below her waist, and her green eyes sparkled as she smiled at Stefani. "Shall we go and join the others?"

"You know about the others, too?"

"Of course," Laurel said, "I have been watching and waiting for you. I can see many things in my scrying pond and, I'm afraid, much of what I have seen is disquieting. Come, we have much to discuss." With a rustle of leaves, Laurel headed toward the grove.

"Wait," Stefani said, remembering the silver ring. "I have something for you. It's from Aurien," she said, pulling the ring out of her pocket and offering it to Laurel.

"Oh, yes," the Treemage said, gazing at the glittering ring in Stefani's outstretched hand. "Would you mind keeping it for me for just a little longer? It will fit your finger better than mine."

"You mean wear it?"

"Yes."

"But . . . but I wouldn't want to lose it," Stefani said, remembering her mother's earrings and cringing inside.

"I'm certain it will be safe with you. And, since it has some magic in it, it will make it easier for me to find you if the need arises."

Stefani gave her a startled look.

"Go ahead, put it on," Laurel said, gliding toward camp.

Stefani stared down at the band of silver,

then carefully placed it on her finger, making sure it fit snugly, before following Laurel.

The others, who had been talking quietly around the campfire, were startled by the appearance of Laurel, but Gamdol hopped to his feet.

"Good greetings, Honored One," he said, bowing formally. "I am Gamdol of the Glimmering. And these fine Lightwings are Captain Kelin Graystar, and Lieutenants Katar Stormlight and Tamel Brightsword. This young person is Robbie, and I see you have already met our companion Stefani. We are pleased to meet you, very pleased."

Tamel and Katar both bowed politely, but Kelin watched the Treemage warily.

Robbie sneezed into his sleeve and Stefani frowned at him. "Sorry," he said, a nasal twang to his voice.

"Good greetings to you all," Laurel replied, opening her arms wide and bowing her head. Her foliage rustled softly when she moved. "I am Laurel Silverbark, Treemage."

She raised her head and smiled. "And now we shall be less formal, for we have much to speak of and there is little time. But first, I see you are in need of something to relieve your discomfort. Do you have a container and fresh water?"

Gamdol produced a cup and Robbie poured some water into it. Reaching up, Laurel pulled several leaves from the top of her head, crushed them between her long fingers and dropped them into the water. A spicy fragrance wafted from the mixture. "Stefani, would you lend me your scarf?"

Stefani gave her a blank look, then realized Laurel meant her bandanna, and pulled it out of her pack. Laurel dipped the bandanna into the mixture, wrung it out, and moved toward Tamel, whose left eye was now swollen shut. The Lightwing flinched as Laurel raised the cloth to her face, but allowed the compress to be applied to her eye. She relaxed instantly and a small sigh of relief escaped from her. When Laurel removed the damp cloth, Tamel's eye was no longer red and the swelling was already fading.

After holding his head over the container and inhaling for several minutes, Robbie's sneezing and sniffling stopped. His oncoming cold seemed to have vanished.

Laurel instructed them to dip the bandanna into the cup and dab the liquid on their insect bites. In moments, Stefani's itching stopped. She smiled and handed the cloth to Gamdol.

"I know you seek the Nelig Stones," Laurel said. As she spoke, Stefani rubbed self-consciously at the ring on her finger. "I also know that another seeks the stones. One, the Skystone, has already been found. It was used to cause the storm that hindered your journey through the swamp."

"I knew somebody had ordered rain," Robbie said with disgust.

"I have gazed into the scrying pond for more, but my seeing has been blocked by a power I do not fully understand. I know the power is born of dark magic, and this worries me greatly, for I cannot tell from where it comes or who is directing it. I can tell you that our journey will likely be dangerous as well as difficult, and we must move quickly."

Kelin still seemed uncertain about Laurel, but he paid attention while she spoke. His eyes grew wide when she told them that she held one of the Nelig Stones in her possession. She reached inside her robe and pulled out a fine silver chain, displaying a dark red stone wrapped in silver wire.

"This is the Twilight Firestone," she said. "It is so named because every evening at dusk it casts a light as bright as flame. It also has the power to control fire." Her voice was tinged with a mixture of fear and reverence. "It has been in the care of the Treemages for eons," she continued, "as fire is the element our kind fears and respects more than any other. The High Ones of Learning, wisest of all Treemages, gave the stone into my protection many years ago. It has been my task to keep it safe. And now, a darkness reaches for the stones."

Laurel tucked the stone back inside her robes. "Aurien has sent you in search of the Nelig Stones to open the Gate between our Worlds, and I am willing to help you return to your home, but we must also protect the land."

Laurel led them to her glade near a deep quiet pond where she provided them with provisions for the next part of their journey. The

Lightwings stayed apart, but seemed less wary of Laurel than they had been.

Stefani offered to fill the water bottles and carried them down to the edge of the pond. She knelt on the bank and dipped a flask into the water, watching as the fluid surface rippled outward. Tiny waves caught the sunlight in glittering flashes. The reflected light danced on the air around her, and then the water grew still and the surface of the pond became silver. Stefani saw herself gazing up from the pond, like seeing her reflection in a mirror. But instead of sky and trees, she saw dark rock and a stone wall behind her that shook and trembled. The wall cracked and black smoke rose up. She caught her breath and dropped the flask. It plopped over with a slurp and bobbed in the water. The surface of the water undulated and the vision disappeared.

Trembling, she grabbed the flask and gazed out across the water. The pond sat dark and still. She saw nothing except a few stray leaves that floated on the water's quiet surface. It must have been a dream. She must have dozed off. She wiped her face with a wet hand and finished filling the water bottles, then hurried to rejoin the others.

Laurel, Gamdol and Robbie pored over the map, which was spread out on a flat rock in front of them. "We will have to travel to the Port of Imbol and from there take a ship along the coast to Felsun Bay. There is no faster way," Laurel said, tracing her finger across the map.

At the news they would be traveling by boat, Gamdol grew stiff. His mouth turned down in an unhappy frown, but he said nothing. He folded the map and stowed it in his pack. Stefani handed him his water bottle, smiling as he took the leather flask by its strap and hung it over his shoulder. "Bigger ships are safer," she said. He walked away without answering.

CHAPTER NINETEEN

In a wide valley, resting between jagged mountains, fire raged. Black smoke billowed up and spread across the sky, covering it in a dark cloud that dropped hot glowing cinders on the ground below. As the embers struck the valley floor, more flames erupted, engulfing fields and farms.

A dozen dragons flew in and out through the dark smoke, scales ruddy in the light of the red-orange flames. They carried huge canvas sacks filled with water from a nearby lake. One after the other, they dumped the contents of the bags onto the hottest parts of the fire, dousing the searing flames. Clouds of hissing steam rose up, mixed with smoke and ash.

King Emris perched on a nearby ridge. His golden scales flashed red, reflecting the fiery flames of the inferno. A muscular dragon smudged with soot stood at attention before him.

"What is your report, General Veld?" the king asked.

"Sire, the flames are nearly contained. The fire patrol arrived shortly after a sentry spotted the smoke. The land damage was severe, but only minor civilian casualties have been reported. One of our younger fire dousers was overcome by smoke when he flew too low, but the healers have assured me he will be fine."

"And the cause of the blaze?"

"According to witnesses, Sire, the fire was started by a group of renegade Fireworms. I have a platoon out searching for them."

"Fireworms, eh? I wonder what could have caused them to break their truce." King Emris rubbed his chin with a foreclaw, his eyes narrowed in thought. "Not that they generally need an excuse to cause trouble, but this is the third fire in the past two weeks. Any ideas what they're up to?"

"No, Sire. The fires seem to be carelessly set. There isn't any gain to be had by them that I can see. The worms just seem to be causing random destruction."

CHAPTER TWENTY

Robbie ducked as a large, gray seabird swooped down, just missing his head, and landed on a nearby piling. A three-masted ship, sails furled, lay moored at the end of the pier. The harbor bustled with business and sailors toted boxes and barrels up the ship's ramp, storing them in the hold.

Even though the tall ship dwarfed the nearby fishing boats, Stefani was certain they would have trouble convincing Gamdol that sailing at sea would be safer than the trip they had taken through the rapids. Nevertheless, although his knees trembled, Gamdol marched proudly behind Laurel all the way up the gangplank.

They set sail with the afternoon sun shining brightly on the rippling water. Stefani stood at the rail, staring out across the open sea. She was thinking of going below when Laurel came out onto the deck, and stood with her arms extended up toward the sun.

"May I ask you a question?" Stefani said.

"Certainly." Laurel dropped her arms to her sides.

"Why do you stand like that?"

"To gather strength and energy from the sun," Laurel said. "The way you gather it from the water."

"I do?"

"Can't you feel it?" Laurel asked.

Stefani thought for a moment before answering. "I guess so," she said. "I thought I was just looking at it, but it does make me feel stronger somehow. I mean, bigger. Like there's more to me than who I am. Does that make sense?"

"Of course." Laurel smiled. She raised her arms again and Stefani went back to the railing and let the peaceful sea fill her with strength.

The next morning, the ship sailed into Felsun Bay and drew up to a wide wooden pier. After buying supplies for the next part of their journey, Laurel secured rooms for the night at an inn near the outskirts of the city.

At dinner that evening, Stefani pushed her food around in her bowl, eating only a few bites.

"You okay?" Robbie asked between huge mouthfuls of stew.

Something heavy seemed to have settled onto her shoulders, and she wanted to tell him how she felt, but it wasn't something she could put into words. She shrugged and he left her alone. Afterward, she sat apart, curled in a big chair near the fireplace until it was time for bed.

Laurel woke them at dawn and after breakfast they set off for the Oban Plains, a flat, empty expanse that, according to Gamdol's map, began a short distance from Felsun Bay.

"We seek the Caverns of Lorn where the Nelig troll's workshop is rumored to have been located," Laurel said. Stefani wondered why, if Laurel knew where they were going, the Treemage stopped so often to ask Gamdol to consult the map. Gamdol would stand straight and, speaking with confidence, point to where they were and how far they had come since their last stop. He seemed somehow older to Stefani. Less chatty. More mature than he'd been when they'd first met at Hole-in-the-Rock.

The glaring sun scorched the plains during the day, so they traveled at night, the waxing moon lighting their way. During the hottest part of the day, they camped under a rough lean-to built with the light poles and canvas Laurel had purchased in Felsun.

Stefani found it more and more difficult to sleep in the heat. This place was even hotter than June in Arizona. Plus, ever since she'd had the menacing dream at Laurel's pond, something had been bothering her, scrabbling at the back of her mind, but no matter how hard she tried she just couldn't quite figure out what it was. It felt like she had the answer to a really important test question squiggling deep inside her brain, but she just couldn't get it to the surface. Both Robbie and Laurel asked her if she was okay, but she didn't know how to explain what she didn't understand herself, so she kept quiet, hoping she would figure it out.

Several days after leaving Felsun Bay, they lay beneath the lean-to, resting while Katar stood watch. But Stefani couldn't sleep in the unbearable heat. After tossing and turning for what seemed like hours, she crept out from under the lean-to. She spoke quietly with Katar, who was standing watch, assuring him she wouldn't go far. Then she walked away from camp.

The Oban Plains looked a lot like the desert Stefani was used to, only without the cactus. Two nights ago, they had passed through an area of hard packed sand where they hadn't seen a living thing for miles. During the night, however, they'd begun to see the shapes of short, gnarled trees, stunted and unhealthy.

Stefani sat in the shade of one of the deformed plants, feeling sorry for the way it struggled to grow out here on the hot plains with so little water. Picking up a scraggly stick, she scratched at the sandy soil. She thought about everything that had happened since Hole-in-the-Rock. She thought about her mother and suddenly realized that she missed her. She tried not to cry, but this time she couldn't stop the tears. Salty droplets ran down her cheeks and plopped into the dust.

She wiped her eyes with the back of her hand and dropped the stick with a start. Beside her, scratched into the dirt, were the same markings she'd seen right before Robbie had torn around the corner and ploughed into her that day so long ago. Had she made those markings in the dirt just now? She'd thought she'd just been aimlessly moving the stick back and forth in the loose dust. But there they were.

A shadow stretched across the ground toward her and she looked up. Robbie stood beside her.

"Hi," he said. "Are you okay?"

"I just couldn't sleep."

"Me neither." He stuffed his hands into his pockets. "Pretty hot, huh?"

"Yes," she said, staring at the ground.

"What's that?" Robbie squatted down next to her and pointed at the marks.

"I don't know," she said, "but it looks just like the writing I saw at Hole-in-the-Rock before you bumped into me. It's like some sort of picture writing, don't you think?"

"Yeah, I guess so." He shrugged. "Anyway, it's time to go. Everybody's awake and getting ready."

Stefani scrambled up. She had been sitting by the twisted tree longer than she'd realized and evening shadows stretched across the land.

She gazed at the markings, then scuffed her foot across the dirt, wiping them out.

CHAPTER TWENTY-ONE

Summoned like a common servant! Greenback gritted his teeth and grumbled all the way to the council chamber. Outside the room he paused, donning the mask of obedience before entering. "You wanted to see me, Your Prodigiousness?"

"Yes, Greenback. I want a report on your progress." Ashkell stood near the rough fireplace, playing idly with the Skystone. He moved it this way and that, peering at the polished azure surface. "What news have you?" he asked, without bothering to look at

Greenback.

It was all Greenback could do to answer without sputtering in anger. “The High King,” he said, unable to resist the opportunity to remind Ashkell that Emris still sat on the throne. “I mean, your brother, is still fighting fires. Our troops keep him well occupied, striking in the predawn hours and leaving before the Anorian legions can be summoned.”

“I want to be certain.” Ashkell continued to toy with the stone. “I don’t want anything getting in my way. Do you understand me?”

Greenback seethed with ire, but nodded his head and hid his feelings. How dare Ashkell play with the Nelig Stones as if they were mere trinkets. They didn’t belong to Ashkell! They belonged to him, Greenback, the only one who could control them and wield their power. He kept telling himself that it was only a matter of time, but bowing to Ashkell became harder and harder to do.

“Where are my other stones?” Ashkell asked, grinning and dangling the blue gem. He sneered at Greenback’s discomfort.

“Our seekers are in the process of securing them as we speak,” Greenback lied, and hoped it would soon be true.

Suspicion showed in Ashkell’s eyes. “So you keep telling me. But I am still waiting. And I wonder why you have not yet brought me the Great Stone.”

"I have found little more information regarding the Great Stone, Your Endlessness. But our searchers continue to comb every possible hiding place. I am sure they will find

something soon."

Ashkell moved in close, narrowed his eyes and peered down at Greenback. "How could something so grand and powerful be so well hidden? Why has it not been found? Where would one keep such a mighty treasure, I wonder?"

Greenback tried not to squirm. Ashkell had no way of knowing about his plans, but his employer was clearly suspicious. "Patience, Your Unlimitedness, you will have the stones soon," he said in a silken voice.

"I want them now!" Ashkell glared at Greenback. "Emris could spoil everything if he marches on us before we are prepared. And that would make me very unhappy."

Greenback backed away. "Your Colossality, you have nothing to be concerned about. Who would dare to go to war against such a powerful and mighty lord as you? If he weren't so afraid of your fierce strength and power, your brother would surely have come against us by now. Only someone stupid would test our—your—armies."

"Perhaps," Ashkell said. He knew he was being flattered, but he was pleased by the praise. "You are probably right. No one would dare to go against me, not even someone as stupid and addle-brained as my weakling brother." He sneered. "And even Emris, with all the armies in Anoria, will not stand a chance once I have control of the Nelig Stones." He pictured himself sitting on the high throne and smiled. "Make haste, Greenback," he said in a low voice, "I want those stones in my claws within the week."

"But, Your Sturdiness, that isn't much time." Greenback licked his lips.

"Plenty of time for someone as capable as you. Surely with your vast knowledge and learning you will be able to deliver the stones by then."

"Yes, certainly, Your Comprehensiveness," Greenback said. He knew better than to argue with Ashkell. Besides, a week would give him time to think of an excuse if he failed. And once he had possession of the stones, Ashkell would no longer be a problem.

"See to it that you do, or I shall find myself another advisor." He raised the Skystone up to the window. Splashes of colored light flickered about the room, reflecting off his dark scales. "You may leave me now and see to your duties."

Greenback choked down his rage. He bowed slightly and backed out of the room, eyes glued to the glittering gem, resisting the urge to rush over and seize it. There must be something I am missing in one of the ancient texts, he thought as he slithered down the hall to his study. Perhaps he should send scouts to search the Caverns of Lorn again. It was odd they hadn't found anything the first time. He had been so certain of his deductive reasoning.

Out of the corner of his eye, Ashkell watched Greenback leave. Then, he lumbered over and tossed the Skystone into an ornate box on the table. "Happily, I won't need that cowering idler much longer," he grumbled. "Soon I will be all-powerful." The idea filled him with glee and the echoes of his laughter resounded off the chamber walls.

CHAPTER TWENTY-TWO

Relief flooded over them when the foothills of the Iron Teeth Mountains finally came in sight. The parched desolation of the Oban Plains had been even more exhausting than the insect-ridden Sestol Swamp. The fierce heat had sucked the energy out through the bottoms of their feet.

With the hills beckoning them, they moved rapidly, traveling through the scorching midday heat, in order to finally leave the dehydrated plains behind.

They camped in a shallow valley between low sloping hills. After the dusty plains, the sparse grass felt like plush carpet to Stefani.

"I thought we'd never see the last of that place," Robbie said with a sigh.

"It was far and dry," Gamdol said. "Very dry."

"Gamdol," Laurel said, "let's take another look at that map."

Gamdol spread out the map and Laurel pulled a scroll from her pack, unrolled it and placed it beside the map. She studied the two documents, squinting in the last rays of the setting sun. "Ahhh," she said at last, pointing to a place on the map. "That's it. Just west of here. Gamdol, mark that spot, please. That's where we're going first thing in the morning. Right now, we all need a good rest." Gamdol made a mark on the map before the fading light disappeared.

"These hills are filled with many caverns," Laurel told them, "but only the Lost Cavern will lead us to the workshop of the ancient Nelig Troll."

Robbie struck two rocks together, dropping sparks onto a pile of tinder. Gamdol had been teaching him about venturing, and Robbie was a quick learner. Stefani sat with her back against a rock, watching the fire come to life under Robbie's care. It blazed brightly, casting shadows that danced and stretched along the sloping valley.

Despite their exhaustion, everyone seemed more relaxed than they'd been for days. Stefani could see it in their faces and the way they talked in low murmurs around the flickering campfire.

The weary travelers fell asleep under the

moon's soft glow, cradled by the sloping hills.

In the morning, sunlight glazed the sides of the hills a buttery yellow. Laurel hurried them through breakfast, impatient to get moving. After a short hike, they reached the place Gamdol had marked on the map. They watched and waited while Laurel pried behind large rocks and poked into the earth with her long fingers. After a thorough search of the area, she stared at the map and wrinkled her forehead in thought. "I need everyone to remain still and quiet for a moment."

She faced the sun and raised her arms over her head, stretching her fingers up toward the sky and spreading them wide. Closing her eyes, she sunk her feet deep into the earth.

It's like she's growing roots, Stefani thought.

Laurel's body swayed slightly. Although there was no wind, the leaves on her head rustled as if a light breeze blew through them. Finally, she dropped her arms and opened her eyes.

"How silly of me." Laurel let out a quick laugh, pulled her feet out of the ground and shook the dirt off them. She practically ran over to a large boulder near the center of the vale and stopped in front of it. Eyes closed, she breathed deeply. Then she lifted her arms over the rock chanting strange words.

Stefani's skin broke out in gooseflesh as tingling energy rose up from the ground. The boulder vibrated and shivered, and a low rumble filled the air.

Laurel continued to chant and the rock

rolled slowly away, revealing a dark hole in the earth. Laurel stopped chanting and opened her eyes. “The entryway to the Lost Cavern,” she said, gesturing toward the opening.

Gamdol stared in awe. “I have never seen such magic before.”

“It is important to speak the language of the land, or of the rocks, if that be the case,” Laurel told him.

Stale air rose from the opening, but the tunnel appeared dry inside. Steep steps led down into darkness. Robbie squinted, trying to see into the gloom. “It’s pretty dark down there,” he said.

“We’ll have to do something about that, won’t we?” Laurel said. She dug in her pack and produced two long tapered sticks. Touching their tips together, she spoke a single word. The ends of the sticks glowed. She handed one of the sticks to Robbie and, carrying the other, led them down into the earth.

They followed her down the narrow steps that plunged into the heart of the mountain. The light from the glowing tapers barely pushed away the deep shadows, casting only a small pool of illumination around them. The air was still, as if it hadn’t been disturbed in hundreds of years, and the only sound was the fall of their footsteps. Stefani brushed against the cold rock wall and jerked back with a gasp, her hand tangled in sticky spider webs. She wiped her hand on her pants with a shudder.

Rocks and dirt littered the tunnel. In places,

the piles reached nearly to the top of the passageway and they had to dig with their hands to clear the way.

Finally, the passageway widened out and leveled off. Robbie found he could hold both arms out, fingertips extended, without touching the walls on either side. "Wait here," Laurel said, finally. Her voice echoed in the dark expanse and her glowing taper grew smaller as it moved away from them.

"Here," she called out, her voice faint. The glow flared, becoming a bright flame as she lit a torch that illuminated a vast cavern.

The torch jutted out from a pillar carved with swirling designs and studded with huge gems that sparkled in the torchlight.

On the far side of the cavern stood a yawning stone furnace, a massive forge that had once been used to smelt and refine heavy ores into precious metals. Covered in soot and connected by a large pipe, the great bellows that had once fanned the coals stood silent and lifeless. "This was used by the Nelig Troll," Laurel said in awe. "This was his workshop, the place where he wrought the gems of the earth and created the legendary Nelig Stones of Anoria."

Tools covered the workbenches. Hammers and tongs and anvils. The cavern walls glittered in the torchlight. "It's beautiful," Stefani whispered.

"He chose his workplace well." Laurel ran her fingers along a sparkling emerald vein. "He didn't have to travel far for the materials he needed to create his treasures." She surveyed the room. "Search for a hiding place," she told them, poking through the dust-covered tools and peering onto the shelves that had been carved into the walls.

Stefani checked the places she thought would most likely hold something precious while Robbie tapped on the walls hunting for secret doors and panels. The Lightwings buzzed around the top of the large room, carefully checking each nook and cranny. They'd been searching forever and Stefani thought they must have checked every possible hiding place at least three times when Gamdol squealed in excitement.

"See here, see here," he said. "Behind the fire pit! Behind." He pointed to a spot where he'd scraped away the accumulated ash and soot from a long crack in the cavern wall.

Robbie grabbed a long stick and poked it into the hole. It went in more than two feet without hitting anything. "Whoa," he said. "This goes really deep."

He helped Gamdol remove the deeper layers of ash from the crevice. They worked quickly and soon had it completely unblocked. The opening was barely large enough for a Lightwing to squeeze through.

Katar volunteered to go inside. Taking one of the glowing tapers, he slipped into the crack and disappeared from sight. The others waited breathlessly, watching the glow of the taper flicker in the mouth of the crack, growing dimmer and dimmer. Suddenly, it went out. Stefani caught her breath and Laurel called to the Lightwing, but he didn't answer.

"What if he's hurt?" Robbie gave voice to their fears.

Just then, light flickered once more in the narrow crack, then grew brighter. They breathed a sigh of relief when Katar reappeared and stuck the taper out of the crack, handing it to Gamdol. He squeezed the rest of the way out of the narrow space, hefting a worn leather pouch on his back.

"Are you all right?" Robbie asked. "What happened? We thought you were a goner when the light went out."

"It didn't go out," Katar said, swatting the dust off his uniform. "I dropped it when I tripped over this bag." He passed the pouch to Laurel, who opened the bag and dumped the contents into her hand. Light sprang back at them from a faceted green gem.

Robbie let out a loud whoop. "We did it! We found one of the stones!" His shouts reverberated through the cavern.

"Yes," Laurel said quietly, "but there are still three missing and remember, we aren't the only ones searching."

"Oh yeah." Robbie's enthusiasm melted away just as his shouts echoed into silence.

"Does this one have a name?" Stefani asked unable to drag her eyes away from the glittering gem.

"I believe we are holding the Earthstone." Laurel held the jewel up to the flickering torchlight, causing droplets of color to dance around the cave.

"What magic does it hold?" Gamdol asked. "What power?"

"Its power would have aided me in the task of moving that boulder from the opening of the passageway," Laurel said. "It holds minor magic over earth and rocks and can affect the growth of plants. I have always wanted to hold this stone in my hands." She stroked the gem with her fingers. "However, it is not a good idea to keep the stones too close together. Their power may be difficult to control, especially without the great stone to act as a grounding point. Robbie, would you be willing to take possession of the Earthstone for me?"

Robbie's eyes went wide. He nodded and held out his hand.

Stefani wanted to protest. Why shouldn't she carry the Earthstone? She touched the silver ring on her finger and remembered what Queen Karissa had said about accepting the way things were, rather than always trying to have her own way. She kept quiet, watching as Laurel passed the beautiful jewel to Robbie. He placed the chain around his neck, tucking the gem safely inside his shirt.

"We have been successful here, but we still have much to do," Laurel said. "Gamdol, quench the torch, please. We must get moving."

CHAPTER TWENTY-THREE

They scrabbled out of the tunnel, blinking in the pale evening light. Dusky shadows stretched across the low hills, and early stars flickered in the darkening sky.

"Perhaps, we should camp here tonight," Laurel said. "We can get an early start in the morning."

Robbie felt the hardness of the Earthstone against his chest. His new responsibility made him uneasy. He pressed his hand against the stone, wondering if there was anything else about it that he should know. He was about to ask Laurel, when the sky above them erupted with blazing light. A swirling fire surrounded them and a foul stench filled the vale.

"Fireworms! Fireworms!" Gamdol squealed.

"Back into the cavern!" Laurel shouted.

They turned to run, but a snarling beast dropped from the air blocking the mouth of the cave. It flapped its leathery wings and snapped at them with vicious teeth. Stefani backed away. The hulking beast lunged at her, hissing and spitting.

Stefani screamed and tried to run, but more of the reptiles swooped down from the sky belching fire at the Lightwings, who dodged the flames and disappeared into the shadows.

From behind a boulder, Gamdol watched as Robbie, Stefani and Laurel were herded into the little vale. He wanted nothing more than to rush out and rescue his friends, but there was nothing he could do alone against an entire clutching of Fireworms. He needed help.

Stefani shuddered as writhing creatures surrounded them. The largest worm slithered close to the three captives. A puckery scar ran along the full length of his body.

"Greetingsss, puny animalsss," he snarled. "I am Longssscar. I guide you now for ressst of your journey."

Robbie and Stefani huddled close to Laurel, eyeing the Fireworms. Fear showed in Stefani's face. Robbie resisted the urge to clutch protectively at the Earthstone.

Laurel reached out a reassuring hand to each of them. "How gracious of you, Longscar, but we don't need a guide," she said calmly. "We are just returning home from a short retreat. Thank you for your offer, but no thank you."

"Isss not offer." Longscar said. "Isss command. Lord Asssshkell, demandsss presssence hisss palassse. Order of High Lord isss not ignored. You come with usss. Now."

"Ashkell? High Lord?" Laurel said in contempt. "He holds no authority in Anoria. Be gone and leave us in peace!" She raised her arms in the direction of Longscar.

The towering beast belched fire, singeing the hem of Laurel's robe. "Beware, sorceressss!" he said menacingly. "We know your weaknessss. Attempt to ussse magic again, we burn you. Fassst. Easssier to bring ashesss to High Lord."

Laurel lowered her arms and glared at the Fireworm. "Very well," she said, but her eyes were filled with defiance.

Gamdol watched in frustration as the Fireworms herded his friends away. Their silhouettes quickly merged into the darkness. He had no idea what could be done, but he knew he must follow. He crept out into the open.

"Psssst!"

Gamdol jumped. Kelin hovered in the moonlight. Relief filled the Glimmering's chest. "I am glad to see you," he whispered. "Are the other Lightwings all right?"

"Yes," Kelin murmured. "I've sent them ahead to see where the Fireworms are taking the others. We'll follow behind and watch for a chance to rescue them."

"Good." Gamdol said, hoping he sounded more confident than he felt. "Do you have a plan?"

"No," Kelin replied gruffly. "But we will find a way."

CHAPTER TWENTY-FOUR

"Do you think Gamdol and the Lightwings are all right?" Robbie asked in a whisper.

"I hope so." Stefani glanced over at Laurel, but the Treemage's face was hidden in shadow. The moon had not yet risen and an inky blackness enveloped them. Robbie and Stefani stumbled in the dark, driven along by their captors. Their eyes stung from the sulfury breath of the Fireworms. The creatures' pale glowing eyes had grown larger as the light grew dimmer, and they slithered along, unhindered by the lack of light, pushing their captives to keep up the pace.

The long night wore on. When the sky grew light once more, instead of stumbling in the dark, Robbie and Stefani staggered from exhaustion.

The Fireworms forced their prisoners to keep moving long after sunrise. Now and then, Stefani sneaked a peek at her compass trying to keep track of where they were going, but without Gamdol's map, she was lost. All she could tell was that their path led westward, away from the Caverns of Lorn and along the edge of the shadowy hills.

Near midmorning, they were allowed to rest for a few minutes, and Robbie and Stefani dropped to the ground in relief. Laurel remained standing, her toes gripping the earth, until a pale yellow worm hissed at her. She sank wearily down to sit beside Stefani.

"Where are they taking us?" Stefani passed her water bottle to the Treemage.

Laurel took a small sip, then shook her head. "I don't know, but if they are working for Ashkell, it can't be good," she said sourly. "His intentions never are, and he is not to be trusted. If you and Robbie have a chance to run, you must take it."

Both Stefani and Robbie started to argue, but Laurel gave them a stern look. "The politics of Anoria are not your burden." She passed the water bottle to Robbie. "Promise me that if the opportunity arises, you will escape." Reluctantly, they both agreed.

Longscar hissed and one of the Fireworms flapped its dark wings. It sprang into the sky and soared rapidly out of sight. Then, the captives were urged back onto their feet and forced to continue their march.

The sun blazed a path across the sky. For the rest of the morning, Laurel kept to herself and Robbie yawned nonstop. Stefani wanted know more about Ashkell, but while the worms didn't seem very bright, she thought better of asking questions in front of them. She trudged on, wrapped in thoughts of ice-cold lemonade and her air-conditioned bedroom back home.

At midday, they came to a murky stream that bubbled up out of the ground and trickled downhill, leaving a muddy rill in its wake. The water from the acrid spring was warm and bitter, but Stefani gratefully washed her face and hands. Robbie drank deeply, trying not to choke on the bitterness, then filled the water bottle.

Longscar halted the party and set out guards. The prisoners were finally allowed to sleep. It seemed like Stefani had barely shut her eyes when, in the dark of the night, she and Robbie were prodded awake by a puckered and wrinkly Fireworm. It snarled, poking them with its blunt tail until they sat up rubbing the sleep from their eyes.

Robbie wobbled on his feet. He sipped from the nearly empty water bottle, then offered it to Stefani. Her mouth was parched, but she shook her head. The vinegary water had already given her a stomachache and if she drank another drop she'd throw up.

A moment later, the water bottle thudded to the ground at her feet, the last of the nasty water splashing onto her legs, and Robbie collapsed in a heap. "Laurel, help!" Stefani dropped to her knees beside him.

The Treemage was already there, her long fingers resting against Robbie's forehead. "He's fainted," she said. "Too much bitter water, and not enough food."

Longscar lashed his tail. "Get moving!"

Laurel and Stefani tried to wake Robbie, but his pale face remained slack, his eyes shut tight. "The boy cannot walk any further," Laurel said. "He needs rest and clean water. And some decent food wouldn't hurt, either."

"Get him up, or we leave him for the ssscavengersss."

Laurel stood and faced the repulsive Fireworm. "We will not leave without the boy." She crossed her arms. "He'll have to be carried."

Longscar hulked over her. "Then carry him."

"We haven't the strength to do it ourselves," Laurel said.

Longscar let out a burbling hiss and two Fireworms slithered toward Robbie.

"No! Don't hurt him!" Stefani tried to bar the way, but Longscar swept her aside with his tail. Stefani sprawled in the dirt and Laurel sprang to her side. "It's all right," she said, glaring at the worms. "They're not going to hurt him."

The Fireworms squished Robbie between them. They wriggled and contorted until they had wrestled him onto one worm's back. Then, Longscar leaned down and hissed in Laurel's face. "Ssstrap him in place," he ordered.

"Stefani, hand me your coil of rope, please." Laurel held out her hand.

They wrapped the rope around Robbie and the worm. The worm writhed and squirmed and Stefani flinched every time her she touched its gross, sticky skin. It felt like touching a damp marshmallow. Finally, with Robbie secured in place, they moved on. The worm undulated awkwardly and Stefani and Laurel walked alongside to keep Robbie from slipping off.

Weak light filled the eastern sky and, about the time Stefani thought she couldn't take another step, a crumbling castle appeared on the horizon. The ruined fortress spilled out from the base of the black mountain like it had oozed there.

When they reached what was left of the broken stone walls, they were herded through rusted gates and into a grim-looking courtyard littered with debris. As soon as Laurel and Stefani had loosened the rope, the Fireworm arched its back and dumped Robbie roughly onto the ground. Then it slithered off, burbling and fizzing like a leaky radiator

Robbie groaned and sat up. "Where are we?" he asked, his voice a hoarse whisper. He rubbed his hands together, and tried to wipe off the sticky stuff that clung to him.

"We are in the southern keep of Ashkell, brother to the High King," Laurel said. "I knew his underlings had been causing trouble for the king. I even suspected he might be the one searching for the stones, but I didn't expect him to know about the caverns. He must have someone very learned in the lore of Anoria working with him. I still have not been able to discern who it is, but we will find out soon enough, I'm afraid."

Uneasiness crawled inside Stefani's belly, but despite her fear, she was so exhausted she couldn't keep her eyes open any longer. Beside her, Robbie was already snoring softly as she drifted off to sleep.

Once again, she found herself running in a dark dream. This time, a huge shadow chased her. She ran and ran, but the shadow stayed right behind her, hot breath scorching the back of her neck. She woke with a start, relieved to find that it had just been another bad dream. Wispy daylight filled the room, but she couldn't shake the dread that squirmed inside her.

"Laurel—" Stefani stopped. A slithery sound came from outside and the wooden door swung open.

CHAPTER TWENTY-FIVE

"Come," Longscar said, thrusting his ugly head inside the room. Stefani jostled Robbie to wake him, and the three captives followed the Fireworm through the desolate courtyard to the inner keep.

The Fireworms pushed and shoved them down a dim corridor. They herded them into the center of a large chamber where they huddled together.

Weak sunlight dribbled in through narrow slits set high in the walls. On the far side of the room loomed a dark fireplace filled with ashes and soot. There were no furnishings except for a few tattered tapestries hanging limply from the rough walls.

"What do you want with us?" Laurel glared at their captors.

Their guards only hissed and gurgled.

"I demand to know why we have been brought here," the Treemage said.

"Tell me, Sorceress," came a cool voice from behind them, "do your magic powers fail you? Or have you merely become dimwitted in your old age?"

Stefani and Robbie turned toward the door. A dragon, at least eight feet tall, stood in the passageway just outside the room. Stefani let out a small yelp and covered her mouth with her hands. Robbie stepped back and gaped up at the imposing bulk of pale green scales. The dragon chuckled, clearly delighted at their fear and surprise.

"Greenback!" Laurel exclaimed. "What are you doing here?"

"So your faculties have not left you completely. I am flattered that you remember me." He ambled into the room, his huge feet clomp-clomping on the stone floor and his scaly tail slithering behind him.

"How could I forget?" Laurel replied, her tone flat and unfriendly. "You were one of my finest students before you chose to follow your own ways into the darker arts."

"Not my ways, witch. The ways of the ancient mages. I found their obscure texts and discovered how you had twisted the knowledge you gave me to suit your own beliefs about magic. The books of the ancient mages showed me a purer form of power. A hidden form. The dark form."

"You're a fool, Greenback. No one has the power to control the dark magic. Why do you think all that remains of the dark mages is their texts?"

"You're wrong," Greenback growled. "I have the ability to control that power. You are weak and have no understanding of dark magic, but I am strong, as you will soon see. Give me the stones!"

"You may be powerful, but you are truly a fool, Greenback, if you think that one mage alone has the power to unleash and control the power of the Nelig Stones."

"I don't think, I know." He thrust out his claw and strode toward her, razor-sharp talons extended. "Now give them to me."

"No! Give them to me!"

Greenback spun around to face a huge black dragon that towered even over him. "That is what I meant, of course, Sire." Greenback bowed and scraped before the bigger dragon.

Stefani gripped Robbie's arm. They stared up over Greenback's head at the enormous dragon lumbering toward them.

With a vicious swipe of his claw, Greenback tore the Firestone from Laurel's neck, then extended it toward the other dragon. "Here you are, Your Gargantuousness."

Laurel sneered. "So, you're not even your

own master," she said, "merely Ashkell's servant." She laughed.

Greenback growled. "Where are the others?"

"The others?" Laurel asked, her face an innocent mask.

"Yes." Greenback's tone was menacing. "My spies have been watching. You would not have returned to the surface so soon if you hadn't found what you were seeking in the Caverns of Lorn. Give me the stones. Or do you need persuading?" He extended his blade-like talons toward Stefani.

"Robbie, give him the stone," Laurel said.

Robbie's eyes flicked from Greenback to Laurel. He gripped the stone beneath his shirt.

Greenback reached for Stefani, who let out a tiny shriek and backed away. Robbie's face grew pale, but he stepped between Stefani and the dragon.

"Go ahead, Robbie. He can't do anything with it anyway. He doesn't have the Great Stone. Do you, Greenback?"

"Don't be so sure," Greenback snarled.

"No," Laurel said, "if you already held the power of the Great Stone, you wouldn't be so urgent. Perhaps your hirelings captured us too soon. Now, you'll have to keep searching." She smiled coldly.

Robbie dragged the Earthstone from beneath his shirt.

Greenback snatched the gem. "We shall see."

"Greenback!" Ashkell commanded. "Bring me those stones!"

"Yes, Sire," Greenback replied. He walked purposefully over to the huge black dragon and held out the two dangling jewels.

"Now, what was that about the Great Stone?" Ashkell took the gems, eyeing them with an evil grin.

"Ah . . . well, S—sire," Greenback stuttered, trying to maintain his composure. "We have not, as . . . um . . . yet, retrieved it. But we are close," he added quickly. "Very close."

Laurel let out another laugh and Greenback glared sharply in her direction. She met his gaze without fear.

"You have until tomorrow to deliver it, or I will find a new advisor." Ashkell's words rang out harshly. "In the meantime, these stones will remain locked in my personal chambers, along with the others."

Greenback glared at him for an instant before gathering his wits. "As you wish." He nearly choked on the words. "Take the prisoners to the dungeon," he told the guards. "I will deal with them later," he added, his eyes locking on Laurel's.

The Fireworms led them away, jostling and shoving them down a steep stairwell that led through darkness to the prison cells deep beneath the keep. They were taken to one of the cages and pushed inside. The rusty door clanged shut and the guards retreated back up the passageway.

The cell was damp and smelled of moldy garbage. It reminded Robbie of the city dump.

He wrinkled his nose in disgust. Stefani held her breath and stood still, trying not to touch anything.

Laurel searched for a weakness in their prison. She tried the lock, but it was strong and well forged. She tested the bars, but they were thick and sturdy. She even tried using her magic, but without the Firestone and with the castle's foundation blocking her connection to the earth, her powers were weakened. "It seems that Greenback isn't as big a fool as I had hoped," she said. "He's put a spell on the lock to counter my magic. I may be able to get us out of here, but it will take some time." She stood with her feet firmly planted on the stone floor, set her jaw and began slowly gathering energy for the task before her.

While Laurel worked at the spell, Stefani and Robbie sat quietly on the driest pile of moldy straw they could find. A veil of dim torchlight penetrated the shadows in the passageway, and they could just make out Laurel's silhouette. Stefani hugged herself and shivered.

They had been waiting quietly for what seemed like forever when Robbie jumped up.

"What's wrong?" Stefani leaped to her feet and looked around in the dark, trying to see what had spooked him.

"I thought I saw something move," he whispered.

"Something? What kind of something?" she asked, afraid of what the answer might be.

"I don't know," he said, trying not to sound

worried. "It was small, I think, but it was quick."

"Do you think we should tell Laurel?" Stefani glanced around, expecting something nasty to jump on her at any moment.

"It was me." A whisper came from the darkness just outside the cell, startling them both.

"Gamdol!" Robbie nearly shouted. "What are you doing here?"

"Shhh!" Stefani said. "Those creepy Fireworms might hear you, and Laurel's still working on the spell."

"It's okay. Okay," Gamdol said. "The key. I have the key." He held out his hand. A ring of keys caught a glint of torchlight and glittered against the darkness.

"How did you get those?" Robbie and Stefani asked together.

"I followed the guards after they left you here. Followed when they went away. Watched when they hung the key on the wall. I waited until they left and then I took it. I was quiet. Very quiet."

"Well done, Gamdol." Laurel, roused from her magic by their voices, sounded tired but relieved. "Now we must find a way to retrieve the Nelig Stones and escape."

"The Lightwings have gone after them. Soldiers have gone to get the stones," Gamdol said, unlocking the cell door. "Brave Lightwings. Tamel listened. Listened outside when the stones the were taken. That's how we knew. Knew you'd be down here. That's how I knew to come. Would have come sooner, but we had trouble finding the back door. Hidden. The back door was hidden. We are to wait here for Lightwings. Lightwings will bring the stones."

"All right then," said Laurel, "but stay alert. We don't want to be recaptured." They locked the cell door and hid in the shadows at the end of the corridor. Stefani, stiff and alert, jumped at every noise.

Finally, a blur of shadow flickered in the dim torchlight at the bottom of the stairs. They stayed still, crouching in the shadows until the three Lightwings came into full view. Each carried what was for them a large bundle.

"You found them," Stefani whispered excitedly. She stepped out of the shadows. But when the Lightwings reached her, the ground quivered beneath her feet.

"What's happening?" Robbie asked. The earth trembled again and loose stones rattled from the walls.

"By leaf and stem!" Laurel said. "Stefani, where is the Great Stone?"

"What?" The ground shook harder and Stefani reached out to brace herself.

"The Great Stone," Laurel repeated. "Where is it?" The ground heaved and outside the castle a powerful wind began to blow. It whistled through the cracks in the thick stone walls, all the way down to the damp lower levels of the keep. "I know Robbie doesn't have it," Laurel continued, "or the Earthstone would have reacted when he touched it. So that leaves you or Gamdol." Gamdol shook his head vigorously.

"All I have are these rocks I picked up at Papago Park before we ever came here," Stefani protested. She reached into her pocket and pulled out the rocks she'd been carrying, holding them out in her hand. The black stone grew warm and throbbed like a heartbeat. The strange symbol she'd seen in the park and had later traced in the sand of the Oban Plains appeared on the stone's surface, glowing and fading. She gasped in astonishment, dropping the other rocks and staring in disbelief at the gem that pulsed in her hand. It was now glossy black with a glowing symbol clearly etched into its smooth surface.

"Be careful," Laurel said. She moved past Stefani to take the Firestone from Tamel. "Robbie, take the Earthstone from Katar. Kelin, give the Moonstone to Gamdol, and bring the Skystone with you." The earth gave another heave and the castle shuddered and groaned. Rocks and mortar fell from the ceiling.

"I didn't expect to have all the stones together without some help to control their power," Laurel shouted over the noise. "We must get out into the open. Move quickly, but don't get too close to one another."

"This way!" Tamel zipped into the darkness.

CHAPTER TWENTY-SIX

Greenback's head snapped up and he sniffed the air. The castle trembled. Wind buffeted the walls of the keep and thunder crashed overhead. He rushed into Ashkell's chamber. The box stood open. The Nelig Stones were gone!

Snarling in frustration, he rushed through the groaning castle to the lower levels. The raging wind outside grew wilder as he stormed into the dungeon. The cell too was empty. The sound of running feet echoed up the dark passageway. With a roar of frustration, he charged after the escaping prisoners.

They ran through twisting corridors, trying to hurry, but the passage slanted upward and rocks and debris tumbled down on them. Each time they got too close together, the castle gave another violent lurch. Stefani's heart battered against her ribs. She wanted to scream. She was breathing hard, and twice she tripped and nearly lost her balance. Behind her, Kelin urged them to hurry.

"Give me the stones!" Greenback roared, suddenly right behind her.

Drawing his sword, Kelin turned in mid-air and faced the dragon. Greenback swatted at him like he would a bothersome insect. Kelin dodged the dragon's fierce claw and moved in closer, trying to stab at Greenback's eyes, but the Skystone weighed him down.

Katar and Tamel flew quickly into the fray. The others stopped running and watched in fear as Greenback spun around and around, growling and hissing, lashing out with his razor sharp claws. He tore at the air, trying to knock the Lightwings away. The valiant Lightwings dodged in and out, striking at the mighty dragon, pricking him with the points of their swords.

A deafening roar erupted from the dark passageway and Ashkell bore down on Greenback. The Lightwings streaked out of the way.

"Get out of my path, you fool!" Ashkell snarled at Greenback, shoving him hard against the stone wall.

"No!" Greenback shrieked. "The stones are mine! It was I who learned their secrets, I who ferreted them from hiding, and I who will rule the land with them!" He lunged at Ashkell, raking his claws across the bigger dragon's black-scaled chest.

Ashkell howled in pain and rage. The two dragons attacked, ripping and shredding one another. Blood gushed from torn flesh. The hallway echoed with their bellowing. Massive tails and bodies crashed against the walls of the passageway as the storm continued to shake and batter the castle.

Greenback moved with lightning quickness. He dodged and lunged, slashing at Ashkell, but he lacked Ashkell's strength and experience. Thrashing his powerful tail, Ashkell advanced, forcing Greenback against the wall. With a mighty roar, Ashkell raked his gleaming claws across Greenback's underbelly. Greenback howled in pain. Then Ashkell sunk his teeth deep into Greenback's neck.

Robbie stood stunned, wide-eyed and open-mouthed. Gamdol yanked at his sleeve, pulling him along the passageway. Stefani and Laurel were already scrambling away from the fighting. With the Lightwings urging them on, they darted up the passageway and dashed out into the howling storm.

The earth shook and heaved. Thunder clapped. The ground roiled and the screaming wind tore at them. They spread out and staggered away from the keep. The wind tossed the Lightwings to and fro like leaves in a gale.

They tried to move away from one another, but the earth rippled and the storm buffeted them, pushing them back and bunching them together. With an ear-splitting crash, the ground buckled and the section of castle wall above the exit collapsed. Huge chunks of stone and debris tumbled outward, rolling toward them.

"Run!" Stefani screamed. The wind whipped away her words in a wild torrent.

Ashkell flew out of the gaping hole in the castle wall, blood dripping from tooth and claw. Driven by his lust for power, he tore after the fleeing group, his shrieks louder than the screeching wind. They were no match for a dragon on the wing.

Ashkell climbed high into the air and dove steeply at them, but the driving wind forced him back up and away. Bellowing in anger, he circled overhead, preparing to attack once more.

Suddenly, the ground gave out a groan like a dying giant. The earth heaved and cracked open. A deep chasm yawned before them. Stefani staggered to a halt. Turning away from the gaping wound in the earth, she stumbled back toward the ruined castle.

Ashkell roared in triumph. He had them trapped! He circled back and came hurtling out of the sky.

Stefani spun back toward the fissure, clutching the glowing stone to her chest. Terrified, she ran on, unable to see through the swirling dust. The ground lurched and swayed.

She stumbled. The gaping chasm yawned in front of her. She reared back, arms pin-wheeling, and regained her balance. But the earth bucked and she fell, sprawling in the dirt. The stone flew from her hand and rolled toward the abyss, its strange symbols glowing with a deep blue light.

Ashkell saw the glowing rock. Finally, the Great Stone was his! He pulled in his wings, shooting like an arrow toward the stone.

Stefani stumbled to her feet and grabbed the pulsing gem. She sped away from the edge of the pit. Ashkell plunged down, extending his huge claws to grab her. In a flash, Robbie was there, pushing her aside. The swooping dragon narrowly missed her as she crashed onto her hands and knees.

Stefani lay panting as Ashkell circled overhead. There was nowhere to run. She had to keep Ashkell from taking the stone, had to keep him from destroying Anoria and everyone in it. But if she did that, she and Robbie would never be able to go home. She would never see her mother, never have a chance to change things between them. She bit her lip, and stared at the Great Stone glowing in her hand. She drew in her breath, pulled back her arm and threw the stone as hard as she could. It landed a short distance from the edge of the chasm, bouncing toward the crevasse.

"No!" Robbie watched in horror as the Great Stone rolled slowly toward the edge of the gaping pit and teetered on the brink. The key that could send them home glittered darkly, balanced on the edge, pulsing with power.

With a thundering roar, Ashkell wheeled and dove. The earth shuddered, tumbling the black rock into the abyss. In a screaming fit of rage Ashkell flew after it, clutching at the air where it had been. The earth gave one last heaving groan and the chasm slammed shut with a crash, imprisoning Ashkell and the Great Stone forever.

A sudden silence enveloped everything. Stefani lay on the ground, afraid that at any moment the earth would open up again and swallow them all. A few stray leaves fluttered soundlessly to the ground. In the awful quiet, she could hear her own breathing, the pounding of her frightened heart, and the echo of her mother's voice calling her name.

Then, with a flutter of wings, a tiny bluebird flew out of a high castle window. With a chirrup of joy, it winged into the sky and disappeared.

CHAPTER TWENTY-SEVEN

Robbie woke to sunshine spilling across a large bedchamber. He bathed and dressed in clean clothes before searching out his companions.

King Emris and his loyal followers had routed the band of renegade Fireworms and followed them back to Ashkell's keep, arriving to find the castle in ruins and the remaining Fireworms frantically fleeing into the mountains.

Emris, himself, escorted the weary companions to the King's castle at Dragon's Tor. On dragon-back, the trip took only a few hours, but the travelers had been exhausted. As soon as they had been shown to rooms, they'd fallen into a deep slumber.

Robbie found Gamdol and the Lightwings sitting in the royal garden, talking quietly beneath a blue and white canopy surrounded by dark green trees and flowering plants. They greeted him with huge smiles and he sat down beside them on a carved wooden bench.

"Where are Stefani and Laurel?" he asked.

"Laurel went to wake Stefani," Gamdol said. "Wake her for the big feast. We thought you would never wake up. Thought you would be sleeping ever."

"It's only nearly two days," Kelin said with a smile. "Not that anyone's counting, of course."

"As if you hadn't slept so much," Gamdol chided. "As if you didn't sleep so much yourself."

"Well said, friend," Kelin responded, with a grimace. Then he laughed light-heartedly, and the others laughed with him.

"So, when do we eat?" Robbie asked. "I'm starving!"

"Soon enough," Laurel said from behind him. She and Stefani wore glittering gowns, Laurel's a rich green and Stefani's a deep purple. Stefani looked different to Robbie, quieter, almost solemn.

The sound of gay voices and laughter drifted out of the banquet hall. Stefani took a deep breath, inhaling the perfumed air. She felt as if the terror of Ashkell and the storm had been nothing more than one of her bad dreams.

Only it hadn't been a dream. The Great Nelig Stone was lost forever, locked deep in the earth, and now she and Robbie were locked here in Anoria, forever.

Stefani felt suddenly miserable at the thought of never seeing her mother again. There were so many things she wanted to tell her, but she would never get the chance now.

Her throated tightened as she choked back her tears. She didn't want to say anything to Robbie, didn't want to ruin the celebration. There would be plenty of time after the banquet to worry about what they would do and where they would stay, how they would live. Anoria was a beautiful country, after all, and everyone they met treated them like heroes. But that didn't make her feel any better.

She sighed heavily, forced herself to smile, and followed the others into the main hall where they joined the celebration.

King Emris shimmered in the light of the blazing torches, speaking with them and listening intently as they told of their adventures. He was a mighty dragon. His blue eyes matched the glittering Skystone, which now hung from a heavy chain about his neck. A gift he had graciously accepted from the weary travellers upon their arrival at Dragon's Tor.

In spite of her worry, Stefani ate hungrily, sampling everything that passed her way, savoring the magnificent flavors of the main dishes and relishing the sweet fruit-filled desserts. After their sumptuous meal, the king rose and the revelers grew quiet.

"My friends." His clear voice carried to every corner of the hall. "We owe a great debt to this band of heroic travelers. During their quest, these brave souls encountered many grave dangers, even daring to face one who threatened to destroy the land of Anoria and all who dwell here." A sound of exclamation erupted from the crowd.

"These fine heroes," continued King Emris, "defeated those who would destroy our land and way of life and we owe them our gratitude." A loud cheering rang out in the hall. The king gestured for quiet and a hush fell over the crowd. "We have chosen to reward these fine companions as befits their heroism. Kelin Graystar, Katar Stormlight and Tamel Brightsword, stand before me."

The three Lightwings leaped up into the air and flew around the end of the table, landing before the king and bowing low. King Emris reached out a golden claw and touched each of them on the left shoulder in turn. "Kelin Graystar, Katar Stormlight and Tamel Brightsword of the Lightwings, you have proven yourselves to be true and valiant soldiers. For this you are given the honor of knighthood. Rise, Warriors of Anoria." The three Lightwings raised their heads up proudly and returned to their places, clearly pleased.

"Now," the king resumed, "I call forward Gamdol of the Glimmering." Gamdol stood before the towering dragon, touching his forehead with his hand and bowing, the Glimmering's most respectful salute. "Gamdol of the Glimmering," the king said. "You have proven yourself both brave and loyal. Your actions have shown that you are wise beyond your years, and you have passed trials more demanding than any Second Cycle Ritual requires. For this your people have asked me to present you with this Staff of Cycles. May you notch it well." He handed Gamdol an ornate wooden staff with several notches carved into one end.

"Thank you, Your Majesty," Gamdol said, taking the staff and holding it with pride. He returned to his place, his shoulders squared and head high. Robbie smiled and cheered for his friend, giving the Glimmering a high five.

"Laurel Silverbark," the king said. Laurel rose and made her way before the king. At her throat, the Firestone sparkled in the candlelight. "I am grateful to you for your aid in this quest. You, of all the companions, understood the dangers best and yet were not deterred. For your devotion and perseverance you are granted a permanent place within this court. We would be honored if you would remain with us to teach and guide us."

With a rustling of leaves, Laurel bowed low. "It would be my honor, Your Majesty."

Robbie waited excitedly, wondering what the king would give him for his part in their adventure. Would the High King give him his own Staff of Cycles like Gamdol's? Maybe he would be knighted. Sir Robbie of Anoria sounded pretty awesome.

Stefani remained quiet. The only reward she wanted was to go home, but with the Great Stone lost, that was impossible. She was glad to have helped save these people and their land, but her heart dragged in her chest. She barely heard her name when Emris called her and Robbie up to the dais.

"First and foremost," she heard the King say, his voice sounding far away, "I name you both Protectors of the Realm. Your names will be carved on the Anorian Stone of Heroes that stands at the top of Dragon Tor." A cheer went up from the crowd.

Stefani wished she could share in their joy, but all she felt was sadness and loss. She wished with all her heart that the last words she'd said to her mother had not been such angry ones. She stood before the High King, lost in her own thoughts, barely listening. Her head jerked up in disbelief as his words broke through to her.

"It will be a sad parting for us," he said, "but you have been away from your homes too long and must miss your people very much."

"Did you say home?" Stefani asked.

"Yes. Did I not speak clearly?"

"I . . . I'm sorry, Your Majesty," Stefani said. "I thought I misheard you. With the Great Stone lost . . ." she let her thought trail off.

"I was saying," the king said in a kind voice, "that being High King of Anoria does have some advantages. As I am sworn to the land, so it is sworn to me. Now that the Great Stone is locked within its heart, and with the aid of Laurel Silverbark and the holders of the other Nelig Stones, I can command the Gate of Worlds to open and give you passage home."

Stefani's heart bounced and she nearly wept with joy, and then with sorrow as she realized they would have to say good-bye to their companions. She gazed at each of them and they looked back at her with sadness, but there was also pride in their eyes and the knowing looks of companions who have travelled together on a difficult quest. Then their faces shimmered and blurred.

Stefani blinked her eyes trying to see them clearly, but they were gone. She found herself staring at the side of Hole-in-the-Rock where she could just make out a mark scratched into the rock. She was no longer wearing a formal gown, but was back in her torn jeans. Shocked, she stood still, heart pounding. Had it all been a dream? She glanced quickly at her hand. The silver ring on her finger glinted in the bright desert sunlight.

Beside her, Robbie started to say something when a tall, red-faced kid came puffing around the corner and stopped in front of them. "So," the dark-haired kid said, panting, "thought you'd get away from me, huh? Now, give me that skateboard!"

Robbie's gaze bounced between Brad and Stefani. Then he turned back to the other boy, planted his feet and thrust out his chin. "Get your own skateboard, Brad."

Brad's jaw dropped. "What?"

"You heard me," Robbie said, He stomped down on the end of the skateboard, flipping it up and catching it like a pro.

Brad sputtered and narrowed his eyes at Robbie, as if seeing him for the fist time. Then, without another word, he turned and tromped down the path, shaking his head and muttering under his breath.

Robbie smiled at Stefani. "Let's go home," he said.

ABOUT THE AUTHOR

SHARON SKINNER grew up in a small town in northern California where she spent most of her time reading books, making up plays, and choreographing her own musicals (when she wasn't busy climbing trees and playing baseball). She has been writing stories since fourth grade, filling page after page with fantastical creatures, aliens, monsters and, of course, heroes. She loves reading, drawing, arts and crafts, sewing, and costume-making (especially Steampunk). She lives in Arizona with her husband and four lovable cats. Her website is www.sharonskinner.com.

ABOUT THE ILLUSTRATOR

KEITH DECESARE has been a freelance illustrator for several RPG companies since 2001. His client list includes WotC, Kenzer Co. and Atlas Games. Born and raised in Arizona, Keith continues to hone his artistic skills ever since scribbling on a white wall with a black permanent marker. He uses a computer to do all his scribbling now with a leaning toward the fantasy/steampunk settings. You can check out his website at www.kadcreations.com!

NOTES

While this book is a work of fiction, some of the places are real.

HOLE-IN-THE-ROCK (PAPAGO PARK)

Located in Papago Park in Phoenix, Arizona, and formed of red sandstone, Hole-in-the-Rock is a cave-like natural rock formation caused by erosion. The original sandstone was formed around 6-15 million years ago.

Visitors to Papago Park can enjoy hiking through the Sonoran Desert habitat, or visit the Phoenix Zoo or the Desert Botanical Garden.

MOGOLLON RIM

Also mentioned in the book, the Mogollon Rim (locals pronounce it Muggy-own) is a rugged escarpment in a beautiful forested area in northern Arizona that begins just east of the New Mexico border and stretches two thirds of the way across Arizona. The area, often referred to as the Rim, includes Payson and its smaller neighbors, the communities of Pine, Strawberry and Christopher Creek.

17612871R00102

Made in the USA
Charleston, SC
19 February 2013